THE GUIDE TO

MYSTERIOUS SKYE
AND LOCHALSH

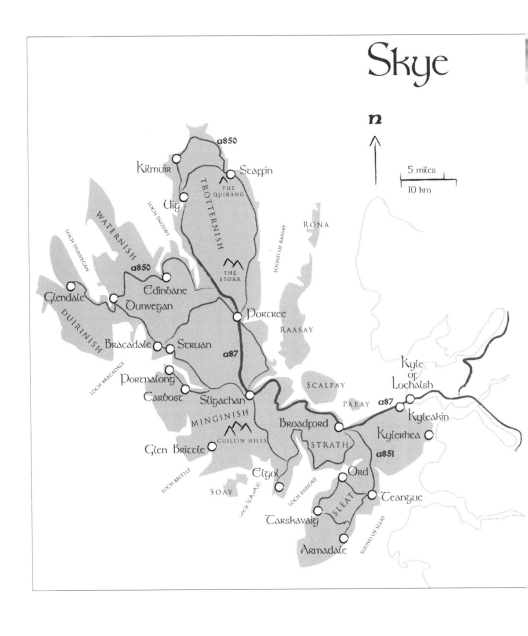

THE GUIDE TO
MYSTERIOUS SKYE
AND LOCHALSH

GEOFF HOLDER

To Alyson, Jodie and Lydia, the Three Weird Sisters.

And RIP my pair of walking boots, which after many years'
faithful service finally gave up the ghost somewhere in Trotternish.

First published 2010

The History Press
The Mill, Brimscombe Port
Stroud, Gloucestershire, GL5 2QG
www.thehistorypress.co.uk

Reprinted 2016

British Library Cataloguing in Publication Data.
A catalogue record for this book is available from the British Library.

ISBN 978 0 7524 4989 0

Typesetting and origination by The History Press
Printed in Great Britain

CONTENTS

ACKNOWLEDGEMENTS

I would like to thank the following for their assistance: Peter MacAskill of the Giant Angus MacAskill Museum, Dunvegan; the High Pasture Cave archaeological team for a guided tour of the cave; Ann-Marie Peckham, Assistant Curator at the MacDonald Study Centre in the Museum of the Isles, Armadale Castle; Maureen Byers, Curator, Dunvegan Castle; The Eilean Bàn Trust, and Barbara Walters, a volunteer with the Trust; Catherine Shearer of Skye Serpentarium; Roman and Armin Kiser from Switzerland; Dr Colin MacLeod of the School of Biological Sciences (Zoology) at the University of Aberdeen, for the identification of the Ord water-horse, and Jennifer Downes, Curator of Aberdeen University Museums; Matilda Richards and Beth Amphlett of the History Press; and of course Ségolène for keeping the show on the road.

Jenni Wilson produced the map. The image of the Loch Alsh monster is © Duncan Macpherson Collection, Dualchas Heritage Service. Two of the photographs on pages 28 are by Ségolène Dupuy. All other photographs are by the author, with digital improvement (including removal of a phenomenal amount of raindrops on the camera lens) by Ségolène Dupuy.

Lastly I would like to thank the number of anonymous drivers who kindly stopped to pick up a footsore and often rain-soaked author; may all your journeys be pleasurable and productive.

This book is part of an ongoing series of similar titles. If you would like to share any stories of the weird and wonderful, or wish to find more information, please visit www.geoffholder.co.uk.

INTRODUCTION

The island is pervaded by a subtle spiritual atmosphere. It is as strange to the mind as it is to the eye. Old songs and traditions are the spiritual analogues of old castles and burying-places and old songs and traditions you have in abundance. There is a smell of the sea in the material air and there is a ghostly something in the air of the imagination … You breathe again the air of old story-books.

Alexander Smith, *A Summer in Skye* (1885)

This is a guide to all things supernatural and strange, folkloric and fantastic, and weird and wonderful in the Isle of Skye, Raasay, and parts of the Lochalsh mainland. Here can be found ancient sites, haunted places, fairy hills, Celtic mythology, holy wells, folk magic and witchcraft, not to mention recent reports of phantom cars, sea-serpents and bizarre and unknown animals. Skye is the place where a community went on a Victorian water-monster hunt, where a policeman was attacked by a squid, and where Bonnie Prince Charlie psychically impressed his good looks onto an unborn child. This book will tell you how to find the skeleton of a water-horse, where to bathe in a fairy pool, and which route to take to enter a cave into Hell. Here too are tales of the clans, case studies of second-sight, descriptions of every castle, stone circle and standing stone, and unusual episodes from the lives of the famous mountaineer Norman Collie and Gavin Maxwell, author of *Ring of Bright Water*.

The book is organised geographically. Everything spooky, surreal and strange about one village, castle or mountain is collected in the same place, and the individual chapters can be used as gazetteers, so you can proceed from one place to another on a logical route by car or foot. Cross-references between locations are shown in SMALL CAPS.

THINGS TO SEE AND PLACES TO VISIT

If you're looking for mysteries, spookiness or unusual and strange experiences, you could do worse than visit:

A Castle – Castles were centres of clan power and the loci of legends and dark deeds. DUNVEGAN and EILEAN DONAN are deservedly popular paying attractions, although for a wilder and muddier time head for the ruins of DUN SCAICH, BROCHEL or DUNTULM.

A Museum – STAFFIN for dinosaur bones, ARMADALE for Clan MacDonald history, and KILMUIR and BORRERAIG for artefacts of everyday life; the best museum, however, is the one dedicated to THE GIANT ANGUS MACASKILL in Dunvegan.

A Visitor Attraction – For something different, head for the reptile-tastic SKYE SERPENTARIUM in Broadford or the utterly bonkers MACURDIE'S BARN OF LAUGHS at Bornesketaig.

A Church or Graveyard – Ghosts, saints, and gravestones carved with warriors or skulls: what more do you need? The graveyard of the ruined church at TRUMPAN contains a standing stone that is still the focus of living folklore, while SKEABOST and EYNORT are both evocative and beautifully situated.

A Prehistoric Monument – Choose from the ritual (standing stones and stone circles), the defensive (forts, brochs and duns), or the just plain odd (souterrains). See The Context – Archaeology section on page 16.

The Giant Angus MacAskill Museum, Dunvegan. The best museum on Skye dedicated to a giant.

How can you resist a sign like this? Bornesketaig/Kilmuir.

Above left: The Priest's Stone, a prehistoric standing stone in Trumpan churchyard. Visitors are still leaving coins in the stone's crevices.

Above right: Skulls, hourglass ('time is running out') and the mort-bells (the bells rung at funerals) on a gravestone in St Mary's, Dunvegan.

A Holy Well – The best spring associated with a saint and miracles is Tobar Ashaig at BREAKISH.

Weird Geology – Enter a different reality in the mountain dream – or nightmare – scapes of THE STORR and THE QUIRAING, or explore the otherwordly qualities of THE FAIRY GLEN.

A Monster – See the skeleton of a water-horse at ORD.

A Cave – Dark, damp, dangerous and difficult to get to. Explore with care.

MAGIC AND THE SUPERNATURAL – KEY CONCEPTS AND EXAMPLES

Liminality – That which is betwixt and between, a transition, a threshold. Liminality is a key concept in supernatural thinking. Dusk and dawn are liminal times, as is Hallowe'en. Liminal places include a boundary between two properties, bogs and rivers, graveyards – and caves. Caves reach into the Underworld, even to Hell, and on Skye are often connected with treasure, fairies, monsters and mermaids. Several Skye caves (such as at BORNESKETAIG and GRESHORNISH) have the legend that a piper entered playing his pipes – and that after a time the music ceased, and he was never seen again. Fairy hills – of which there are many on Skye – are liminal sites, the gate between mundane reality and the Realm of Faery. Water is a key liminal element, and many freshwater lochs on Skye – such as LOCH NAN DUBHRACHAN – are home to the demonic Celtic monster known as the water-horse. Water-horses could appear as a fine stallion or a handsome young man, the latter giving away his supernatural origin through the sand and shells in his hair. Water-horses lived to drag unsuspecting humans down into their watery lair for culinary purposes; for some reason water-horses could not digest hearts and lungs, for after an abduction those organs were always found floating on the surface.

Apotropaic – That which protects against evil. The Cross or Bible is often used apotropaically. In 1891 William MacKenzie reported to the Gaelic Society of Inverness that even fervent Protestants would make the sign of the cross on the ground if they met an 'untoward person' suspected of possessing the Evil Eye. In the early twentieth century, Mary Julia MacCulloch collected a number of Skye folktales, including one of a girl who prevented a water-horse from following her by rubbing her crucifix along the road she would have to take, while another resourceful damsel kept a water-horse at bay by standing on a hurriedly-drawn cross inside a protective circle. When MacCulloch moved into her new house a local man told her to sow the path with salt to keep away witches. He also gave her a piece of old iron to bury at the gate, which she duly did. Iron traditionally worked against supernatural beings of all denominations; when a former minister in Trotternish insisted on still visiting his cattle fold after his death, an old man laid the ghost by shaking hands with it – but using an iron ploughshare rather than his hand. The story is in J.G. Campbell's *Witchcraft and Second Sight in the Highlands and Islands of Scotland*. Rowan trees warded off witches and fairies, which is why you see so many rowans on the site of deserted villages. Both wise men who cured animals, and midwives attending a birth, would walk three times deasil around the patient, that is, in the direction of the path of the sun (these days we would say clockwise). Presumably this somehow invoked the power of the sun to keep evil influences at bay. Silver coins in water negated the Evil Eye, especially when a charm was spoken that invoked the Father, Son, and Holy Ghost. Apotropaic actions have continued into the modern era, with photographs of the FAIRY FLAG of Dunvegan being carried during the Second World War.

Magical thinking – Together apotropaism and liminality contribute to Magical Thinking, the thought process that allows belief in magic to operate. A great deal of magical thinking depends on Sympathetic Magic, which comes in two main forms. Things once connected are supposed to have a sympathy between them that means they are linked forever. So, for example, water used for baptising a boy would somehow retain the 'maleness', and if then used to baptise a female infant, the girl would grow a beard in later life. In the *Celtic Magazine*, the Revd Alexander MacGregor recorded a case of this at a Skye baptism a little before 1878, when the girl's grandmother snatched the bowl out of his hands and poured the water away, muttering aloud in Gaelic, 'Goodness forbid that my lassie should have a beard.' Similarly, as recorded by Martin Martin in 1695, a snake-bite could be cured by applying to the wound the adder's tongue steeped in water, or the severed head of the serpent. And MacCulloch told of a woman who wrapped together a cow bone, certain flowers and broken glass, and threw it into her sister-in-law's byre with the words, 'Another cow dead for you.' Sure enough a cow died; presumably the bone in the package was from the same herd, or perhaps it was enough that it was of a cow. Obviously the glass was the means of the magical killing, but what were the flowers for?

In the second kind of 'sympathy', all is needed is for two things to resemble each other. Up until at least 1911, as witnessed by MacCulloch, some Skye people were making clay images of their enemies and sticking pins into the vital parts. This Hebridean equivalent of the Voodoo doll was also mentioned in the Revd J.A. Macculloch's *The Misty Isle of Skye* (1905) – Lord Macdonald's factor, Mackinnon of Corrie, had found an image of himself in a barn near his house, deposited there by a crofter with a grievance. In his 1904 book *Scottish Reminiscences*, Sir Archibald Geikie tells how the geologist John Macculloch (1773-1835) stayed as an honoured guest with Mackinnon of Corriehatachan, near Broadford, and then published what Mackinnon thought were derogatory remarks.

A protective rowan tree marking the site of a cleared township near Drinan, Strath.

On his next visit to Glasgow the chief took a portrait of Macculloch and had it copied onto a set of chamber pots, which he distributed to friends around Skye. Thus every time nature called, John Macculloch's face received the insult.

WITCHCRAFT

Was there ever an island that harboured so many witches as the Isle of Skye?

Alasdair Alpin MacGregor, *Over the Sea to Skye*

Unlike many other parts of Scotland, Skye saw no trials that condemned people to death during the period that witchcraft was a capital crime (1563-1735). There are, however, endless tales of local witches, and many of them are given in this book. Some – such as those about transforming into cats or hares, sinking ships through spells, or zipping off to distant parts on a stalk of grass – are found all over the country and belong to the folkloric tradition of 'spooky tales told at ceilidhs'. There are, however, several records that show many islanders genuinely believed some of their neighbours were witches. Whether or not their magical powers were real or not is a moot point – the important thing is that people believed the magic was authentic, and acted accordingly. Campbell's *Witchcraft and Second Sight in the Highlands and Islands of Scotland* (1902) gives two real-life examples from the nineteenth century. A party of women were preparing cloth in an old woman's house when one went into the barn and found many herrings hanging from the roof. The old woman was accused of obtaining them by witchcraft, and was angry and ashamed when she was exposed. And somewhere in Trotternish a bull was put on the top of a suspected witch's house 'to bring back the stolen mill'. One wishes there was more detail of this intriguing-sounding case. How was the mill stolen? And how do you get a bull onto the roof?

In 1773 the Revd Donald McQueen told Dr Johnson that when he first took up his post as a minister in the north of Skye, women were frequently accused of stealing milk from cows by means of witchcraft. It is not clear from the report whether these accusations were informal jibes shouted out in a quarrel, or whether they were formally brought before the Kirk Session. However, the Revd Macculloch stated that cases of witchcraft were being heard at the Session as late as 1775. Macculloch, writing in 1905, also mentioned that he personally knew two witches (see PORTREE). One was of the 'white' variety, who largely confined her activities to telling fortunes and healing, but local people genuinely believed the other had darker powers.

Witches in Victorian and Edwardian Skye tended to 'overlook' things with the Evil Eye, which caused cattle to lose their milk and horses and humans to sicken and die. The cure involved taking water from a stream dividing two properties – a liminal boundary – and pouring it into a vessel containing gold or silver and seven cutting implements (to 'cut' the spell). A charm was pronounced and the vessel passed deasil round the flame of a candle. Special water, precious metal, iron, holy words, fire and a sunwise direction – this was a battery of apotropaic actions. If the bewitched patient was human, the water was drunk; if a cow, it was thrown over the animal's back and placed in its mouth, accompanied by the words 'In the Name of Jesus Christ'. Through sympathetic magic any remaining water now contained the 'evil', so it was thrown out onto a stone. If it was not carefully disposed of, any human or animal who drank or passed over it would contract the disease.

THE FAIRIES

If you were seeking an entry to the Realm of Faery, Skye would be a good place to start. There are at least a hundred sites on the island with fairy place names or associations with fairy encounters, an astonishing number. Many fairy dwellings are prehistoric cairns, brochs and duns (see the Contexts section on Archaeology, below). Others are set in natural mounds, often identified by the name sidhean or sithean, the Sithe (pronounced 'shee') being the fairies themselves. In *The Land of the Hills and the Glens* Seton Gordon reports that Skye fairies wore blue bonnets and clothes coloured crotal, a brown or yellow dye made from lichen. Like most Scottish fairies, the Skye variety are never the cute winged Tinkerbells of Victorian fantasy and modern children's stories. Instead they are of all different sizes, from the height of a garden gnome to the form of a grown human. They steal children and substitute for them sickly fairy changelings; they dance and feast in halls where time proceeds at a fraction of the pace in the outside world, and where abducted humans can labour as slaves for decades; they harvest crops but expect payment, often in an inconvenient form; they proffer home-made buttermilk and food but get angry if it is refused, often handing out sickness and death in retribution; they can be helpful, or mischievous, or cruel and vicious; and they can have sexual relations with humans, although the union is usually between a fairy woman and a mortal man, not the other way round (see, for example, DUNVEGAN CASTLE and MACLEOD'S MAIDENS).

In 1958 Mona Smith, the Skye-born wife of an Edinburgh minister, sent a letter to the great folklorist Katherine Briggs. In it she described an episode from the 1830s, when her father, his sister and another little boy were taken by an elderly friend of their grandmother to see something special. It was an autumn evening, and in the gloaming they went to the side of the burn – 'And there on the hillside, all dressed in green, were the fairies dancing in a ring round a fire.' Smith was told the story many times by both her father and her aunt, and in 1956 she met the third witness, now an old man, who still had a vividly clear memory of that enchanted moment. The old woman was credited with second-sight, and she and all the children had been holding hands; there are many cases where second-sight has been recorded as being temporarily transferred from the seer by deliberate physical contact, so perhaps that is what happened here. The episode is in Briggs' 1961 article 'Some Late Accounts of the Fairies'.

SECOND-SIGHT

Virtually everyone who has written about Skye has commented on the faculty claimed by some inhabitants of seeing visions or receiving portents of future or distant events. In *Highland Superstitions* Alexander Macgregor summarised the typical subjects of these visions: 'funerals, shrouds, the appearance of friends who were at the time in distant countries, the arrival of strangers, falls from horses, the upsetting of vehicles, bridal ceremonies, funeral processions, corpses, swamping of boats, drowning at sea, dropping suddenly dead, and numberless other subjects.' Seventeenth- and eighteenth-century writers tended to believe in second-sight, while Victorian commentators were often scathingly dismissive, citing coincidence, credulity and imposture as explanations. But as Alexander Smith noted in *A Summer in Skye* (1895), you had to take care with expressing such doubts: 'These stories are devoutly believed in Skye, and it is almost as perilous to doubt the existence of a Skyeman's ghost as to doubt the existence of a Skyeman's ancestor.'

One thing that many agree on is that the second-sight facility – if it exists and if so whatever it might actually be – decreases with distance from Skye. A classic example of this is in a very strange book, *Ghost Land, or, Researches into the Mysteries of Occultism* by Emma Hardinge Britten, published in 1876. Britten was a noted Spiritualist and occultist and a founding member of the Theosophical Society. The book claims to be the reminiscences of an anonymous European occult adept, which Britten translated and edited. It is equally possible that she wrote some or all of it herself. In one episode an occult expert had gathered together psychics from a number of northern lands, with a view to conducting experiments in parapsychology. Among the group was a seer from Skye: 'Panoramic representations of future events, with all the vivid imagery of well-defined persons and circumstances, would be presented to this man's waking vision, like a picture daguerreotyped on the atmosphere.' Unfortunately, the removal of the man from his native soil had suspended his ability, and he could not 'perform' – except in one case, when he saw himself drowning in a shipwreck. For this reason he refused to return home, and eventually took up work as a gardener, far from the sea. He was subsequently convicted of theft and sentenced to be transported to Australia; the convict ship sank in a gale, and he perished.

MYTHOLOGY

Long before King Arthur and his Knights, Ireland had a fully-developed mythological cycle of heroism, betrayal and magic, the tales of Fingal and his warrior-band the Fingalians. When the Gaelic people known as the Scots moved from Ireland to the north-western edge of Britain, they brought with them the oral tradition of the Fingalian mythos. Soon skilled storytellers were anchoring the Irish tales in the local geography of what became known as Scotland, and so place names related to Fingal can be found all over Skye. Examples include KYLERHEA, KENSALEYRE, PORTREE and many other sites.

Often the Fingalians are characterised as giants. One of the typical tales told of them is that, like Arthur and other hero-giants, they lie sleeping in the earth, waiting to return when they are most needed. A blacksmith found the locked door that kept them secure and forged a key to match the lock. Within, the giants slumbered, until he picked up an enormous whistle and gave two blasts. On the first the Fingalians shook from head to toe, and on the second they started to wake up. But so terrifying were the behemoths that the smith could not stand to summon them with the third call, so he ran from the chamber, locked the door behind him and threw the key into the loch. So, somewhere on Skye, Fingal and his warriors sleep still, and somewhere at the bottom of a sea-loch is the key that can release them. This version of the tale is given in the Revd J. MacDougall's *Waifs and Strays of Celtic Tradition* from 1891. Another mythological Irish culture hero, Cu Chulainn, turns up at DUN SCAICH.

SAINTS AND CHRISTIANITY

There are dozens of legends about saints and other holy men, and their interactions with the fairies, water-horses and demons that swarmed around Skye. Christianity seems to have reached Skye in the late seventh century, although the documentary sources for the early missionaries are fragmentary and contradictory at best, so it is difficult to be certain of anything. The best-known saint associated with the island is Columba. There are two reasons for Columba's fame: a) he was clearly an effective leader whose spiritual and temporal power enabled him to found the famous abbey on the isle of Iona and inspire several generations of monks to evangelise the wild lands of the north and west of Scotland; and b) he had a great marketing campaign. About a century after Columba died, Adomnan, third Abbot of Iona, produced his *Life of St Columba*. It is a superb book which set the benchmark for later hagiographies (the biographies of saints). Adomnan's work can be mined on several different levels, but its main value for a guide to mysterious Skye is that it is a great slab of Dark Ages magic, replete with wizardry, psychic powers, demonology, curses and much else. The *Life* gives two occasions when Columba visited Skye (although they may be two episodes from the same visit). An example of Columba's powers of prophecy – or second-sight – is given in the section on SKEABOST. The second episode is entitled 'How a wild boar was destroyed through his prayers':

> On one occasion when the blessed man was staying some days in the Scian island [Skye], he left the brethren and went alone a little farther than usual to pray; and having entered a dense forest he met a huge wild boar that happened to be pursued by hounds. As soon as the saint saw him at some distance, he stood looking intently at him. Then raising his holy hand and invoking the name of God in fervent prayer, he said to it, 'Thou shalt proceed no further in this direction: perish in the spot which thou hast now reached.' At the sound of these words of the saint in the woods, the terrible brute was not only unable to proceed farther, but by the efficacy of his word immediately fell dead before his face.

Boar-slaying by voice-command aside, Adomnan does not state why Columba came to Skye, and there is no mention in the *Life* of any church being established here. Nevertheless,

A sign promoting the sanctity of the Sabbath at Inverarish, Raasay.

there is a persistent tradition in the north of the island that the great man founded several religious sites, including EILEAN CHALUIM CHILLE, SKEABOST and FLADAIGH CHUAIN. None of these foundations can be confirmed by any evidence we have available. Certainly the number of sites supposedly founded by the saint around Scotland is greater than even a man like Columba could have achieved. One possibility is that the missionary active on Skye may have been the later St Colm, whose name was understandably often confused with, and eclipsed by, that of his more illustrious predecessor.

South Skye seems to have been evangelised by the eighth-century St Maelrubha, who was based at Applecross on the mainland and whose major dedication is at the holy well in BREAKISH. The other principal saint associated with the island is Chaon/ Comgan. Through the efforts of these men, and other missionaries whose names are now lost, Skye was probably completely Christian by the end of the eighth century, at least nominally. At this point the pagan Vikings turned up, which may have put a dampener on further Christian expansion. In 995 the Norwegian king, Olaf Tryggvasson, forced his subjects, including the Norse settlers on Skye, to accept Christianity, although it is likely many remained at least semi-pagan for generations.

Although Catholicism was outlawed at the Reformation of 1560, many Catholic practices – such as visiting the holy well at LOCH SHEANTA – continued for generations. In 1843 the Presbyterian, Established Church of Scotland was rent by a dispute over doctrine and patronage. The resulting Disruption created, after some further schisms, unions, reconciliations and splits, two additional congregations, the Free Church of Scotland (known colloquially as 'The Wee Frees') and the Free Presbyterian Church of Scotland (inevitably dubbed 'The Wee Wee Frees'). Both these denominations, noted for their austerity, have many adherents on Skye, and have strong views on topics such as the profanation of the Sabbath. The official website for the Free Presbyterian Church of Scotland states that one of their core beliefs is, 'Everyone is guilty of sin and deserves to be punished in Hell for ever,' although salvation is possible through accepting Jesus Christ.

THE PHYSICAL SETTING AND GETTING AROUND

Long chains of high inland cliffs, awesome summits, sculpted corries, hexagonal basalt columns and pavements, table-top mountains, spectacular coastal arches and rock stacks – all these and more make Skye one of the most scenically stunning places in Britain. Spreading out from a mountainous core, large peninsulas such as Trotternish and Sleat are separated by deeply indented fjord-like sea-lochs which typically forge mighty glens between the hills. Roads are limited and distances longer than they seem on the map, largely because of hills, bends and loch-skirting detours. Many roads are single-track and require care and patience when negotiating passing places with oncoming traffic. Outside the Armadale-Broadford-Portree corridor, public transport is limited and frequently non-existent, so if you are not bringing a car, plan accordingly. By its very nature much of Skye is not wheelchair-friendly; the degree of access to the various attractions is given in the respective sections.

> The cold, cheerless rocks, the treeless desolation, the perpetual tendency of the clouds to rest, as if it was their home, on the tops of the hills, the great corries into which the weather has hollowed one side of most of the mountains, the utter want of natural verdure, the grey, benty colour of the always drenched pasture, the absence of villages and of all human appearance, these things mark Skye as the asylum of dreariness.
>
> Lord Cockburn, *Circuit Journeys* (1888)

On a good day Skye can feel like the best place on earth; on a bad day, as his lordship clearly thought, it seems like the worst. Expect rain any day, any season. Bogs and mud are very much the order of the day once you leave the road, the coast is often slippery and windswept, the moors are lonely and frequently mist-bound, and the summits and precipices of the Cuillins kill people regularly. For all these reasons, good kit and appropriate outdoors behaviour is essential. Many sites are not easy to find, so I have given Ordnance Survey grid references. Skye, Raasay and Lochalsh are covered by the 1:25000 OS Explorer Maps 407 to 413; don't go walking without them.

THE CONTEXT – ARCHAEOLOGY

Not only are archaeological sites of interest in themselves, covering as they do everything from prehistoric religion and burial practices to defence, they also have a significant role in folklore. Many cairns, brochs and duns are supposedly fairy dwellings, while stone circles were often associated with the Fingalian giants. A story repeated by Donald Mackenzie in *Footprints of Early Man* (1909) tells of a Skye sorceress who used her wand to transform a standing stone into a warrior, and then back to stone again. The spirit of the long-dead warrior was held in the stone, waiting for release by someone with the correct magical skill. The Highland Folk Museum in Newtonmore, south of Inverness, has a hollow bronze prehistoric axe head from Skye that had been used as a cup for drinking whisky. Almost certainly some kind of 'luck' must have been associated with supping from this unusual vessel.

There are relatively few Neolithic or Bronze Age standing stones or stone circles on Skye, the best probably being at BORVE and KENSALEYRE. These ritual places date from around 3000 to 1000 BC. In terms of funerary sites, there are several large Neolithic chambered cairns, with RUBHA AN DÙNAIN the finest to visit – and crawl into, if you want to visit the chamber where the dead were deposited. Most of the smaller round burial mounds and cairns are probably Bronze Age, although few have been properly excavated.

Skye's richest prehistoric harvest comes in the Iron Age, which began around 750 BC and continued until the first centuries AD. The most prominent monuments are the brochs, tall fortified dwellings with a gallery running between the outer and inner walls, the whole resembling modern cooling towers in shape. There are more than thirty in the area, with the best-preserved at GLEANN BEAG by Glenelg. Duns were also fortified structures but lacked the internal passages of the broch. Some duns were built on top of earlier forts – larger, more open spaces defended by a boundary wall. Confusingly, many brochs are given the place name 'Dun'. The usage adopted here is that 'Dun' with an initial capital D is a place name, while 'dun' with a lower-case d refers to the monument type.

The strangest Iron Age monuments are the Souterrains or 'earth-houses', underground passages probably used for storage of food, although this is disputed, with some people suggesting a ritual purpose. There are many in the area, the easiest to visit being at KILVAXTER and CLACHAN on Raasay. Souterrains are tremendously atmospheric (and dark and dirty). Even more potent, but not open to the public, is the ritual site of HIGH PASTURE CAVE.

The Romans never touched Skye, so the Iron Age moved straight into the Pictish period, which roughly starts in the fifth or seventh century AD. Skye was part of the kingdom of the Northern Picts, but the small number of carved Pictish stones that have been found, combined with the distance from the Pictish powerbase in northern and north-eastern Scotland, suggests Skye was very much on the periphery.

The best book on the subject is Ian Armit's *The Archaeology of Skye and the Western Isles*. Also highly recommended is the Canmore website of the Royal Commission on the Ancient and Historical Monuments in Scotland, www.rcahms.gov.uk. Most of the otherwise unattributed archaeological information in this book has been taken from this authoritative source. Something more freewheeling can be found at www.themodernantiquarian.com, the splendid user-generated site inspired by Julian Cope's book *The Modern Antiquarian*.

Dun Borrafiach, Waternish – a typical Skye broch, now much reduced.

THE CONTEXT – A BRIEF HISTORY

THE DARK AGES AND THE VIKINGS

The early history of Skye is like the Cuillin on a rainy day: you know it's there, but it is only visible in brief glimpses. Generally, Skye has been the possession, victim or cat's-paw of various competing power blocs based elsewhere. From the 790s onwards the island was battered by raids from the new power in the West, the Vikings. Soon afterwards the Norse took entire possession of Skye, presumably driving out the native Pictish elite. By the twelfth century the entire western seaboard was a Norwegian sub-kingdom, much fought over by the regional players – Ireland, Norway and Scotland (by which is meant the mainland, and more usually the Lowlands). The majority of place names on Skye – particularly on the coastal and fertile areas suited for settlement – are Norse. The native population was not wiped out, however. After 450 years of domination, Norse power was annihilated in 1263 at the Battle of Largs in Ayrshire. With the Scandinavians expelled, Gaelic made a strong comeback on Skye.

THE LORDSHIP OF THE ISLES

Into this power vacuum emerged the Lordship of the Isles, a maritime kingdom in all but name, encompassing all the Hebrides and beyond. The Lords of the Isles, and their neighbouring clans, both allies and enemies, were largely of mixed Gaelic and Norse descent, with strong cultural links to Ireland. Nominally, the Kings of Scotland owned the Hebrides, having wrested them from Norway. So the Lords of the Isles owed allegiance to their feudal superiors in the Lowlands, at least in theory. By and large, however, the Hebridean leaders were hostile to Scotland – even allying with England on occasion – and centuries of conflict followed. Eventually, the balance of power shifted and the Scottish crown extinguished the Lordship in 1493, although rebellions and failed attempts at maintaining political autonomy continued for another half century.

THE CLANS

The Lords of the Isles were usually MacDonalds, although the actual Lordship was a shifting miasma of clan alliances and enmities. From the thirteenth century onwards, the political structure of the clans had been established as a military aristocracy. Labouring peasants were bound to the elite members of the clan through ties of kinship, while the same ties required the leaders to protect their people. Martial aristocracies tend to be violent and aggressive, and when the Hebridean clans were not fighting the Scots, they turned on their neighbours, usually in disputes over territory (and the wealth that went with it, such as cattle, crops or fishing). The centuries up until about 1600 are clogged with endless tales of butchery, rape, church-burnings and torture.

  The principal clans associated with Skye are the MacLeods and MacDonalds, locked for centuries in a perpetual dance of alliance and treachery (as Alexander Smith phrased it in *A Summer in Skye*, 'putting wedding rings on each other's fingers, and dirks into each other's hearts'). Their exact territories changed with the winds of war, although Sleat was usually a MacDonald possession while the MacLeods held Duirinish and Waternish. Trotternish swung between the two. Each clan built strongholds to stamp their authority on the political scene, and today these castles – especially DUNVEGAN (MacLeod) and DUNTULM, ARMADALE and DUN SCAICH

(MacDonald) – are some of the most interesting sites on Skye. The best book on the subject is *The Mediaeval Castles of Skye and Lochalsh* by Roger Miket and David Roberts. A smaller clan, the MacKinnons, occupied Strath, while a separate sept of the MacLeods held Raasay.

The eventual cowing of the rebellious clans brought the chiefs into the political and economic mainstream of Scotland, with the result that the ties of kinship with their people became loosened, to be replaced by relationships more commercial in nature. Already, by the seventeenth century clan leaders were on their way to being transformed from chiefs to landlords, although the wholesale exploitation and abuse of their tenants did not commence until the clan system was suppressed after the Jacobite rebellion of 1745.

THE JACOBITES AND BONNIE PRINCE CHARLIE

In a curious reversal, once the Skye clans were overcome by the Scottish Stuart kings – principally James IV and V – they demonstrated intense loyalty to the House of Stuart. During the Civil Wars of the seventeenth century, they turned out in force to fight for Charles I and then Charles II. In 1688, the Catholic Stuart, King James VII, was ousted and replaced with the Protestant William of Orange, and for three generations Jacobite forces attempted to regain the British throne for the Stuarts (the term Jacobite comes from Jacobus, the Latin for James). The clans fought for James VII at the Battle of Killiecrankie in Perthshire (1689) and for his son James Edward Stuart at the Battle of Sherrifmuir near Stirling (1715). In both cases the rebellion was unsuccessful, although the island chiefs continued to intrigue through the 1720s and 1730s. One of the casualties of these plots was Lady Grange, kidnapped and imprisoned for fifteen years with the connivance of her own husband and the MacLeod and MacDonald chiefs (see TRUMPAN).

By the time James VII's grandson, Charles Edward Stuart – usually more romantically referred to as Bonnie Prince Charlie – turned up in 1745, it would have seemed a foregone conclusion that the MacDonald and MacLeods would join the fray. Indeed the prince was counting on their extensive forces to help him carry the day against the Hanoverian army. But it was not to be. The chiefs sent their regrets, but they could not participate in the uprising.

What had brought about this abrupt change of heart? One word: blackmail. A few years previously MacLeod of Dunvegan and MacDonald of Sleat had arranged to sell hundreds of their own inconveniently abundant tenants as virtual slaves. Men, women and children were kidnapped from Skye and forced onto a ship bound for the West Indies. When the vessel put into an Irish port the story got out and the enslaved peasants were liberated. MacLeod and MacDonald were never prosecuted, but their cruelty to their own tenants – the very people they were sworn to protect – had dealt the Government a powerful hand. If the chiefs came 'out' for the Jacobites, their involvement in the scandal would be made public. No chief could have withstood such a humiliation, and so they stayed at home when Bonnie Prince Charlie came calling. As it was, a number of clansmen independently joined the Jacobite cause, and the MacLeods of Raasay, not having been involved in the slavery scandal, also gave their support (and suffered for it).

Despite initial military successes, the Jacobite dream ended in disaster at the Battle of Culloden in April 1746. The prince went on the run, and even though he had a huge bounty on his head, he was never betrayed by chief or clansman. As part of his extensive wanderings as a fugitive, Charles was brought to Skye disguised as the maid of Flora MacDonald, a kinswoman of the MacDonald chiefs. During his few perilous days on the island he moved from one 'safe house' to another, landing on the west coast of Trotternish, staying briefly on Raasay, and finally getting to Elgol, from where he departed to Mallaig. He was eventually picked up from the mainland by a French ship in September 1746, and never saw Britain again.

The Hanoverian kings may have been unattractive, but arguably having Charles as monarch (and a vassal of France) would have been even worse. But whatever his failings as a leader, and his anti-modern, almost medieval view of the role of kings, as a fugitive Charles displayed fortitude, courage and grace. Out of his three months as a hunted man, he spent only six days on Skye, but this brief episode became the stuff of legend. His shoes, possessions, gifts and a lock of his hair were preserved as relics. His very presence had a powerful psychic impact on pregnant women (see BALMEANACH). Flora MacDonald became a Jacobite heroine whose virtues could be heartily saluted by the arch anti-Jacobite Dr Johnson. Her grave and memorial can be seen at KILMUIR. The entire episode, told and re-told again and again, has contributed greatly to the notion of 'Romantic Scotland'.

THE CLEARANCES

Much less romantic is the grim recounting of the breakdown in the relationship between the chiefs and their tenants from the later eighteenth century onwards. Money became the presiding motive. Rents were raised again and again, peasants were impoverished by the removal of their animals, and eventually many people were unable to survive and so emigrated. At which point, the chiefs breathed a huge sigh of relief, as they could now flood the empty lands with profitable sheep. In some cases tenants were evicted with force and cruelty. In the 1880s a number of crofters fought back, resisting the detested estate factors and imported police forces alike. Some ended up in jail, to become heroes on their release. The callous and arbitrary power exerted by some chiefs and their factors shocked the Victorian public, and an official Crofters Commission addressed some of the main issues. A monument to the crofters' resistance is at COLBOST. The legacy of the Clearances is to be seen everywhere in the form of abandoned villages. In many cases the sites can only be identified by the presence of rowan trees which now have outlived the buildings they were intended to protect.

JOHNSON & BOSWELL

In 1773 Dr Samuel Johnson, probably the most famous English intellectual of his day, accompanied by James Boswell, his gadabout fan-boy and amanuensis, toured the Western Highlands and Islands. At the time, the Hebrides were as exotic and little-known to the inhabitants of London as the islands being visited by Captain Cook on his pioneering voyages in the Pacific. For the elderly, corpulent Johnson, travelling through a land where the majority of the uneducated people spoke only Gaelic, in weather conditions bordering on the atrocious, and where few members of his class had ventured before, must have been a daunting challenge. Yet the duo were treated hospitably wherever they went, and in truth so famous was Johnson that the journey was the eighteenth-century equivalent of a modern celebrity's television travel documentary. Johnson was the original Grumpy Old Man, a learned scholar and moralist with an acerbic wit and an armoury of opinionated arguments designed to pinion anyone who verbally wrestled with him. Boswell assiduously wrote down Johnson's conversation and behaviour, including his occasional *faux pas* and boorishness. In 1775 Johnson published *A Journey to the Western Isles of Scotland*, which contains such observations that second-sight – which Johnson thought was genuine – was believed in by everyone except the clergy, and that the ordinary people of Skye had a horror of eating eels or pork. The eel taboo may have arisen because the fish were believed to be generated from horse-hairs. Boswell's racier and more gossipy *The Journal of a Tour to the Hebrides with Samuel Johnson, LL. D.* came out a decade later. Together they opened up Skye to a hitherto unsuspecting readership, and unwittingly set off the first tourist boom.

WHISTLERS BEWARE!

A party of ladies and gentlemen lately spending their holidays in Skye one evening went out to sea for a sail. It got so calm that the boat made no progress. One of the gentlemen, in fun, said that they should whistle for wind. An old fisherman on board, with the greatest earnestness of gesture, interposed, saying that it was not 'canny' to whistle for wind. He had before then experienced the worst consequence of such. Laughing him to scorn, they whistled away, but ere long a tremendous hurricane of wind came on, so that it was with difficulty they reached the shore. The man having got ashore with his life, was more convinced than ever that whistling for wind is a dangerous thing.

Cathal Kerr, 'Fishermen and Superstition' *Celtic Magazine* (1888)

DEATH BY SCONES

The following appears in a delightfully odd book from 1909 by Ernest Suffling, *Epitaphia: Being a Collection of 1300 British Epitaphs Grave and Gay, Historical and Curious*:

Donald Jones. Isle of Skye.
Here lies the bones
O' Tonald Jones,
The wale o' men
For eating scones.
Eating scones
And drinking yill,
Till his last moans
He took his fill.

I have been unable to locate this gravestone, and doubt that it actually exists. There's a cream tea on offer if you know different.

SOURCES AND FINDING OUT MORE

Anyone writing about Skye soon realises they are standing on the shoulders of giants. As well as the indispensable Johnson and Boswell, there is a plethora of excellent works on the island, including the following, all of which are quoted extensively in the text:

- Martin Martin, *A Description of the Western Islands of Scotland Circa 1695* (1703). Martin was a Skye man, and although a tad credulous at times, he was the first to write extensively about Skye.
- Theophilus Insulanus, *Treatises on the Second-sight* (1763). This was the pen-name of the Revd D. McLeod of Glendale ('Theophilus' was a learned or academic individual mentioned in the New Testament; '*Insulanus*' is Latin for 'of the island'). It republished several existing pieces on second-sight, and was largely arranged in a series of 'case studies'.
- C.F. Gordon-Cumming, *In the Hebrides* (1883). Constance Fredereka Gordon-Cumming was a wealthy and intrepid adventurer and prolific author who cruised the Hebrides in a yacht and managed to pick up a boatload of stories.
- Alexander Smith, *A Summer in Skye* (1885). A sheer delight to read even today, this lyrical work is bathed in Victorian optimism and filled with folklore.
- Revd J.A. Macculloch, *The Misty Isle of Skye* (1905). An insightful work from a Portree minister, replete with tales of the supernatural.
- Mary Julia MacCulloch, 'Folk-Lore of the Isle of Skye' (1922-3). Her four long articles in the journal *Folklore* reflected the large number of tales she had collected in the years before 1911.
- Alasdair Alpin MacGregor, *Over the Sea to Skye* (1926). This, and Seton Gordon's *The Charm of Skye* (1929), are probably my favourite books on Skye. Both authors were leviathans in their field.
- Derek Cooper, *Skye* (1970). A combination of a gazetteer and an anthology of previous writings on the island; also very funny.
- Jim Crumley, *The Heart of Skye* (1994). The best attempt to capture the emotional and intellectual impact of the Skye landscape.

The Skye folklore book par excellence, however, is *Skye: The Island and its Legends* by Otta F. Swire of ORBOST. 'Classic' is an over-used and much-abused word, but this is a genuine classic. First published in 1952, the 2006 edition comes with an erudite and helpful introduction by the Gaelic scholar Ronald Black.

All these works, along with the other books, specialist publications, newspapers and websites referred to in the text, are listed in the Bibliography.

ONE

THE SOUTH: STRATH

KYLEAKIN – KYLERHEA – BROADFORD – ELGOL – SOAY

Superstitions of every kind – witches, the evil-eye, omens, mermaids, fairies, kelpies, sacred waters, trees and stones – were at the very core of the Skye man's life.

Gavin Maxwell, *Raven Seek Thy Brother*

Much of Strath was owned by Clan MacKinnon, whose forces, never a challenge to the duopoly of the MacLeods and MacDonalds, nevertheless sometimes formed a buffer zone between the two great power blocs. Where alliances were made, they tended to be with the MacDonalds. The MacKinnons often played one side off against the other, hence their reputation for duplicity, which from a survival point of view looks like simple good sense.

KYLEAKIN

Once the port for the ferry from Kyle of Lochalsh on the opposite side of the narrow Kyle Akin strait, the village is now bypassed and overshadowed by the Skye Bridge, and in terms of atmosphere is all the better for it. There are displays on local history, wildlife and geology at the Bright Water Visitor Centre on the pier, which is also where tours for EILEAN BÀN are booked. Typically the centre, which is free and has good disabled access, is open 10 a.m. to 4 p.m. Monday to Saturday from Easter to the end of September. A footbridge from the main car park leads to South Obbe on the opposite side of the river, from whose road-end a path runs east to the shattered ruins of Caisteal Maol standing prominently on the headland (NG75802634). Here at this powerful strategic location dominating the narrows, once stood Dunakin, a fortress named after the Norwegian king Haakon (and hence Kyleakin is pronounced Kyle-AH-kin, not Kyle-EE-kin). The two stark fingers of stone are all that remain of a modest fifteenth-century tower house built by the MacKinnons when they moved here from DUN RINGILL near Kilmarie in the fifteenth century. The castle was abandoned in the seventeenth century. In 1951 a hoard of seventy sixteenth-century Scottish and English coins was found in a chink in the masonry.

Legend has it that around AD 900 an early MacKinnon chief married a Norwegian princess who has gone down in history under her nickname 'Saucy Mary'. There is nothing in the tradition that indicates how exactly her sauciness was expressed. It seems an unlikely name for a Norwegian; possibly it is a corruption of a difficult-to-pronounce

Scandinavian original, or a twisted version of a Gaelic alternative. I also suspect that if she had been called something less salacious her fame would not have survived. Mary allegedly operated a toll on shipping through the sound, running a heavy chain from the castle to the mainland. To describe this as unfeasible in engineering terms is to underplay the meaning of the term 'ludicrous'. In the nineteenth century, visitors were shown a pillar on the shore that allegedly bore the marks of the chain. Recently, claims have been made that the barrier was not an actual metal chain but a line of ships linked together; it is difficult to see how such a construction could be sustained in the face of the strait's strong currents and storms. Mary is supposedly the princess buried on BEINN NA CAILLICH near Broadford. There is no documentary or archaeological evidence for Mary's existence; folklore however claims otherwise.

In 1884 diggers at a peat moss near Kyleakin uncovered a prehistoric bronze cauldron; nearby at the same level, 7½ft (2.3m) below the surface, were several wooden kegs filled with what is termed 'bog butter'. A number of these barrels containing dairy produce have been found in mosses throughout Scotland. One of the Kyleakin examples is in the National Museum of Scotland in Edinburgh and has a capacity of about 6 gallons (28 litres); the wood has been carbon-dated to between AD 225 and AD 401. The items were deposited in a watery site, and may have been votive offerings, that is, things left for the gods. Bogs and marshes were often seen as liminal sites, with the water providing access to the underworld. The cauldron was a high-status object and would have been the equivalent of, say, sacrificing a Harley-Davidson motorbike. In 1857 a report in the *Transactions of the Society of Antiquaries of Scotland* described a double stone circle at 'Taynandruineach', apparently about 2 miles (3km) west of Kyleakin. No one else has ever found this circle, which may have been a mistake on the part of the author, D. Gregory.

Otta Swire describes the origin of the boulder Clach Chraigisgean, which is somewhere near Kyleakin. The giant Na Craigeain saw a witch stealing milk from a cow and threw the rock at her. Unfortunately, he overestimated his own strength and buried the cow as well. Presumably the skeletons of the woman and the animal, along with the crushed remains of the milk pail, are still beneath the boulder, awaiting their discovery by a future archaeologist. Two female giants, Grein of Skye and an associate from Raasay, fell out over the exact ingredients of a face lotion. During their catfight they threw several stones at each other, which now form the skerries and islands between Kyleakin and the mainland.

Another of Swire's stories takes place in the woods between Kyleakin and Broadford. Here a priest from PABAY was met by a group of the Daoine Sithe, the fairies, who asked him to pray for them so that they could once again become children of God and recover the souls they had lost when they fell from Heaven. (One of the traditions concerning the Little People is that they were once angels who were expelled from God's presence at the time of Lucifer's rebellion; the evil angels plunged into Hell and became demons but those whose sin was less merely fell to earth and became the fairies.) The priest however, refused to absolve them, saying 'as soon would my stick become a tree again as God forgive you.' The sound of the fairies' grief-stricken wailing followed him as he departed. Having completed his task elsewhere – the baptism of a new-born child – he then realised he had left his staff in the forest. He returned to the spot where he had

A sculpture of an otter at play, outside the Bright Water Visitor Centre, Kyleakin. In the background is the ruin of Caisteal Maol.

encountered the fairies – and found his wooden crook had become transformed into a great ash tree, taller than all its companions. Recognising that his unlikely prophecy had come true, he tried to find the fairies again, but instead only heard distant wailing. Thereafter he lived in the woods as a hermit, praying for the redemption of the Daoine Sithe, but never again meeting them. This is a curious tale, which seems to overlay a Christian veneer on a story whose core message is the power of fairies as nature spirits.

South of Kyleakin is Gleann na Bèiste (Glen of the Monster, NG748251), which leads into the sea-loch Loch na Bèiste (Loch of the Monster). The loch can be glimpsed from Caisteal Maol. In *Raven Seek Thy Brother*, Gavin Maxwell summarised what little was known about this evocatively-named place. In some accounts the monster was described as having a head covered with a mane, while other people apparently refused to give any description for fear of breaking the taboo associated with the creature. On one (undated) occasion two fishermen in a rowing boat claimed their boat was almost swamped by an animal about 20ft (6m) long. They said it had a mane on its neck and was as thick as a man's thigh. Getting to the area is not easy. You could try the pathless moorland south of Caisteal Maol, or else head west from Kyleakin for about 2 miles (3km) to a forestry track that leaves the A87 at NG734258. Walk south along this then turn left (east) at a junction. When the track runs out continue east along the firebreak associated with the power line. It is tough going in places.

Somewhere near Loch na Bèiste was the impromptu dwelling of Tom Leppard, the Leopard Man of Skye. For twenty years the ex-soldier lived alone in an abandoned and barely weather-proof bothy more than two hours' walk from Kyleakin. He would canoe across the strait to Kyle of Lochalsh to shop and pick up his pension. He was an easily recognisable figure because the *Guinness Book of Records* lists him as the world's most tattooed man, with 99.2 per cent of his body tattooed, mostly with a leopard-skin pattern. The tattoos helped him eke out a living from occasional appearances in the media, for which he also commissioned a set of custom-made fangs. Other than that, the ex-soldier simply decided he liked living a gentle existence alone in a place far from people.

The view from Caisteal Maol to Loch na Bèiste, supposedly home to some kind of monster.

Tom garnered some unwelcome publicity in 2001/2 when he was linked to German murderer Manuela Ruda, who, along with her husband Daniel, was convicted of slaughtering a man 'for Satan'. Manuela had become fascinated with Leppard's lifestyle while working at a hotel in Kyleakin and after returning to Germany kept up a correspondence with him. Leppard was horrified at the negative nature of her letters, and was appalled at her actions. Scurrilous press reports hinting that Leppard 'inspired' Ruda were well wide of the mark. She simply latched on to him because of his outsider status. In 2008, at the age of seventy-three, the Leopard Man finally admitted he could not face another Skye winter, and took a one-bedroom dwelling within sheltered housing in Broadford. For following his own unusual, solitary and peaceful path, unencumbered by social norms or the expectations of others – Tom Leppard, we salute you.

In *Raven Seek Thy Brother* Gavin Maxwell gave an example of precognition. Two men, talking in a shed on Kyleakin pier, heard a great crash as if two boats had collided. They rushed outside to find nothing amiss. A few days later an old fisherman had his boat at anchor in the sound. Being partially deaf he did not hear the MacBrayne steamer *Loch Ness* approach. Just before the impact, someone on the ship threw him a rope, to which he hung on for several minutes before being hauled up. In the meantime the steamer sliced the little launch in two, with a sound similar to that previously heard by the two men.

EILEAN BÀN

As it soars over the straits, part of the Skye Bridge comes to rest on this special place. The 'White Island' was once owned by Gavin Maxwell, celebrated otterphile author of the *Ring of Bright Water* trilogy and other works, and is now owned by the Eilean Bàn Trust. A wildlife hide is sometimes open, but access to most of the island and its Maxwell Museum can only be arranged through the Bright Water Visitor Centre on the pier at Kyleakin; telephone 01599 530040 or see www.eileanban.org to check exact details and book a tour (Easter to September). Note that there is very limited impromptu parking outside the gate giving on to the island from the bridge, and the speed of traffic makes stopping and turning hazardous; if you can, it is easier and safer to walk from Kyleakin onto the bridge. Wheelchair access to the island is reasonable but the wonderful nineteenth-century lighthouse cannot be reached with wheels, and some of the paths require help from an assistant.

Gavin Maxwell bought the former lighthouse cottages in 1963 – three years after *Ring of Bright Water* was published – although it was not until 1968 that he moved here, following the destruction by fire of his house south of GLENELG (for much more on Maxwell, see SANDAIG in Chapter Nine, Lochalsh). Maxwell lived in the converted cottages for the last eighteen months of his life. When he died in September 1969 – of cancer largely brought on by an incessant cigarette habit – he left behind Teko, the last remaining of his otters. Teko himself passed away shortly after Maxwell, and his grave is marked by a simple inscribed stone on the island.

The museum is Maxwell's 'long room', three cottages converted into one space, and is filled with mementos and possessions commemorating the famous – but difficult and some say dislikeable – author. His wonderful writing desk is carved with nine miniature human and eight beast heads, and there is a pair of harpoons from his days as an annihilator of basking sharks (see SOAY). A mysterious portrait painted by Maxwell of an unidentified androgynous individual divides visitor opinions – about half identify the sitter as female, the other half say definitely male. My belief is that it is a portrait of a European chess genius who sat for Maxwell while the two were lovers in the 1950s. Tomas (we do not know his surname) was said to have resembled the glamorous society beauty Clement Glock, who was noted for her blonde hair. This suggests Tomas was androgynous and blond, as is the person in the painting.

In *Raven Seek Thy Brother*, the third part of his otter trilogy, Maxwell described the apparent paranormal phenomena associated with Eilean Bàn. He spoke to a former lighthouse keeper who described how low-pitched muttering voices could be heard in argument from outside the cottages, sometimes associated with loud metallic clangs. The voices were heard solely in the small hours, and only then in the autumn and winter. Another keeper, a Gaelic-speaker who had lived there seven years, said the language of the voices was not Gaelic. A relief keeper who spent eighteen months on the island followed the advice of his predecessor: when he heard the voices for the first time he asked loudly, 'Who's there?' – and the sounds ceased and never returned. Early in 1966 Morag MacKinnon stayed in the house and heard the voices only once, about 8.15 on a Sunday morning. They were low-pitched, faded and increased in strength, and spoke in a language neither English nor Gaelic. In 1964 Maxwell engaged Richard Frere to bring the cottages up to a habitable state, but did not tell him about the voices. To complete the job effectively, Frere sometimes stayed on the

Above: The carved human and animal heads on Gavin Maxwell's writing desk, Eilean Bàn. (Photo: Ségolène Dupuy)

Left: Otter bench, Eilean Bàn. Close by is the memorial to Teko the otter. (Photo: Ségolène Dupuy)

Below: The Skye Bridge from its footprint on Eilean Bàn.

island alone. In January 1965 he was awakened at 3 a.m. by a metallic clang, followed by muttering voices moving along the north side of the house from west to east. It seemed to Frere the voices were those of an ancient raiding party, although he could hear no footsteps – just the incoherent voices and the occasional clang. That first time the phenomenon seemed to last about ten minutes. He heard it several times thereafter, but only up until March, after which nothing more occurred. In all the time he was there, Maxwell never encountered the voices.

In 1976 Frere published a memoir of this period, *Maxwell's Ghost* (the title referred to Frere's physical resemblance to Maxwell, and his being mistaken for his former employer after the author's death). At one point Frere, working on the conversion, was assisted – if that was the word – by Brewster, whom he describes as a runaway juvenile delinquent that Maxwell had taken under his wing. In the biography *Gavin Maxwell: A Life*, Douglas Botting more charitably characterises Brewster as a former assistant keen to put to good use skills recently learned on an outdoor adventure course; he also calls the youth Philip Alpin, so presumably 'Brewster' was a pseudonym. Maxwell had already suggested Brewster/Alpin was the focus of the poltergeist phenomena at SANDAIG, and on Eilean Bàn the young man heard the voices frequently – and they frightened him. As Frere put it, 'Brewster was terrified because he had come into range of the island's psychic wavelength, and his subconscious mind had been invaded.' Frere thought that Brewster's unsophisticated and wilful personality somehow made him more susceptible to the voices – the panic-stricken lad refused to be left alone at night with what Frere termed the 'captive echoes' of the 'timeless companions'. Eventually, Brewster left, much to Frere's relief, as in terms of the conversion work the young man had been more of a hindrance than a help. Interestingly, Frere describes how the voices were more prominent when he was bored or tired; work, an erotic fantasy or a gripping novel kept them at bay.

Frere gives a few other examples. Estate agent Bruno Dereham holidayed on Eilean Bàn when the island could only be visited by boat; it was very isolated. Alone of all his family, the ex-Army man picked up the voices, and became very frightened. And a practical-minded friend of Frere's, Gordon Mackintosh, saw the apparition of a man walking on the path to the 'Cathouse' (so called because one of Maxwell's companions once kept Scottish wildcats in it). Frere thought the sighting – which had a powerful impact on Mackintosh, because the figure simply vanished – was unconnected to the voices, partly because it was an apparition, and partly because it took place in June, outside the voices' usual time-range. Other strange occurrences are given by Botting: on two midnights in May 1969 Simon Maclean, a lighthouse man, saw a light moving outside the house and around the lighthouse and bay. Several people in Kyleakin saw a lamp burning in the window of the cottage even though the house was empty and locked. Maxwell heard footsteps and the opening and closing of doors in unoccupied rooms – his only experience of anything strange on the island. Botting also mentions 'ships that vanished into thin air', but gives no details.

Given that the voices were heard by numerous individuals – from lighthouse keepers to Frere, Brewster and Maxwell's guests – there is reason to suppose the phenomenon had objective reality. The seasonal and time-specific behaviour of the phenomenon suggests there was something in the natural environment that was producing sounds that were interpreted as human voices. Were the sounds coming from birds, or animals, or noises travelling from further afield across the waters?

The current live-in custodian has reported nothing. Perhaps the building of the Skye Bridge has dislocated whatever was present in the local environment and the voices murmur and plot no more. I also suggest that the non-voice phenomena – the lights, noises and apparitions – may have somehow been a psychic side-effect of the events on the island at the time. During his residence Maxwell – always a difficult character – was increasingly ill, and engaged in tempestuous rows with his usual companions and almost anyone who came to visit. Some of these visitors – such as the poet Kathleen Raine – were themselves strong personalities (see SANDAIG for proof of this); perhaps the volcanic emotions on display somehow manifested in external phenomena. Since Maxwell's death, nothing strange has been noticed.

KYLERHEA

Here, the closest point to the mainland, was once the principal crossing route for both humans and animals, and a bijou car ferry still operates in summer (a notice just east of Broadford, at the start of the 7-mile (11km) minor road to Kylerhea, tells you whether the ferry is actually running that particular day). In the old days, of course, no one bothered with this pantywaist ferry nonsense: the Fingalians, recalled from a hunting trip by a domestic emergency, simply crossed the strait by using their swords as poles. Sadly one of the band, Mac an Reaidhinn, drowned – even magical Celtic heroes have their off days – and thus gave his name to Kyle Rhea (pronounced Kyle-RAY).

A large but damaged cairn can be seen close to a building south of the ferry slipway (NG78692054). To the north is Sithean a' Choire Odhair (Fairy Hill of the Dun-coloured Dell, NG773239) and Beinn na Caillich (NG771229, the Mountain of the Old Woman – or Witch). The latter is the grave of the giantess Grein (or Grainne), wife of Fingal. According to Otta Swire, Grein was buried above an earthenware crock filled with gold and jewels donated by her husband's warriors. Just to confuse matters about where exactly the mythical giantess is buried, to the west is Beinne na Grèine, Grein's Mountain (NG752223).

At the summit of the road to Kylerhea is Bealach Udal (Pass of Odal, 915ft/279m above sea level). John Gregorson Campbell's *Witchcraft and Second Sight in the Highlands and Islands of Scotland* (1902) states that when the public road was built about 1840 the pass was haunted by the Biasd Bealach Odail, the Beast of Odal Pass:

> This thing, whatever it was, did not always appear in the same shape. Sometimes it bore the form of a man, sometimes of a man with only one leg; at other times it appeared like a greyhound or beast prowling about; and sometimes it was heard uttering frightful shrieks and outcries which made the workmen leave their bothies in horror. It was only during the night it was seen or heard. Travellers through the pass at night were often thrown down and hurt by it, and with difficulty made their way to a place of safety. It ceased when a man was found dead at the roadside, pierced with two wounds, one on his side and one on his leg, with a hand pressed on each wound. It was considered impossible these wounds could have been inflicted by human agency.

BREAKISH

This scattered township east of Broadford is mostly notable for the holy well of Tobar Asheig by the shore at its eastern end (NG68672426, with good access by road). The site is associated with St Maelrubha, an eighth-century missionary who apparently regularly travelled to this point from his monastery at Applecross on the mainland. 'Asheig' is derived from *aiseig*, the Gaelic noun for ferry. Maelrubha is one of several 'surfing saints' on the West Coast of Scotland – when no suitable boat was available, he would simply step on a stone and it would carry him over the sea to Skye. The legend of the well is that when Maelrubha was an old man he leant on a tree for support. The tree collapsed and water issued out. There was once a building over the spring but this has long vanished. A good restoration in the 1990s has left the well stone-lined and enclosed in a fence, with access by a gate. The spring is still flowing and the water can be easily sipped – there is even a separate enclosure for cattle to drink from.

Finds from the well included an early medieval ornamented bronze strap-end – possibly part of a book-binding – and a cross-marked stone was found nearby. One of the lintels over the water channel is carved with a small lozenge; this may be a piece of prehistoric rock art reused in the building of the well. Was this just a piece of good-quality stone chosen for simple practical purposes, or was the fact that it bore a pre-Christian carving of some significance for the people who constructed the well in the Dark Ages? We cannot know. Similarly, a Neolithic axe found in the well could have simply been left behind about 4,500 years ago, or it could have been deliberately deposited during the Christian era – prehistoric axe heads had been valued ever since Roman times, and were often regarded as talismans against bad luck or 'thunderstones', which gave protection against lightning-strike.

Above left: Tobar Asheig holy well, Breakish. The well feeds the cattle drinking trough in the background.

Above right: A carved prehistoric lozenge or diamond found on a reused stone in the holy well. Did it have any significance for the well's users in the Dark Ages?

Anonymous sailors found
off Skye after the sinking of
HMS *Curacoa* near Ireland,
Breakish cemetery.

The immediate environment bears several markers of the Maelrubha legend. On the other side of the river, below the aerodrome runway, is Creag an Leabhair or Hubhuir, 'the Rock of the Book', claimed to be the pulpit from which the saint preached the Christian message to the pagans. Maelrubha's church, now vanished, was at the centre of the modern cemetery immediately west of the well. Here too was a tree on which hung the holy man's bell, which would ring of its own accord to announce Sunday Mass. When the bell was removed to a later church in Strath it lost its self-ringing powers, and its former treehouse withered and died. The 27 August used to be celebrated locally as La Maolruidha, the feast-day of St Maelrubha.

The burial ground contains a number of stones in the standard format of war graves, some of them anonymous ('A Sailor of the Second World War – Known to God'). The details inscribed on the stones only hint at the associated tragedy. In 1942 the liner *Queen Mary*, acting as a troopship, was being escorted by the cruiser HMS *Curacoa* some 37 miles (60km) north of Ireland. While taking zigzagging paths to avoid U-boats, the *Queen Mary* hit the *Curacoa*, cutting the smaller vessel in two. All 338 hands were lost, many of the bodies being carried by the tides to the west coast of Scotland. There are more *Curacoa* graves in Portree, and at Arisaig and Morar on the mainland.

In *Over the Sea to Skye*, Alasdair Alpin MacGregor noted that 'Neil MacInnes of the Bow', a great archer of the eighteenth century, attributed his invulnerability in battle to a charm performed on him by a resident of Breakish. Before leaving Skye to join the British Army, Neil obtained this 'life charm' from a wise man named Patrick. Thereafter he was convinced he could not die in combat. The charmer was presumably the same man described by Gordon-Cumming as saving soldiers in the Napoleonic Wars:

> There was a blind man in Broadford who was able to put the charm upon them. On each in turn he laid his hands, and they went away looking straight before them. One man half turned his head and saw his own shoulder – an evil omen – and sure enough he lost that arm; but though the balls fell round the others as thick as peas, they were nowise hurt, but returned as living proofs of the blind man's power.

BROADFORD

The 'Capital of South Skye' has much of interest. A large tumulus beside the road north to the youth hostel at Corry is Liveras chambered cairn, a Neolithic burial mound which is the focus of many a strange story (NG64162378). Otta Swire says that fairy music was heard coming from the mound and the little people would dance nearby. In the 1841 edition of *The Gentleman's Magazine*, a gentleman named as J.W.B. related how in the autumn of 1839, on a two-and-a-half day visit to Skye, he engaged a number of local men to dig into the mound: time was short and the weather awful, and nothing was found. Mr B. – actually John William Burgon, the Dean of Chichester – was encouraged in his precipitate actions by meeting a poor girl who, a few years previously while aged nine, was sitting on the mound when part of it gave way, revealing a hollow chamber. Some local men subsequently conducted a haphazard search. It is this first exploration that is the subject of much legend-mongering. The men were said to have entered armed with pistols, and to have abandoned the search for fear of ghosts – possibly when they found a stone-lined cist (grave) containing human bones. A local man told Burgon the cairn was a prison which once held nine Norwegians. So that makes fairies, ghosts and Vikings – a fine haul of folklore. Finds included an urn and two stone wrist-guards, while Burgon says the girl saw an amber bead. These days the mound remains impressive, although in summer any features are obscured by the trees and vegetation.

The dean was also told about a subterranean passage that had been discovered during ploughing in a field called Goirtean nan H-uamha (Field of the Cave) a few years earlier. Explorers crawled along it for about 100ft (30m) in the direction of the sea, arriving at a circular chamber which contained sheep bones, cinders and a quern. This was clearly an Iron Age souterrain, but unfortunately all knowledge of this particular structure has been lost, even its very location. On his short visit, Burgon also learned that the area south-west of Broadford and west of the Broadford River, known as Goir a' Bhlair (Field of Battle), was traditionally the site of a conflict involving either the Vikings or the Mackinnons. The presence of two Neolithic chambered cairns in this area may have amplified the tradition, prehistoric burial mounds often being mistakenly regarded as the sepulchres of the recent noble dead. The pair of cairns is in a clearing in

The interior of Liveras Chambered Cairn in Broadford, as seen by John William Burgon in 1839. The fairies, ghosts and Vikings are not shown.

a forestry plantation between Broadford and Old Corry, accessible via the power-line fire-break (NG639237), but they are in poor condition. Another chambered cairn stands at Achadh A'Chuirn, in Waterloo at the east end of Broadford (NG66422343). The grass-covered mound is on private land but can be seen at a distance from the road.

In *The Ghost Book*, Alasdair Alpin MacGregor tells of the experience of an Edinburgh doctor holidaying in Broadford sometime around the year 1950. Walking along the beach at twilight he saw a glow in the bay, which he initially took to be a distress flare from a boat, until it moved steadily and speedily towards the shore. When it reached the water's edge the light briefly vanished, to be replaced by an apparition of a cloaked woman carrying a child. She hurried across the sand in front of him and then vanished. Describing his adventure back at the inn, he was told by the host that a shipwreck several years ago had cast ashore the bodies of a woman and child at the very spot. I have searched the records of shipwrecks in the area, and have been unable to find a candidate for this supposed calamity.

Norman Adams' *Haunted Scotland* mentions that the Broadford Hotel on the main road has been the site of minor poltergeist activity consisting of the appearance of a shadowy figure and a strange mist that is apparently an old housekeeper searching for her favourite chair. The hotel is the original home of Drambuie liqueur; the tale that the secret recipe was gifted to his host Captain John MacKinnon by a grateful Bonnie Prince Charlie in 1746 is a lie of the most overt kind, being an advertising gimmick designed to boost sales.

The Skye Serpentarium at The Old Mill (open Monday to Saturday 10 a.m. to 5 p.m., same hours for Sunday in July and August, admission charge, good disabled access) is a wonderful visit on a rainy day, being (a) dry and hot and (b) full of very cool reptiles, from iguanas and tortoises to lizards and boa constrictors, as well as various tropical amphibians such as tree frogs. Snake-handling sessions are regularly held. Star animals include the African giant land snails, the bearded dragons, a monitor lizard, and a corn snake that is amenalistic (the reptile equivalent of albino). All the animals were rescued, bred by the Serpentarium team, or seized by Customs & Excise as illegal imports. There are cast-off snake skins for sale, displays on the appalling illegal trade in reptiles, and a replica of a dinosaur egg.

In his 1881 book *Notes on the Folk-Lore of the North-East of Scotland*, Walter Gregor gave the story of a wise woman who lived near Broadford about 1843. A man from the mainland near Strome Ferry was dangerously ill, and so his two brothers took him to Skye to be cured. At Broadford he was lifted into a cart and driven to the woman's house. Just before the party arrived the woman came to meet them, addressing the patient by name, even though he and his family were complete strangers to her. She told the sick man that had he delayed coming for a further three days he would have died, and then invited the visitors in for a simple meal of bread, butter and milk. Other than saying the invalid would be able to walk home from the boat, the wise woman engaged in no healing practices. She did, however, identify the cause of the illness as being the ill-will of a neighbour, and gave instructions on how to counter the magic. The three brothers returned to the mainland, and the sick man did indeed walk home. They then boiled milk over the fire and, as predicted by the Broadford sage, in a short time a female neighbour arrived in great haste, asking desperately to be allowed to put her hand in the milk. This was the witch who had cast the spell. The patient soon recovered his health and lived to a ripe old age. When the wise woman was on her death-bed she wished to transfer the secret power to her daughter. The daughter, however, refused it, saying that she intended to live unmarried, and would therefore have no one to pass the gift on to. So when the wise woman died, so did the power.

From Mary Macdougall, one of her servants, Mary Julia MacCulloch learned the story of the maid's great-aunt. The lady had recently died, and hence the episode could now be safely related. The woman had a brother working in Broadford, and every week she would walk 30 miles from Skirinish near SKEABOST with his clean linen. One night she stayed over, lying down by the kitchen fire. Suddenly seven women appeared. They transformed into cats, ran up and down the chimney, then back in human form brewed up some hellish concoction, which they washed down with drams of whisky. One of the witches thought the old woman was faking her sleep, and threatened to stab her to death with pins. But the chief witch, who happened to be the mistress of the house, stated that the sleep was genuine, and soon the women left, the mistress going to bed. The next morning Macdougall's great-aunt left at first light and never returned to the house. The motif of women shapeshifting into cats, and then threatening a person faking their sleep, is found in several other Skye folktales, such as at BAY and BLÀBHEINN.

Treatises on the Second-Sight describes how several sailors on a ship from Harris to the mainland saw a vision of two men hanging from the ropes that secured the mast. When the weather forced them to seek shelter at Broadford, they found Sir Donald Macdonald dispensing justice. He sentenced two men to death, and they were hanged using the ropes and masts of the very ship.

On 12 January 1952 Constable John Morrison came across a large creature lying half out of the water on the shore near Broadford. He gave it a kick, whereupon a 6ft (1.8m) tentacle shot out and gripped him by the left ankle. The officer slipped his boot off and killed the animal with rocks and garden shears. The cephalopod was later identified as a Red Flying Squid (*Ommastrephes bartrami*), an occasional visitor to these waters, although it could have been a giant-sized common octopus (*Octopus vulgaris*). The episode is in George M. Eberhart's *Mysterious Creatures: A Guide to Cryptozoology*.

BEINN NA CAILLICH

This 2403ft (732m) high mountain dominates Broadford and all around it. At the very top (NG60182337) is a stupendous cairn of stones. This has never been excavated, so archaeology is silent as to whether it covers a grave or is simply a collection of summiteers' souvenirs. Folklore, however, knows otherwise. The 'Caillich' or Old Woman of the name is universally regarded as being Norwegian. In some versions she is Saucy Mary and has been confused with the giantess of the other Beinn na Caillich further east (see KYLEAKIN). In others she is a princess whose dying wish was to be buried at a place that felt the winds from Norway (this is the most popular option, as it combines romance with royalty). In yet other variant she is not the actual princess, but the Norse nurse. On a clear day the cairn can be seen to create the simulacrum of a nipple atop what, from some angles, is a distinctly breast-shaped mountain.

STRATH SUARDAL (THE ROAD TO ELGOL)

Note: the sites as far as Cill Chriosd can be visited by taking the well-made path that follows the old marble quarry railway line and runs from just south of Broadford parallel to, and east of, the road. After that, walkers will have to take to the tarmac and dodge the cars.

The conspicuous mound on the west side of the road at NG62722203 is known as Aant Sithe, a corruption of An Sithean. In *The Misty Isle of Skye*, Revd Macculloch says it is 'where the good people still come out on moonlight evenings, and dance to elfin music on the green turf.' In *Over the Sea to Skye*, Alasdair Alpin MacGregor noted that local people still avoided the spot at night. The mound is actually a Neolithic chambered cairn, although only one standing stone remains upright and the cairn itself is badly damaged. Some 70yds (64m) east are a pair of circular enclosures marking the sites of prehistoric huts. The low rise to the north, at the treeline, is called An Sidhean, another fairy hill.

If you follow the track north-west from the road you come to Coire-chat-achan. The road from here to the A87, passing through Old Corry, was once haunted by a very tall woman known to have resided in life at a nearby farm. She was dressed in a long black coat and a white mutch (cap), and was seen in the gloaming and at night. Those who summoned the courage to speak to her received a stony stare. Her description is given in *Over the Sea to Skye* – prior to 1926 she had been 'revived' by someone wandering round in a sheet and pretending to be the ghost.

Above left: Cill Chriosd church, Strath Suardal.

Above right: The carving of a gun on a gravestone in Cill Chriosd church.

Cill Chriosd or Kilchrist Church, by the roadside to Elgol (NG61722072), is a roofless post-Reformation parish church built on the site of a medieval predecessor, itself possibly replacing a much more ancient structure. The Ordnance Survey map shows a Rocking Stone to the south at NG617203. My inability to locate it was explained to me by a passing archaeologist: one day the workers at the nearby marble quarry tipped the stone off its pedestal. Remains of the quarry workings can still be seen east of the road.

Both *The Misty Isle of Skye* and *Over the Sea to Skye* have a 'ghost' story which no doubt grew in the telling. In his retirement, Neil MacInnes of the Bow, magically-charmed hero of the Napoleonic Wars (see BREAKISH), would come to Broadford to draw his pension, get drunk, and regale audiences with his heroic deeds. Several sceptics decided to test the boastful ex-soldier's courage, so on his way home they waylaid him at the graveyard, leaping out in white sheets and going 'Woooo!' in the approved ghostly fashion. According to MacGregor, Neil's response was: 'Spooks, or whatever ye be, if it's a fight you're wanting, you can have it now, for Neil, the son of John, the son of Ewen has more friends lying in the churchyard of Kilchrist than you're thinking!' He then proceeded to beat them with his stick, and when they retreated he returned home with a bounty of a dozen sheets.

Immediately west of the churchyard is Loch Cill Chriosd, in whose reedy waters once lurked a terrible monster with a penchant for snacking on women and children. According to Otta Swire the water-horse was expelled when St Maelrhuba blessed the loch. Frederick Sillar and Ruth Meyler's 1973 book *Skye* has a slightly different version. The water-horse thought he saw a girl wandering near the loch and rushed to seize her. Unfortunately for the short-sighted creature, his intended victim was a monk, who promptly took the monster off to EILEAN CHALUIM CHILLE in Trotternish and converted him into a good Christian.

Loch Cill Chriosd, once home to a maiden-devouring water-horse.

HIGH PASTURE CAVE

This incredible site is the most significant Iron Age ritual location ever discovered on Skye, and one of the richest in Scotland. An Iron Age excavation in the Hebrides typically produces enough finds just to populate a matchbox; here the discoveries would fill an entire museum, and many are unique in Scotland. In addition, the nature and setting of many of the finds – from animal and human skeletons to unusual collections of domestic items – makes it clear this was a significant ritual site at which religious ceremonies took place for around 800 years. There is very limited parking on the south side of the road around ⅔ mile (1km) west of Loch Cill Chriosd. If there are vans here, work is probably going on at the excavation. From here an uphill path, rough and slippery in places, leads south for 330yds (300m) to the excavation site at NG5943I971. No dogs should be brought onto the hill. Visitors are welcome, but the site is unstaffed. Please do not step beyond the barriers – you may damage the fragile archaeology, and the site is full of holes and other dangerous elements. There is no public access to the cave itself, which is a serious, cavers-only affair. The year 2010 is the last of six seasons of digging; after this the entire site will be backfilled and reverted to its original pre-excavation state. A single covered vertical access will remain; a narrow and hazardous descent, only suitable for those with suitable caving equipment and experience.

The archaeology of Uamh an Ard Achadh (High Pasture Cave) was accidentally discovered in 2002, although the cave had been known to the speleological community for three decades previously. It is the second longest cave complex on Skye, with around 350yds (320m) of accessible passages. A gully leads to the cave entrance. After a dry passage the lightless cave joins an underground stream, a potently liminal place where the sense of being in contact with the powers of the underworld is palpable. Initially, the cave seems to have been used just as a rubbish dump, but around 800 BC that all changed and some form of ceremonies regularly took place in the 'forecourt' in front of the cave. Whatever these ceremonies were they clearly involved fire, as a huge ash heap grew up on the spot. Eventually this ash heap grew so large – over 13ft (4m) high – that it blocked the entire cave entrance, and a stairwell was cut into the rock down into the entrance to maintain access. Clearly no one considered the easier task of removing the ashes, so this ceremonial hearth and its rubbish must have been of some importance.

Around about this period there was an explosion of ritual activity, with hundreds of items buried in and around the cave – beads, spindle whorls, bronze and bone pins, antler picks, stone tools, pots, metal items, an apparently graffitied scratch-marked stone, tuning pegs from a lyre, and much more. One of the more unusual finds was a collection of quern stones, the stones used for grinding corn. Was this deposition somehow connected to fertility? By far the most amazing find was that of two cows. The first was probably killed on the site, with the skull being cut in half along the central line – a highly unusual practice. After the meat was removed the entire skeleton was then buried in a pit in the cave floor. The second cow is missing its head and feet but its location is astonishing – the bones were placed on a rock shelf high up near the cave roof, some 45yds (40m) along the section of the cave with the underground stream. The sheer logistics of taking most of a cow along a difficult-to-access unlit cave are impressive – this was clearly an important offering to the gods.

The stairwell cut into the rock down into the entrance to the Iron Age ritual site of High Pasture Cave.

Around about the same time, a massive burnt mound was built up above ground. This contained thousands of stones that had been placed in fires and then used to heat water. Clearly more ceremonies were going on here, possibly akin to the saunas of Lapp shamans or the sweatlodges of Native Americans. Pits were dug and filled with ritual deposits, and the several holes where posts once stood possibly suggest carved posts, or something like totem poles. There is also extensive evidence of metalworking on site.

Around 40 BC, however, everything stopped. The end-sequence is speculative, but it may have involved a massive feast where the main food was pig meat. Studies, both anthropological and archaeological, have shown that feasting on pigs often has a ceremonial function – pigs are relatively difficult to raise in northern Scotland, and investment in farming and then consuming them may represent a kind of high status 'conspicuous consumption'. Unusually, the pigs were butchered laterally – that is, great effort had been expended in cutting through their skulls and vertebrae along the line of the animal. This very unusual butchery technique was also used on the cow in the cave. Perhaps splitting the animal laterally meant that one side was for humans, the other side for the gods? After the feast the pig bones were deposited in the cave. Then the stairwell was filled with boulders and earth and, as a closing ceremony, three humans were buried at the very entrance. One was a woman between twenty-five and forty years old, the other two being a foetus and a newborn or very young infant. Both the latter were mixed with the bones of a foetal pig. It is tempting to speculate that the woman was a priestess or noble, that one or both of the children were related to her, and that the great feast was prompted by her death, but there are of course many other narratives that could be constructed around the remains. Whatever happened, with the revered bones acting as a magical barrier to the sacred cave below the whole site was sealed off and forgotten.

What does it all mean? Clearly the vast assemblage of artefacts will keep archaeologists busy for years, constructing theories and engaging in various interpretations. One notion that has gained initial favour is that this was a site dedicated to the popular Celtic goddess Bride. Bride's sacred animals were cattle; she was associated with springs and water; she was patron of metalworkers; and she was a goddess of fertility. All of which fits with the morphology and archaeology of the site. Her popularity was such that when the Celtic peoples were Christianised, she was converted into a saint, St Bride or Bridget. To cap it all, the township just to the west is called Kilbride, the Church of Bride. There is no doubt many more exciting discoveries to emerge from High Pasture Cave. I recommend their comprehensive website www.high-pasture-cave.org for deeper investigations.

KILBRIDE

Here we have a standing stone, holy well and ancient church, although all but the first are frustratingly elusive. To reach the tall finger of Clach na h-Annait take the minor road west towards Kilbride/Camas Malag. After about 500yds/m, walk north up the drive to Kilbride House and ask permission to visit the stone, then enter the field opposite. The 7ft 9in. (2.4m) high stone is north of the small white building (NG 58942030). Otta Swire states the Brahan Seer (see GLENDALE) prophesied, 'Here the raven will drink his fill of blood from the Stone' and reports a tradition that

Clach na h-Annait standing stone, Kilbride. A holy well is nearby.

the stone was once an unlikely 30ft (9m) tall. In front of the shed a clump of trees and vegetation probably hides the holy well Tobar na h-Annait. In the early twelfth century this was enclosed in a circular stone structure, but these days a visit in summer merely promotes a close relationship with brambles. Martin Martin states that the well contained a single trout: 'the natives are very tender of it, and though they often chance to catch it in their wooden pails, they are very careful to preserve it from being destroyed.' The term 'Annait' means 'Mother Church' and indicates this was an important early Christian site. Sadly, St Bridget's or St Bride's Chapel has long since vanished and even its location is uncertain. In 1870 a stone baptismal font and a hand-bell surmounted by a cross were dug up here. One gets the sense that Kilbride was once a place of great significance, but it has escaped archaeology, history and even folklore, and thus remains largely unrecorded.

SUISNISH & BORERAIG

A splendid coastal walk south from the car park at the seaward end of the Kilbride/Camas Malag road passes a number of places of archaeological interest, as well as visiting Suisnish and Boreraig, two deserted townships whose inhabitants were 'cleared' with vicious brutality in 1852-4 by Lord MacDonald's factor. Near where the good track briefly turns inland up Glen Boreraig is a pile of rocks marking the site of a prehistoric hut circle (NG59211743). A few hundred paces east is the ruinous galleried dun of Dun Kearstach (NG59641745), and further south are two large overgrown cairns (NG59131732). After the sheepwash at Suisnish the path peters out for a while, then re-establishes itself above the cliffs. Dun Boreraig (NG61511612) is one of the scantiest of duns, but the obvious standing stone at Boreraig (NG61951638) is a worthwhile marker for the end of the walk. A second stone lies on the ground next to it. The stones overlook Loch Eishort and the tradition is that they mark the burial of a body washed ashore. Otta Swire claimed there was once the ruin of a little Celtic church, Teampuill Chaon, nearby, but no one else has seen this 'Chapel of St Congan'. From here walkers can retrace the route or take the boggy path north across the moors back to CILL CHRIOSD, passing the marble quarry workings on the way.

TORRIN

Just east from where the road crosses the river at the head of Loch Slapin, a path leads north to Clach Oscar, a truly enormous boulder (NG564226). Oscar, one of the Fingalian giants, flicked the stone here from a neighbouring summit during a moment of levity. Above the stone is Loch na Sguabaidh, home of a maiden-devouring water-horse. South of Torrin, Dun Mor and Dun Beag (NG57402015 and NG57511984 respectively) are too ruinous to garner much attention.

KEPPOCH

Swire describes another giant-tossed boulder, Clachan Fhuarain (Well Stone), near Druim an Fhuarain. This one was chucked here from Soay by one of Cu Chulainn's mates (see DUN SCAICH for more on Cu Chulainn). This stone is probably somewhere near Tobar Ceann (Well of the Head, NG56111952), which can be reached by taking an upland path north from the road just east of Allt na Nigheidh, and keeping left at the first junction.

KILMARIE & KIRKIBOST

A side road runs south-east to Cille Mhaire, the Kilmarie Burial Ground (NG55331715), within whose walled grounds the overcrowded graves seem to be making a bid to escape – negotiating the cemetery without stepping on a gravemound is tricky. Some part of the church remained in the mid-nineteenth century, but Otta Swire says the ruins were swept away in a great storm in the 1920s. Apparently, an unknown sailor had been found drowned and buried in the churchyard. Local belief had it that a body taken from the sea should always be buried near the water's edge or the sea will come onto the land to reclaim its own – which is what happened in this case.

Dun Ringill is a prehistoric broch and medieval fortress in one. The bearded flute-playing prog-rocker standing on one leg is not shown.

A small gate opposite the gates of Kilmarie Lodge leads to an ornamental footbridge. Turn right here and follow the coastal path to the ruined but still attractive Dun Ringill (NG56191708). This is a fascinating site; it was originally a prehistoric broch and then reused in medieval times as the home of Clan MacKinnon (they later abandoned it for Caisteal Maol at KYLEAKIN). A scramble along a deep passageway gives access to the interior, and chambers can still be seen within the walls. The rock band Jethro Tull have a track called 'Dun Ringill' on their album *Stormwatch*. The lyrics make reference to the ancient gods, stone circles, and the kings of old. The band's singer, Ian Anderson, used to own the Strathaird estate on which the broch is located. Just after the Kilmarie footbridge the path passes Cnocan nan Gobhar (Hillock of the Goats), a large tree-encrusted cairn (NG55261734).

From the car park on the main road by Cnoc an Taibhse (Hill of the Ghost), take the track west in the direction of Camusunary. Where a line of trees crosses the path at right angles, turn right (north). Cross the stream (at the very least you will get your feet wet) and on the plain in front of you, by the side of a small loch, is a miniscule stone circle, Na Clachan Bhreige (the Lying or False Stones, NG54321768). Otta Swire states these were once regarded as 'Stones of Wisdom', able to foretell the future and decide guilt or innocence. Their current name is a residue of Christian disapproval. Three of the stones are upright, the tallest being 6ft 6in. (2m) in height. Others may lurk beneath the peat.

BLÀBHEINN (BLAVEN)

In *The Heart of Skye*, Jim Crumley calls this great mountain 'the landscape's godliest's gesture' and suggests it was some kind of sacred hill, the focus for the more low-lying ritual sites within its orbit. In *The Charm of Skye*, Seton Gordon gives the story behind some of the place names. Bealach na Beiste (Pass of the Monster, NG540239), is where eons ago a MacKinnon of Strath slew a ferocious beast (possibly the water-horse of LOCH NA SGUABAIDH). And the route up Allt na Dunaiche (Burn of Sorrow, NG5421), passes Airigh na Dunaiche (Shieling of Sorrow or Disaster). Here seven girls and one boy were spending the summer with the animals at their high pasture. The lasses were away at a wedding and as the boy lay in bed seven cats strolled in, had a gossip in human voices by the fireside and then deliberately spoiled the butter and milk. The boy related all this to the girls when they returned. The next night the seven witches revisited in human form and killed all seven girls, inexplicably leaving the boy alive.

ELGOL

The precipitous end of the road, Elgol is the jumping-off point for boat trips to LOCH CORUISK, Loch Scavaig and beyond. According to Otta Swire, Bidein an Fhithich, the hill overlooking the village, was once home to the Raven's Stone, apparently the subject of a prognostication by the Brahan Seer. Any prophecy is now moot, however, as in the late nineteenth century the stone was broken up and – rather curiously, and logistically unlikely – is said to have been used to construct one wall of the church at GLENDALE. There is apparently a cross-incised stone at the roadside 1 mile (1.6km) from Elgol (NG52711449) but I failed to find it. Perhaps the carving has eroded away. Derek Cooper, in his book *Skye*, retells another case of second-sight. A woman 'saw' a funeral procession near the shore of Loch Scavaig. She later died, and shortly afterwards three drowned fishermen were buried *pro tem* by the lochside. Later, they were disinterred and carried to a churchyard – along the very path the woman had described.

A rough path leaves Elgol jetty and proceeds south to Suidhe Biorach (Pointed Seat), an overhang whose resemblance to a gentleman's part makes it clear why childless women sat on the headland hoping to conceive. Just to the east is Prince Charles's Cave, the last refuge for Bonnie Prince Charlie before he left Skye for the mainland and then France, never to return. Swire suggests the cave was the traditional site where a MacKinnon chief slew a fierce wolf by forcing a deer bone down its throat, a story that shows that a) heroic clan societies need heroic ancestors and b) wolves always get a bad press. The cave is above the waterline but can only be reached at low tide – and if you do not leave enough time to explore, you will be trapped. From Suidhe Biorach continue to the next bay, Port an Luig Mhóir, then double back below the cliffs, looking for an irregular vertical entrance about halfway along the shore. If you come across a through cave, you still have a bit to go. Bring a torch.

GLASNAKILLE

A good torch is also essential when exploring Spar Cave, a wonderland of bulbous and tentacular shapes formed from water flowing through limestone. A muddy entrance gives way to a fossilised cataract known as a flowstone staircase, and then a series of dark and cold pools, the last and largest of which was likened by Sir Walter Scott to a mermaid's bath:

The mermaid's alabaster grot
Who bathes her limbs in sunken well
Deep in Strathaird's enchanted cell

'Lord of the Isles'

The cave was once even more spectacular, but Victorian visitors snapped off the stalagmites and stalactites for souvenirs and blackened the ceiling with their candles. The word 'spar' refers to calcium carbonate formations.

The cave has legendary and historical interest as well. Its alternative name is Slochd Altrimen (Nursling Cave). In the twelfth century, so the legend runs, a galley was wrecked in Loch Slapin, the only survivor being the son of the chief of Colonsay. Princess Dounhuila, daughter of one of the lords of Skye, nursed him back to health and, as is the way with these things, found herself pregnant. Unfortunately, the respective families were engaged in a bloody feud, and Dounhuila's father intended to kill the young couple. Before he could do so, however, he was called away to yet another war or expedition. Dounhuila persuaded the jailors to release Colonsay, and when she gave birth the child was secreted in the cave by a trusted servant and guarded by Colonsay's dog. Dounhuila would make her way to the cave to nurse the infant, hence the name. Eventually, the two families were reconciled and Dounhuila, Colonsay and their child lived happily ever after. The tale is given in *The Misty Isle of Skye*.

Although the cave has a definite terminus, it is supposed to be one of the many places on Skye where a piper bravely marched deep into the bowels of the earth, the sound of his pipes eventually giving out when he met a terrible fate (for further versions see BORNESKETAIG, GALTRIGILL and other places). Alasdair Alpin MacGregor also notes that the cave was the hiding place of the Episcopal minister Neil MacKinnon, who, during the religious troubles of the seventeenth century, was in the habit of preaching at Cill Chriosd while wearing a full set of armour.

Getting to the cave is not a casual expedition, and must only be undertaken at low tide. Walk a little south from the road junction at Glasnakille and opposite a byre take a gate on the left (east). The wet and muddy path descends deeply through trees to a rock-strewn inlet on the shore. Here you need to check the state of the tide. Only proceed if you can round the headland to the left, then pass by a second inlet. After this is the main inlet, which is larger than the others and leads into a striking canyon with high walls. A tricky approach over ledges and across slippery rocks brings you to the cave mouth. Here are the remains of a wall built in a fruitless attempt to keep visitors out of the cave. When Walter Scott's group came here in 1814 they used a rope to climb over, but a later tourist with little patience and less sense bombarded the barrier with a cannon mounted on his yacht. Allow enough time to explore the cave and return to the first inlet before the tide returns. The cave is dirty and cold. And on second thoughts, bring two torches.

Dun Grugaig, on the shore east of the road to the south (NG53541229) is worth a visit because part of its massive wall, complete with through-passage, still remains.

A good walk north from the Glasnakille road-end to Drinan passes Dun Liath, now little more than a scattered circle of stones (NG54331427). I was unable to get near the intriguingly-named 'Tomb' shown on the map just to the south. The continuation of the walk north from Drinan to Kilmarie passes several former dwellings whose location is primarily marked by red-berried apotropaic rowan trees.

In 1925, Alasdair Alpin MacGregor was told several supernatural tales from the area. A shepherd from Elgol had jilted a girl, and was returning home from Glasnakille one dark night when a hare crossed his path and made a circle round him. It then changed first into a horse and then a woman who beat and scratched him. She threatened to attack him again if he told anyone about the assault (but he must have told someone, else how would we know of the story?). She also said he was lucky the animal he had with him was a dog. The implication was that if it had been a bitch, it would have joined in the attack. It is not clear whether the shapeshifting witch was the girl the man had jilted, or was merely wreaking vengeance on her behalf. Fairy pipes were apparently still heard from the hillock close to the spot. A couple told Macgregor they had heard fairy music and seen fairies several times on a mound near Glasnakille. Possibly this was the same place. Unfortunately, the road to Elgol passes through a landscape replete with natural bumps and tumps, so it is impossible now to pinpoint this particular fairy hill.

SOAY

Soay is the large relatively low-lying island west of Elgol. In the late 1940s it was owned by Gavin Maxwell, who set up an ill-fated industry to harvest basking sharks. The story of the rise and fall of the enterprise, complete with vivid episodes of danger and drama, is in Maxwell's first book, *Harpoon at a Venture* (1952). The book makes for uneasy reading these days, as much of it is taken up with descriptions of the hunting and killing of these enormous but harmless creatures; the numbers of basking sharks in the area have still not recovered from the slaughter.

Maxwell also recorded the superstitions of his crew and other fishermen: no woman was to be allowed on a boat; some words could not be mentioned – salmon were called 'cold iron', pigs 'those grunting things' and rabbits 'the furry long-eared things'; and once when Maxwell shot some rabbits for food on Soay and brought them on board, the reaction was close to a mutiny. He repeated a tale he must have been told by someone from the island: a Soay man was walking from his croft to his boat when he met an old woman who had something of a bad reputation. He passed her without speaking, then thought better of this, and said, 'Why are you up so early to meet me this morning?' 'Be it according to your faith,' she replied. He ruminated on this – certainly at the moment his faith was in her malevolent powers. At the harbour he found his boat sunk. It had been his fault, as he had overloaded it with stone ballast, and when the tide receded the unsupported boat capsized under the weight of the stones. That, however, was a minor consideration – the obvious cause of his misfortune was the 'witch'. (In 1901 Alexander MacGregor noted in *Highland Superstitions* that when the head of a Soay family died, the custom was to cut off a lock of his hair and nail it to the door-lintel as protection against fairies and witches.)

Maxwell was also alive to the notion that strange things lived in the seas around Soay. He heard of the experience of Sandy Campbell, who as a boy around 1900 was in a boat fishing with two older men when all three saw a neck perhaps 20ft (6m) long emerge from the water, while below the surface they could see a dark shape. Campbell also said that the following summer two men saw a neck some 30ft (9m) in length rise out of the sea near Rhum. In 1917 Ronald and Harry MacDonald saw a tall head and neck poking out of the water at the mouth of Loch Brittle. In his book *Sea Serpents, Sailors and Sceptics* Graham McEwan dismisses these as sightings of a long-necked seal, with the witnesses grossly exaggerating the dimensions of what they had seen.

Issue 10 of the local paper the *Clarion of Skye* (10 November 1951) reported another strange sighting. The previous winter, Ronald MacDonald and Mr MacRae of Soay had been checking lobster creels when they saw an all-white creature around 20ft (6m) long, with no dorsal fin. They wrote to the British Museum, who replied:

> There is no doubt from the astonishingly correct description supplied by Mr MacDonald, he witnessed something very rare in the British Isles. He did see a White Whale, or Beluga (*Delphinapterus Leucas*), and there are less than a dozen records of its visiting the British Isles during the last 160 years.

Laurance Reed, in *The Soay of our Forefathers*, adds that a large sperm whale was stranded on the coast of Loch Scavaig in 1871. Martin Martin stated that just before 1695 a whale had overturned a boat, and devoured three of the crew. In his 1836 book, *Sketches of the Coasts and Islands of Scotland*, Lord Teignmouth recalled that the rowers taking him across Loch Bracadale became greatly frightened by an approaching creature, thinking it was a whale that had been attacking boats in a neighbouring bay. However, although the creature appeared to be 'a fish, apparently sixty feet in length' it proved as it passed to be a pair of porpoises, 'preserving a distance so exact, that they might well be mistaken for a single fish.' Alexander Robert Forbes' *Gaelic Names of Beasts* of 1905 records a Skye sea monster called Biasd na Sgrogaig (Beast of the Towering Horn), which had one horn on its forehead, long legs, and a clumsy gait. He surmised it was an exaggerated account of a narwhal that had strayed from the Arctic seas. Meanwhile, the *Daily Mail* for 8 February 2000 reported that Skye fishermen had spotted three seals that were coloured bright orange, possibly through a coating of some kind of algae.

One of the people involved in Maxwell's basking shark business was Joseph 'Tex' Geddes, a man whom Maxwell described as 'unkillable'. An adventurous action man whose multitudinous stories about himself may have been true (or not, and if not it didn't matter), he purchased Soay from the receivers when Maxwell's company failed. Shortly afterwards, the other Soay inhabitants requested evacuation from the increasingly-isolated island, and the authorities were minded to cut off all postal and telephone services – until Tex persuaded them otherwise by getting his friends to deluge him with telegrams and registered packages (some of which just contained stones). Geddes wrote up his harpooning experiences in a 1960 book, *Hebridean Sharker*, which contained an extraordinary sighting. On 13 September 1959, a calm and bright day, he had been out fishing with a friend, James Gavin, and they had seen some killer-whales and a basking shark, when something else appeared some distance away. To the astonished Geddes it seemed like 'some hellish monster of prehistoric times'. It had a large reptilian head with a broad slash of a mouth, a neck, and a domed back which he estimated at 8-10ft (2.4-3m) in length. The great creature slowly passed within 15-20yds (13-18m) of the dinghy, moving its head from side to side, before diving and re-emerging around ¼ mile (400m) away. Tim Dinsdale later interviewed James Gavin for his 1966 book on water monsters, *The Leviathans*, and Gavin gave a detailed description, adding that the creature made 'loud roaring whistling noises' as it breathed and that he had seen what appeared to be triangular-shaped spines on the back.

This extended sighting by two very experienced mariners has excited much attention. In 1968, Dutch zoologist Leo Brongersma, author of the 1972 book *European Atlantic Turtles*, identified the creature as a loggerhead turtle (*Caretta Caretta*), which can reach known lengths of 3.5ft (1.1m), far smaller than the estimates given by Geddes and Gavin. In a website posting on 4 February 2009, Jonathan Downes, 'ringmaster' of the Centre for Fortean Zoology, suggested the creature was a leatherback turtle (also known as the leathery turtle or luth, *Dermochelys Coriacea*), which can reach 9ft (2.75m) in length. Although they breed in the tropics, leatherbacks have been seen as far north as Norway.

The exact identity of the 'Soay Beast' may forever remain a mystery, but it is certain that giant turtles have been found in these waters. In his book on the Loch Ness Monster, *Project Water Horse*, Tim Dinsdale described how in August 1971 he saw an immense dead turtle in a locked shed in Mallaig. The trawlermen who had caught it had estimated its weight at 'thirteen hundredweight' (1500lbs or two thirds of a ton). Dinsdale, peeking through a cobwebbed window, identified it as a leathery turtle, three times the size of the specimen in the Natural History Museum. Unfortunately, the site was deserted and by the next day, when Dinsdale returned with the means to record and preserve the animal, it had vanished, probably converted to turtle soup.

TWO

THE SOUTH-EAST: SLEAT

ISLEORNSAY – KILMORE – ARMADALE – TARSKAVAIG – ORD

The Isleman ... Death is ever near him, and that consciousness turns everything to omen. The mist creeping along the hill-side by moonlight is an apparition. In the roar of the waterfall, or the murmur of the swollen ford, he hears the water spirit calling out for the man for whom it has waited so long. He sees death-candles burning on the sea, marking the place at which a boat will be upset by some sudden squall. He hears spectral hammers clinking in an out-house, and he knows that ghostly artificers are preparing a coffin there. Ghostly fingers tap at his window, ghostly feet are about his door; at mid-night his furniture cries out as if it had seen a sight and could not restrain itself. Even his dreams are prophetic, and point ghastly issues for himself or for others.

Alexander Smith, *A Summer in Skye* (written in Ord, 1885)

Much of the peninsula of Sleat was MacDonald territory, at least from the late fourteenth century, when they appear to have displaced the MacLeods.

THE A851 ROAD FROM BROADFORD TO SLEAT

In 1859 geologist Hugh Miller recorded what was obviously a well-known folk belief in his book, *The Cruise of the Betsey*. The valley through which this road passes was haunted by a spirit called the Laidag, which ...

... has but one leg, terminating, like an ancient satyr's, in a cloven foot; but it is furnished with two arms, bearing hard fists at the end of them, with which it has been known to strike the benighted traveller in the face, or to tumble him over into some dark pool. The spectre may be seen at the close of evening hopping vigorously among the distant bogs ... and when the mist lies thick in the hollows, an occasional glimpse may be caught of it even by day.

In 1902 J.G. Campbell expanded and changed the story in his *Witchcraft and Second Sight in the Highlands and Islands of Scotland*. The Luideag, as he called it, was apparently derived from the Gaelic word for ragged or slovenly. It was a young woman dressed in rags and wearing a coat about her head. In the 1860s or '70s an exciseman passing along the lonely road spoke to her in both English and Gaelic but she did not answer. A man was then found lying dead at the roadside in mysterious circumstances and, equally mysteriously, the Luideag was never seen again.

ISLEORNSAY & CAMUSCROSS

The scant remains of an old church and graveyard can be visited on the tidal island of Ornsay at low tide only (NG71011239). Wet and muddy access is from the east of the bay. Flowing past Camuscross into Camus Croise bay is Allt na Bèiste, Stream of the Monster. This may possibly be connected with the legend of Loch nan Dubhrachan (see below).

LOCH NAN DUBHRACHAN

This small loch is close to the lay-by on the east side of the main road opposite the turn-off to Ord and Tokavaig (NG675105). Many lochs on Skye are supposedly the habitations of the dreaded monster known as the Each Uisge or water-horse. Loch nan Dubhrachan however, is, to my knowledge, the only one where an actual monster hunt has taken place.

The search for the water-horse occurred in 1870. There are two accounts of the events, and the most detailed is the later one, from Alasdair Alpin MacGregor's *Somewhere in Scotland*, published in 1935. Some years previously MacGregor had interviewed John MacRae in GLENELG; MacRae had been present as a boy at the hunt. The background was that a couple cutting rushes at the loch saw something small and black on the shore. They thought it was either a drowned cow, or 'one of the sea-cows they would be seeing in olden times'. As the man approached the object it swam out into the loch with its head below water. So terrified were the pair that when they reported the encounter a large net was organised to trawl the loch from end to end. Along with his fellows, MacRae had been let off school for the day. He described what happened:

> The net got stuck, and all the gillies got the fear of death on them. So they just dropped the net, and ran back from the loch … A while after they commenced again; and after a while the net came away on a sudden. Well, then, they pulled it in like, afraid all the time what would be in the net … Anyway, there was nothing in the net at the finish but some mud and two small pikes!

The second account is in M.E.M. (Mary) Donaldson's *Wanderings in the Western Highlands and Islands* of 1920. Donaldson was told the story by an old man who had been present on the day (was this John MacRae as well?) and the description adds to the sketch of the day. It was something of a holiday, with people coming from far and wide in carts and traps, and considerable quantities of whisky being downed. The net was dragged between two boats, one at either shore. The snagging of the net, the general melee as everyone fled in fear, and the eventual discovery of the catch of two pike, were all described in the same way.

John MacRae told MacGregor that Lord MacDonald had organised the gillies and gamekeepers and the net. Reasoning that such an event would have left some record, I contacted the MacDonald Study Centre at Armadale Castle. Ann-Marie Peckham, Assistant Curator, kindly checked the catalogue of the MacDonald estate papers and sadly found no reference to either the loch or the water-horse. Her conclusion was that the arrangements for the dragging of the loch were made verbally, and never written down. And so the trail of the Great Water-horse Hunt of Loch nan Dubhrachan goes cold.

Loch nan Dubhrachan, where a large-scale
monster hunt took place in 1870. The
water-horse was not found.

TEANGUE

One day a MacDonald man slipped and only managed to prevent falling into a deadly
drop by holding on to a grass sod. A MacLeod woman heard his cries of desperation.
Contemplating the man's predicament, and recalling that the invading MacDonalds
had recently thrown all the MacLeod men out of Knock Castle, but had kept the
women as rape-slaves, she said, 'Ah well, you've taken everything else, so I suppose you
had better take this with you too.' And with that she kicked the sod and consigned the
MacDonald to his doom.

This tale – which can be found in Miket and Roberts' *The Mediaeval Castles of Skye
and Lochalsh* – perfectly illustrates the complex clan enmities of Knock Castle, the ruined
fortress at the east end of the bay (NG67150872). Once a MacLeod stronghold, then
taken by the MacDonalds in the fifteenth century, then regarrisoned by the MacLeods,
then handed over by a much-despised treaty, then besieged by the MacLeods and ably
defended by 'Mary of the Castle' who inspired her fellow MacDonalds to victory … it
finally found peace in the seventeenth century when it was abandoned. The medieval
building, also known as Caisteal Camus and Caisteal Uaine, has entirely obliterated
its Iron Age predecessor on the site, Dun Thorabhaig (Dun of the Bay of Thor – the
name may indicate it was still in use in the Norse period). To reach it, walk down the
track south of the hotel and past Cnoc Uaine farm. Just before the last house at the
bay, turn left over a bridge then right to follow a faint path along the shore. The real
dun enthusiast can follow the pathless coastline to reach Knock Dunan Choinnich

Above: The stark ruin of Knock Castle was once haunted by a menagerie of ghostly entities.

Left: A modern shrine at the road junction to Upper Teangue. The structure covers a well while the marble figure is of a woman (the Virgin Mary?) sheltering two children.

(aka another Dun Thorabhaig, NG68290834) but the ruins are not worth the journey (although the views are). A curious modern shrine consisting of a domed wellhead and a female sculpture sits at the junction to Upper Teangue.

In *Over the Sea to Skye*, Alasdair Alpin MacGregor states that the area around Knock is 'saturated with stories of the green-attired glaistig or hobgoblin, and a gruagach or long-haired damsel with daemonic propensities'. Saturated is right; generations of writers have added to the storehouse of legend. John Gregorson Campbell, in *Superstitions of the Highlands and Islands of Scotland* (1900) noted that the glaistig was often seen near the Gruagach Stone at dusk, perfectly illustrating the confusion between the two spirits, both of whom are associated with cattle. The glaistig was a fairy woman dressed in green who haunted dairies, and the gruagach a kind of shaggy-haired female cowherd to whom offerings of milk were left in hollowed stones, but much of the folklore has understandably mixed up the two. In 1930 Ratcliffe Barnett's *Autumns in Skye Ross and Sutherland* described the Knock glaistig as a Green Lady who was actually a she-devil disguised as a beautiful woman or a grey goat. Otta Swire notes the Maighdean Uaine ('Green Maiden') was seen at moonrise walking through the ruins. She was the guardian spirit of the dun and was linked to the castle's 'rightful owners' (whoever they might be – MacLeods? MacDonalds? Vikings?)

The 1763 work *Treatises on the Second-Sight* had a local case:

> The Lady Coll informed me that one McLean of Knock, an elderly reputable gentleman, living on their estate, as he walked in the fields before sunset, he saw a neighbouring person, who had been sick for a long time, coming that way, accompanied by another man; and, as they drew nearer, he asked them some questions, and how far they intended to go. The first answered they were to travel forward to a village he named, and then pursued his journey with a more than ordinary pace. Next day, early in the morning, he was invited to his neighbour's interment, which surprised him much, as he had seen and spoke with him the evening before; but was told by the messenger that came for him, the deceased person had been confined to his bed for seven weeks, and that he departed this life a little before sunset, much about the time he saw him in a vision the preceding day.

KILMORE

The interior of the Victorian parish church on the east side of the road (NG65740694) has columns carved with angels' heads, good sculptural monuments with coats of arms, and, in the corridor, a small tapered slab incised with an early Christian cross. There is no other indication of an ancient Christian foundation but Otta Swire states that below the current church is the Sgeir Chaluim Cille, Columba's Stone, marking the spot where the saint allegedly landed and blessed the ground, thereby expelling the resident druids. This appears to be an offshore reef. The roofless church in the graveyard is the seventeenth-century replacement for the now-vanished medieval original, within which the MacIntyres (a sept of the MacDonalds) sought sanctuary after losing a battle with the MacLeods in a field next door. As was standard practice with Skye Christians of the time (see also TRUMPAN) the MacLeods locked the church door, set fire to the thatched roof and burned alive all those within.

Skulls, bones, coffin and gravedigger's spade on gravestone at Kilmore church. The skull on the right has a strange hole in its forehead.

Martin Martin remarked that one night at Ostaig, just to the south of Kilmore, the cows gave blood instead of milk. This was taken as a bad omen, and indeed on that date (27 July 1689) James MacDonald of Capstill and Ostaig was killed fighting for the Jacobites at the Battle of Killiecrankie. Martin concludes, 'The minister of the place and the mistress of the cows, together with several neighbours, assured me of the truth of this.' Boswell and Johnson had a copy of Martin's *A Description of the Western Isles of Scotland* with them when they visited Skye. It was this kind of story that made Johnson regard Martin as credulous and naïve.

ARMADALE CASTLE

(Open April to October 9.30 a.m. to 5.30 p.m. daily; admission charge; disabled access to museum and most of the gardens.) This is the locus of MacDonald heritage on Skye, the Clan Donald equivalent of the MacLeods' DUNVEGAN CASTLE. Apart from the extensive gardens (with statues of a raven and an otter at play), the main items of interest are the ivy-clad roofless shell of the nineteenth-century mansion house – the now-isolated grand staircase hints how opulent this was – and the Museum of the Isles. The latter has displays relating the history of the MacDonald Lordship of the Isles in the Middle Ages, and the subsequent fortunes of the MacDonalds on Skye, including the periods of the Jacobites and Clearances. The first room is focused on a circle of five great standing stones. You are encouraged to touch the several replicas of graveslabs carved with warriors, from Islay and Iona. One replica has a birlinn (a Hebridean galley), two sets of opposed beasts, and a floral pattern. Mention is made of holy wells and the cult of the Celtic goddess Bride who became St Bridget (see HIGH PASTURE CAVE). An audio guide is available in several languages.

Two generations of ruined mansions at Armadale Castle.

Above: The former grand staircase of Armadale Castle, now isolated in a garden.

Right: A memorial stone at Armadale Castle. The butterfly emerges from its chrysalis – a symbol of immortality or resurrection.

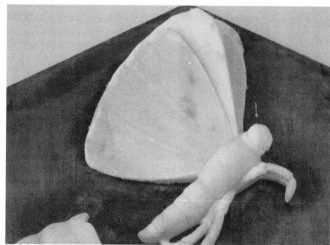

ARDVASAR

In 1986 David Hitchcock and his family quit their dream cottage in Ardvasar because they believed there was a witchcraft conspiracy against them. As described in the *Sunday Express* on 21 December, they had been told someone had placed a curse on the house, Hitchcock's daughter had been accosted by 'two hooded cackling crones,' and workmen building a wheelchair path to the house quit for no reason. More alarmingly, they found a criss-cross pattern of rowan branches outside the front door and human fingernails scattered on their doorstep.

Otta Swire recounts a widespread folktale, as usual given a localised veneer. One night several young fishermen saw a group of seal-maidens at play, the beautiful women having taken off their seal-skins. One youth stole and hid the skins, so that the seal-women could not return to the sea. As an upshot, each 'selkie' married a fine fisherlad and lived in happiness for a year. But after that time the location of the skins was revealed, and all the women, beholden to the sea their great mother, donned their seal-skins and returned to the waves. Their distraught husbands waded out to try and dissuade them, and were turned to stone. But their wives never forget and can still be seen, keeping faith with the stone that stand in the waters of Port na Faganaich (Bay of the Forsaken Ones).

AIRD

Macculloch's *The Misty Isle of Skye* has some spooky, if stereotyped, tales from this area. One stormy night a fisherman's widow saw her recently-deceased husband enter the house in dripping oilskins and remove a brick from the fireplace. He raised his hand in farewell and disappeared. His life savings, kept secret from his wife, were beneath the brick. Another tale tells of a black cat which kept stealing a crofter's precious cream so he caught it and cut off one of its ears. A few days later everyone noticed that an elderly neighbour had lost an ear. Almost the same story is told in MacGregor's *Over the Sea to Skye*, the only difference being that the cat was only caught after several years' depredations, and it was the dairymaid who cut its ear off, not the crofter.

Dun-baggers have three opportunities in this area, Dun Ban (NG60030042), Dun a'Chleirich (NG60590091) and Dun Chlò (NG618015), but all are in very poor condition, especially the last.

In his droll book *The Meaning of Liff*, Douglas Adams, author of *The Hitch-Hikers' Guide to the Galaxy*, takes various place names and assigns to these entirely fictitious meanings. His entry for 'Aird of Sleat' reads, 'Ancient Scottish curse placed from afar on the stretch of land now occupied by Heathrow Airport.'

CARADAL

This deserted township on the west coast is a long way from anywhere else, being reached by an energetic walk along a track that leaves the road about ⅔ mile (1km) south-west of Ardvasar and Calligarry. The situation of Dun Geilbt (NG56750480) is so dramatic – separated from the land by a deep chasm and standing on wave-washed cliffs – it is a shame so little of it is left. Otta Swire says the wood of Caradal or Carradale was home to a giant bird. Somewhere nearby is Lochan na Poite, in which is sunk a brass creel filled with gold. This treasure was once guarded by a monster that was slain – it is not said by whom – and buried in Lagan Inis na Cnaimh (Hollow of the Meadow of Bones). At this spot, says Swire, at an unknown time in the nineteenth century, bones of some prehistoric animal were dug up. All of these sites have sadly eluded me.

THE WEST COAST

The single-track road that loops along the west coast through Achnacloich, Tarskavaig and Ord embraces steep inclines, serpentine twists and sheer drops. Not a place for caravans or faint-of-heart drivers.

ACHNACLOICH

Somewhere near Cnoc An Teampuill (NG59080872) once stood a chapel, now lost (the Gaelic word 'Teampuill' usually indicates a church or chapel). Water that collected in the hollow of the Teampuill Stone, thought to be the old font, was used for the healing of illnesses of the hands. To the south-west and south-east respectively are Sìthean Beag and Sìthean Mòr, the Little and Big Fairy Mounds. Both are natural hills with no trace of a dun or cairn.

TARSKAVAIG

Uamh Tharsgabhaig or Tarskavaig is a fine cave some 65ft (20m) deep with a natural arch in its entrance canyon (NG583109). It is reached by walking past the old church west of Tarskavaig, rounding the point and following the beach northwards.

DUN SCAICH CASTLE

Also known as Dunscaith and Dun Sgathaich, this dramatically-sited ruin commands an outcrop which has been separated from the mainland by the hewing out of a deep and forbidding rock-cut gully (NG59521207). The drawbridge that once spanned this ravine has gone, leaving only its two floorless flanking walls atop the bridging arch, with nothing but gulfs of air between you and the rocks far below. There is a narrow ledge around the edge of the central empty space, but negotiating this is extremely hazardous. Unless you have a yen to emulate Indiana Jones, it's safer to view the pile from outside. The route is along the track from the road, towards the abandoned house, then left over the boggy headland.

The castle, as was often the case, changed hands between the clans, being originally a MacLeod stronghold before becoming the MacDonald headquarters in the fifteenth century; sieges, fratricidal murders and battles followed, with the site being abandoned when the MacDonalds relocated to DUNTULM in the 1600s. On one occasion, a cousin of the occupant, disgusted at the behaviour of the kinsmen of the lord's wife, slaughtered twelve of them and hung them in front of the lady's window before breakfast; he was later assassinated in revenge. Another claimant to the castle, while enjoying the hospitality of the chief, murdered his host in cold blood.

Far more interesting, however, is the castle's role in myth. Here the Irish culture hero Cu Chulainn came to learn the arts of war at what was effectively a finishing school for Celtic warriors. Cu Chulainn's teacher was the warrior queen Sgathaich the

Terrible. That much all the bards and written sources agree on – after that, the stories that circulate around Cu Chulainn and Sgathaich are legion, often contradictory and confused.

Cu Chulainn was persuaded to come to Skye by the wiles of Forgal, the father of Emer, the hero's sweetheart; at the very least Cu Chulainn would be out of the way, and at best, killed by Sgathaich. In some versions, Cu Chulainn later returns from the training camp and marries Emer. In other versions he marries Sgathaich, or Sgathaich's great rival Aoife or Aife, whom he first defeats in battle as Sgathaich's champion; Aife later bears him a son. Or he is besotted with Uathach, Sgathaich's daughter. Alternatively, Cu Chulainn is said to marry Bragela (who may be Uathach) and leave her behind at Dun Scaich, where she pined for him while he was away defending Ireland from its enemies. (Mythology is so confusing.)

It was only when Cu Chulainn had proved his worth by overcoming the castle's various defences that Sgathaich accepted him as her pupil. The hazards, again, vary from story to story, but include: the Bridge of the Cliff, which rose vertically as soon as anyone set foot on it; iron doors within seven walls crowned by iron palisades, with severed heads stuck on the spikes; a pit full of snakes and beaked toads; and fierce dragon-like monsters. In one version, Cu Chulainn makes it to the throne room and threatens Sgathaich's life, so she agrees to teach him. In another version, Sgathaich had a band of 100 Amazons who executed fifty pirates by tying their hair to an oak tree and leaving them to hang until they expired. Cu Chulainn first defeated all of these Amazons, then Sgathaich's daughter, and finally fought Sgathaich to a standstill, each of them being unable to defeat the other. Only at this point did she recognise he was worthy of her tuition.

In a completely separate tradition, Cu Chulainn actually had the castle built himself, commissioning a witch or fairy to complete the task in one night:

Dun Scaich Castle, home of beaked toads, dragons, Amazons, mythical warriors, and multiple murders.

All night the witch sang, and the castle grew
Up from the rock, with tower and turrets crowned;
All night she sang— when fell the morning dew,
'Twas finished round and round.

If the weather is good, a grand view of the castle can be obtained from a seat-shaped rock down on the beach, the perfect place from which to contemplate this cauldron of myth and legend.

TOKAVAIG

North of the township the remains of three cairns flank the inlet of Inbhir Amhlabhaig. The one to the west (known as Druim Dubh, NG60441259) is badly mutilated but the burial cist can just be made out. On the opposite side of the stream are two adjacent cairns, the better preserved specimen still having its stone-lined cist (NG60591264). A complete skeleton was found in the other cairn, the bones being taken to the schoolhouse, the ruins of which can be seen to the south-west. According to Sillar and Meyler's book, *Skye*, the skeleton kept the inhabitants awake with its whistling, so they got rid of it. Another burial cist was reported under the floor of the schoolhouse, but it is no longer visible.

Otta Swire relates that the wood north-east of Tokavaig was once called Doir'an Druidean, which supposedly means 'the sacred grove of the druids'. As a result of this dubious translation a flimsy edifice of druidical nonsense has been constructed, with tales of the worship of an ancient deity in the form of a horse, sacrifices using a silver knife, and the pagans being purged by St Comgan. In contrast to this farrago – which has all the hallmarks of the antiquarian lust to see faux druids around every corner – Alexander Forbes in his 1923 *The Place Names of Skye* states Doir'an Druidean really translates as 'the grove of starlings or thrushes'.

ORD

The highlight here is most definitely the complete skeleton of a water-horse. The bones can be found in the small and delightful garden of An Acarsaid on the shore, where they are mounted on a plinth with a notice describing the creature's habits and possible relationship with the Loch Ness Monster. Of course, this is not an actual each uisge, but the corpse of some marine mammal, probably a small whale. It is, however, still wonderful. The garden is open from 1 April to 31 October, 10 a.m. to 5.30 p.m., and all proceeds from the donation box go to charity. Wheelchair access is limited to the upper part of the garden, with no view of the water-horse.

A little further north along the shoreline is the holy well of Tobar Chaon (NG616135), now covered by a cistern, but a pipe still pumps water out onto the pebbles. Possibly this means the seaweed is imbued with holiness. Otta Swire gives the legend that this well was originally Tobar na Slainte (Well of Health) and flowed beside the chapel called Teampull Chaon on the upper ground a few hundred paces south-west. The well, says the story, was originally a pagan spring until blessed by St Chaon or Comgan (he who also supposedly expelled the druids from the sacred grave at TOKAVAIG). An unbeliever washed his dirty hands in the water to show his contempt for the new faith, at which point the disgusted well promptly decamped to the shore. Time has eliminated virtually everything of the church at Teampull Chaon (NG61831321), along with its pre-Christian Stone of Healing and the spring called Tobar an Domhnaich (Well of the Lord). The area around has faint traces of folklore that suggest this may have been an important Christian centre. Swire says that to the east, near Cnoc na Fuarachad (Hill of Cold) is the River of Cold (or Death), across which the dead were carried for some unknown reason. Two miles (3km) east, spanning the road, is a small wood called Coill a' Ghasgain. According to Seton Gordon in *Highways and Byways in the West Highlands*, this marked the entrance to the sanctuary centred on the chapel. As soon as a man charged with a crime or in fear of his enemies entered St Comgan's Sanctuary he was safe from pursuit for a year and a day. This was certainly the theory; I'm not convinced that a clan culture that frequently burned people alive in churches would have much respect for the concept of sanctuary. A giant called Mòchaidh lived on Sgiath-bheinn an Uird, the hill to the north-east (NG643138); one of the boulders now in the sea at Ord is his handiwork. Ord was briefly the home of Alexander Smith, author of the delightful book *A Summer in Skye*. In it he gives an example of second-sight, as related to him by the local priest, Father McCrimmon. About 1878, a young cowherd claimed he had seen a fishing boat sink as it rounded the point. The sea was calm and the fishermen, the two brothers McMillan, were experienced sailors. No one could believe anything adverse could have happened and the boy had his ears boxed for telling lies. But the men did not come home, and when Loch Eishort was searched nothing was found. So Father McCrimmon consulted 'Old Mirren', a poor woman from Ord who had the second-sight.

The skeleton of a 'Long-Tailed Water-Horse' at An Acarsaid, Ord. Dr Colin MacLeod, a zoologist from the University of Aberdeen, has tentatively identified the skeleton as an adult male Cuvier's beaked whale.

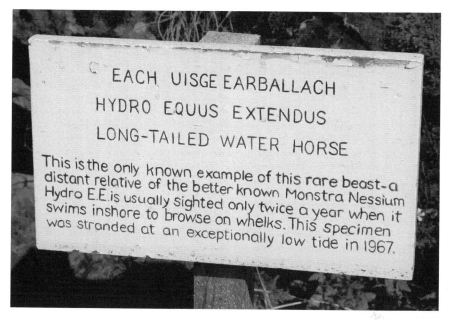

EACH UISGE EARBALLACH
HYDRO EQUUS EXTENDUS
LONG-TAILED WATER HORSE
This is the only known example of this rare beast - a
distant relative of the better known Monstra Nessium
Hydro E.E. is usually sighted only twice a year when it
swims inshore to browse on whelks. This specimen
was stranded at an exceptionally low tide in 1967.

The notice identifying the water-horse, with its nomenclature in both Latin and Gaelic.

'Will they get the bodies?' he asked. Mirren shook her head.

'The bodies are not there to get; they have floated out past Rum to the main ocean.'

'How do you know?'

'Going out to the shore about a month ago I heard a scream, and, looking up, saw a boat off the point, with two men in it, caught in a squall, and going down. When the boat sank the men still remained in it, the one entangled in the fishing-net, the other in the ropes of the sails. I saw them float out to the main sea ...'

McCrimmon continued the tale:

... six weeks after, a capsized boat was thrown on the shore in Uist, with two corpses inside, one entangled in the fishing-net, the other in the ropes of the sails. It was the McMillans' boat, and it was the two brothers who were inside. Their faces were all eaten away by the dog-fishes; but the people who had done business with them in Uist identified them by their clothes. 'This I know to be true,' said the Father emphatically, and shutting the door on all argument or hint of scepticism.

The road from Ord to the main highway skirts the beautiful Loch Meadal (NG658111). Swire gives the amusing story of a young couple who were walking past the loch on the way back from their wedding when a water-horse rose out of the loch. The groom took to his heels but his bride was hampered by her long skirts. As the water-horse caught her she shouted to her husband for help, but he ran off. 'Don't be frightened,' said the half-human creature as he carried her away, 'better half a man than one who is no man at all.' Loch na Doirenach over the moors to the west (NG637107) was also home to an each uisge, which makes three in three successive lochs in this area.

The now piped and covered holy well of Tobar Chaon situated by the beach at Ord.

THE SOUND OF SLEAT

In *Superstitions of the Highlands and Islands of Scotland* J.G. Campbell describes the sea-serpent of Scottish folklore, the Cirein Crôin, the largest of all creatures in the sea:

> Seven herrings are a Salmon's fill,
> Seven Salmon are a Seal's fill,
> Seven Seals are a Whale's fill,
> Seven Whales are the fill of a Cirein Crôin
> And seven Cirein Crôin are the fill of the Big Devil himself.

The stretch of water between Sleat and the mainland has been the setting for some of the most dramatic sightings of sea monsters in the British Isles. A typical example is a very detailed report that appeared in *The Zoologist* journal (No. 92, May 1873), although the first printed account was in the *Inverness Courier* in August 1872. On the 20th of that month the Revd John McRae, minister of Glenelg from 1840 to 1875, plus the Revd David Twopeny, vicar of Stockbury, Kent, along with MacRae's grandson, his two adult daughters Kate and Miss Forbes J. MacRae, and Gilbert Bogle of Newcastle, all saw a huge multi-humped creature swimming close to their boat. At a rough estimate they thought it was 45ft (13.7m) in length, although later sightings increased this guess. The head was rarely seen but seemed to be small. Up to eight humps were seen at one time. There were hints of a fin on the back or neck. The day was calm and bright and viewing conditions excellent. They sighted the animal several times again the next day in Loch Hourn and the Sound of Sleat, and consistently recorded its rapid and smooth motion and the sound of spray as it moved past – MacRae thought it was travelling at 10-12 miles (16-19km) an hour. They were all of the opinion that it was a sea-serpent.

The witnesses were people of substance, and their connections and influence meant they could seek out other people who had seen the creature. The ferrymen on each side of the Kylerhea strait, and Finlay McRae of Bundaloch and several other men in a boat on Loch Hourn, all had sightings on 21 August, as did a telescope-wielding woman from Duisdale on Skye who said she saw a strange object that appeared 'like eight seals in a row'. On either 22 or 23 August, guests aboard Lord MacDonald's ostentatious steam-yacht – the Revd McNeill of Skye and Mrs G.C. Lysons, along with his lordship himself – all spotted the animal. And on both 23 and 24 August Alexander and Farquhar Macmillan of Dornie saw it from a boat on Loch Duich, where they were sufficiently alarmed to speedily head for the shore. Alexander estimated its length as 60-80ft (18-24m). (Something large had also been seen rushing about in Loch Duich in the summer of 1871, but no one got a good look at it.)

The sighting was widely publicised and clearly made an impact locally. When writing *Somewhere in Scotland* (1935), Alasdair Alpin MacGregor was told of it by 'a well-informed lady in the district'. She said the monster 'was as big and as round as a herring barrel, and of great length. And it went wriggling up and down through the water, zigzag, right and left like.' A good account of the events is in Charles Gould's *Mythical Monsters* (1886) but the best is found in *The Great Sea-Serpent* by the Dutch zoologist A.C. Oudemans (1892). Oudemans had tracked down the principal witnesses – some of whom were anonymous in the original reports – and received previously unpublished descriptions from some of them; the accounts are all consistent, and it definitely seems that something unusual was swimming through the Sound of Sleat in 1872.

This giant-sized sea-serpent taking a jaunt in Loch Alsh was created in the 1930s by the photographer Duncan Macpherson of Kyle. Its iconography is drawn from popular ideas about the Loch Ness Monster.

This was not the only encounter. In September 1893 a London physician, Dr Farquhar Matheson, was sailing off Kyle of Lochalsh when he saw:

> Something rise out of the Loch in front of us – a long, straight, neck-like thing as tall as a mast … It was then 200 yards away, and was moving towards us. Then it began to draw its neck down and I saw clearly that it was a large sea monster – of the saurian type, I should think. It was brown in colour, shining, and with a sort of ruffle at the junction of the head and neck.

Matheson compared it to a longer version of a giraffe's neck. It swam west out of the loch, diving and reappearing every few minutes. No body was visible. Matheson concluded: 'It was not a sea-serpent, [a] but much larger and more substantial beast – something in the nature of a gigantic lizard. An eel could not lift up its body like that, nor could a snake.' The most accessible account is in Peter Costello's *In Search of Lake Monsters* (1974).

And to finish on a note of glorious exaggeration, in *The Misty Isle of Skye*, J.A. Macculloch was given a description of the sea-serpent by a man from Kylerhea: 'Yes, yes, one day I saw the fearful head of the beast go down the Kyle, and indeed it was a week after before his tail had passed!'

THREE

THE CENTRE: MINGINISH AND THE CUILLINS

SCONSER – SLIGACHAN – GLEN BRITTLE – CARBOST – BRACADALE

No one who has seen a summer sunset from the Cuillin can fail to sense the nearness of things spiritual. The half-forgotten Celtic Gods, the Fairies or Daoine Sithe, the Spirit of the Hills, the mysterious Spiritforces of the sea – all these are more closely joined to him than the affairs of everyday life.

Seton Gordon, *The Charm of Skye*

This is the heartland of Skye, a land of mountains and moorland, few roads and fewer people.

SCONSER

Several of the stories Mary Julia MacCulloch collected were set in Sconser. Bella Nicolson told MacCulloch that she, her sister and two companions heard sweet music coming from the mission-house late at night. The building was uninhabited at that hour, and so their conclusion was that the sounds were made by spirits.

When a particular man died in the township, his neighbours, as was usual, sat up all night to 'watch' the corpse. For several hours after midnight the dreadful sound of clanking chains was heard, prompting fervent praying. The noises stopped just as dawn broke, and it was widely believed that the prayers of the watchers had prevented Satan from claiming the man's soul.

A woman begged a bed for the night from two sisters, choosing to sleep between them. In the early hours, one sister found that her sibling had been killed and possibly eaten; she fled and managed to cross a stream just as the cock crew. The combination defeated her pursuer, now revealed as a water-horse. The inability to cross running water is a curious taboo for a creature that resides in lochs; this sounds more like an evil spirit or witch than a conventional each uisge.

Another Macculloch, this time the Revd J.A., mentioned a curious episode in *The Misty Isle of Skye*. In 1900 it was proposed that the crofters of Sconser should move to better land in the south of Skye. They objected. One of the reasons, as presented to the Crofters' Commission, was that the intended site was cursed. Evictions had formerly taken place on the spot, and hence the area was marked as a place of evil; nothing would thrive there.

SLIGACHAN

This metropolis consists of a road junction, a campsite and a hotel, the latter being the base-camp for several famous assaults on the Cuillins in the nineteenth century. It was here that the great mountaineer Norman Collie lived out the final years of his life (he died in 1942 and is buried at BRACADALE). Sgurr Thormaid (Norman's Peak) is named after him, a fitting tribute to the first person to effectively map the Cuillins. He was a former Professor of Organic Chemistry and Derek Cooper relates how in 1939 the local rumour was that this frail white-bearded scientist was a world expert on poison gases; he was supposedly staying at Sligachan to work on deadly weapons with which to defeat the Nazis. That wasn't true, but Collie was certainly famous for something else strange: in 1925 he penned an article recounting his 1891 encounter with an apparently invisible entity atop the Cairngorms in North-East Scotland:

> I began to think I heard something else than merely the noise of my own footsteps. For every few steps I heard a crunch, and then another crunch as if someone was walking after me but taking steps three or four times the length of my own. I said to myself this is all nonsense. I listened and heard it again but could see nothing in the mist. As I walked on and the eerie crunch, crunch sounded behind me I was seized with terror and took to my heels.

The experience was probably an extreme example of 'mountain panic', in which strange sounds combine with the sense of the uncanny often felt on high mountains to produce an overwhelming sense of fear. It certainly overwhelmed Collie, despite his vast mountaineering experience. Whatever happened that day, the legend of 'The Big Grey Man of Ben MacDhui' was born, and continues to circulate to this day in Aberdeenshire and Inverness-shire. (For a Skye example of mountain panic, see BACA RUADH.)

During the 1940s and '50s something that took on the form of a phantom car or lorry was frequently seen between Sligachan and Portree, when most of the road was single track. There are several accounts, some of them contradictory, and by the time you get to the internet, the process of 'paranormal Chinese whispers' is in full flow. Probably the best-known reliable report was penned by Seton Gordon for the *Scots Magazine* in October 1959. At an unnamed date he and his wife were driving in broad daylight when they both saw a lorry approaching from beyond a bend. Gordon prepared to pull in to let it pass – but when they rounded the bend, there was no vehicle in sight, and nowhere it could have gone. Gordon then noted that the vehicle had been seen by many people in both the hours of daylight and darkness, and at night appeared as a single bright light that looked like a car rapidly approaching in the middle of the road. In one case the light appeared in the pre-dawn winter darkness to a mail van driver who was faced with a head-on collision – but at the last minute the light appeared to pass right through the van.

Alasdair Alpin MacGregor had earlier recorded several other sightings in his 1953 book *Skye and the Inner Hebrides*. On 10 February 1948, the driver of a lorry travelling from Sconser to Portree saw a car approaching, so he pulled up to let the vehicle pass – only to see the car vanish 60yds (55m) in front of him. Five other men in the lorry also saw the phantom disappear. On 24 March of the same year, five people from Sconser were driving to Portree when they saw a car and a lorry approaching. The larger vehicle passed them, but the car simply vanished. As with Gordon's encounter, this took place during the day.

Peter Underwood's *Gazetteer of Scottish Ghosts* (1974) pushes the earliest report back to 1941. In that year, Dr Allan MacDonald saw a car approaching at a frightening speed, so he pulled over – but no vehicle passed him. Donald MacKinnon from Sconser, and his son Donald John MacKinnon, both saw the speeding vehicle on separate occasions – and the speed was too fast for any ordinary car. Lt Donald Campbell of the island's Observer Corps was driving south to Broadford when he saw the powerful headlights of the vehicle approaching fast – but, again, it vanished. Postman Neil MacDiarmid saw it in the darkness near Sligachan. A chill swept over him in his van as he saw an old Austin travelling very fast. It seemed to have one bright headlight and 'a kind of dim glow' inside the car which allowed him to see there was no driver at the wheel. The vehicle sped off and disappeared.

MacDiarmid's report is the source for the widely-quoted notion that the phantom is a 1934 Austin Seven (although he did not actually identify the year or make). The Austin Seven was a popular marque in production from 1922 to 1939, and several models dated from 1934. Even if MacDiarmid's sighting was of an Austin Seven – and I am not convinced of this – this identification cannot stand for all the encounters. Seton Gordon's phantom, for example, was definitely a lorry. In addition, many of the night-time sightings are only of a single bright light. The vehicle was inferred, but not seen. The sightings have occurred in daylight and darkness, at all times of the year, and in both directions. If all the reports are reliable, it is possible the phenomenon takes a number of different forms, some of which are interpreted as vehicles, while others are fast-moving lights. One possibility is that the phantom is some kind of 'future echo' – cars of today obviously travel much faster than their mid-twentieth-century predecessors, so perhaps the witnesses were seeing ghost-images of cars from their future.

Norman Adams' 1998 work *Haunted Scotland* states that in 1987 the phantom car was spotted by two men out hunting foxes, and by an island policeman driving to Portree after a football match. However, the upgrading of the A87 into a two-lane racetrack seems to have made the phenomenon a thing of the past – unless some readers know otherwise.

Tracking the 'Sligachan Phantom Car' accurately is frustrating because the story irresistibly lends itself to retelling and exaggeration. On 15 April 1966 Elizabeth Byrd, staying at an Edinburgh hotel, was told about the ghost vehicle by Anne, a young maid from Skye. Anne said the car was black, and always sped without a driver or headlights. A local minister was taxiing some women and their children on an errand when he saw the phantom car. He swerved and drove into the waters of Portree harbour, drowning all his passengers. As a result he was confined to an asylum in Inverness-shire. This superb example of a weird episode hyped up into something ridiculously catastrophic is in Byrd's memoir of her supernatural experiences, *A Strange and Seeing Time*. In the same book is a case from 1961 related by 'Ronnie

C'. Ronnie had been on holiday in Skye with two solicitors whom he described as 'stiff-upper-lip Englishmen'. After a walk in thick mist on the first day, one of them left abruptly and returned to London. Two years later he revealed that on the path he had seen his dead wife, wearing the black silk dress she had been buried in some seven years previously. 'She came right out of the mist and looked at me and smiled, so real that I could see the white flowers at her throat.' Possibly the fact that he had been due to marry again had some effect on the experience.

In 1886 J.G. Frazer, author of *The Golden Bough*, the famous compendium of folklore and mythology, contributed a piece to the *Folk-Lore Journal*. His guide at Sligachan the previous year told him of the experience of an acquaintance. This young man, walking home late at night, was attacked by a foal. The struggle continued for some time until the man's dog bit the horse, at which point the assailant spoke to him in a human voice. The foal, it transpired, was a girl he had jilted. As she was a witch she had shapeshifted to wreak her revenge; only the dog's bite had compelled her to reveal herself. The resemblance between this story and a similar adventure at GLASNAKILLE is striking.

THE CUILLIN HILLS – HARTA CORRIE

> This dark gorge … is a place of dread. The ghosts of the slain haunt it; the fairy folk dance in it, and, if all tales be true, make their elfin bolts of the bones of the dead. Here, where the silence is so sacred that it weighs upon you like a heavy load, a great clan fight was fought, grim and great, a whole summer day; the blood of MacDonalds and MacLeods ran like water; and round this massive red boulder, named so appropriately, were piled the heaps of the slain. You shudder as you pause by the stone; in fancy the glen rings with the fierce shouts of the clansmen and the shrieks of the dying; you see the eagles at their ghastly feast, – and you hurry away lest some shape of dread should confront you.

Thus the Revd Macculloch introduced Harta Corrie in *The Misty Isle of Skye*. The valley penetrates deep into the Cuillin massif from the east, and is reached by a long and boggy walk along Glen Sligachan. The boulder Macculloch refers to is the Bloody Stone, on the south side of the Sligachan river (NG48812365), and the battle seems to have taken place around 1395. Tradition claims the MacDonalds were victorious, and that not one MacLeod warrior was left alive. In his book *Psychic Scotland,* medium Tom Rannachan recalls sitting here alone as a small boy and hearing the sound of men shouting and screaming. This was long before he learned about the slaughter.

In November 1956, Oxford geology student Peter Zinovieff and his half-brother Sir Patrick Skipwith were engaged in making the first geological map of the Cuillins. They pitched camp in Harta Corrie, only to be awakened at around 2 or 3 a.m. by the sight of dozens of kilted Highlanders moving purposefully across the mountainside. Accounts vary as to whether the warriors were completely silent or making a noise, but they were definitely apparitions, and made no sign they were aware of the two very frightened men, even though they passed within 50yds (45m) of the tent. After about eight to ten minutes the figures could no longer be seen. Either the following night, or the one after, Zinovieff and Skipwith saw the clansmen again, only this time the band appeared to be in dispirited retreat. The sighting was reported in the press soon after, and Skipwith's aristocratic background seemed to ensure the pair were not mocked. There is a good account in Alasdair Alpin MacGregor's *Phantom Footsteps* (1959). As an aside, Peter Zinovieff is now a pioneer of electronic and computer music, and in the 1960s he invented the famous VCS3 synthesiser, as used on many Pink Floyd records and by other progressive/space-rock groups.

LOCH CORUISK

This large freshwater loch set in its basin of brutally bare mountains was a favourite spot for nineteenth-century visitors in search of the sublime and savage in nature, and its dramatic if sombre charms remain popular to this day. It is usually reached by boat daytrips from ELGOL, while hardier souls walk in from Glen Sligachan or via the path through Camusunary – anyone entering this uninhabited wilderness must be equipped with food and appropriate clothing and equipment. The Cuillins have claimed far too many lives already.

Coruisk was fêted by Sir Walter Scott and other luminaries of the Romantic Movement, and the stark scenery seemed to cry out for tales of the uncanny. The valley at the head of the loch, Coire-nan-Uraisg (these days marked as Coir'-Uisg) was said to be the home of an urisk, described by the Revd Macculloch as 'a fearful shape, half-human, half-goat, with long hair, long teeth and claws.' Somewhere in this corrie was the Cave of the Ghost. In 1883 Robert Buchanan, author of *The Hebrid Isles*, asked about this cave and was told by his guide Hamish that, 'the taisch [spirit] o' a shepherd has been seen in it sitting cross-leggit, and branding a bluidy sheep.' Hamish also knew the story of an old man from Dunvegan who had discovered a source of gold and precious stones near Loch Coruisk. 'It was whispered about that he had sold himsel' to the Deil, at night, here by the loch; and he didna deny it.' The treasure brought the man wealth but not happiness, and on his death-bed he confessed to the priest that his heart had been blackened with greed. He also described the location of the find: an obscure cave with 'strange marks like writing all o'er the walls.' Strangest to tell, however, was that he was not the first man to have accidentally stumbled upon this cave: at the entrance was the coulter of a plough, a pair of rotten brogues – and a set of human bones. Despite these hints that this was a place of bad, dangerous magic, after the man's death his relatives continuously searched for the cave, but never succeeded; and it has eluded modern mountaineers to this day (unless they have found it, and have just not told anyone).

South of where the path from Glen Sligachan passes Loch A'Choire Riabhaich is a small pyramidal monument (NG49882060). The plaque on it reads:

> Erected in memory of Staff Captain A.J. Maryon GHQ India Command who met his death here in July 1946. He lay on this spot for nearly two years and now rests in Portree. This cairn was built by his friend Myles Morrison ex Staff Captain R.E. who served with him in the 1939-45 War.

The remoteness of this location highlights the degree of dedication the former Royal Engineer must have had in erecting this memorial to his friend, who died after setting off from Sligachan. If you're passing, it's worth ascending the hill and spending a few moments in contemplation.

GLEN BRITTLE

Many people use this glen as the jumping-off point for walks and climbs in the Cuillins. About half-way down the glen is the Fairy Pools car park on the west side of the single-track road (NG423258). Opposite from this, a good path follows the Allt Coir' a' Mhadaidh as it heads directly into the overpowering masses of raw rock and scree. The mountain water of the stream is crystal clear and on the gently rising plain a series of small waterfalls has created a necklace of beautiful pools called, naturally, the Fairy Pools – although there is no other connection with the Sithe. These rock-fringed cauldrons of blue water are ideal for al fresco bathing – indeed, many enthusiasts regard them as the best site for outdoor freshwater swimming in the country. The water is cold – very cold – so don't bother pussyfooting around, just jump straight in (do not dive). Following the initial shock your internal central heating kicks in and the experience becomes very pleasurable. The further up the stream you go, the better the pools tend to be. The stream passes through Coire na Creiche (Hollow of the Spoil), so-named for a clan battle from 1602, in which the MacDonalds beat the MacLeods, the fighting lasting all day and into the moonlit night. A sword-fighting sequence from the fantasy movie *Highlander* was filmed on Sron Na Ciche (NG445204).

RUBHA AN DÙNAIN

The long and wonderful walk to this, the southernmost tip of Minginish, leaves from the campsite at the shore in Glen Brittle. The route crosses several fords so if the rivers are in spate, do it another day. The 'Roo' itself is a boggy moorland replete with several thousands years' worth of archaeological sites, and it can be easy to lose your bearings. However, the entire headland is cut off by a wall running through a miniature glen called the Slochd Dubh (Black Pit), so no matter where you are, head in the direction of the Cuillins and you will eventually hit this wall.

From the wall follow the north coast below Carn Mor to reach the tiny Loch na h-Airde, only a little higher than the adjacent sea, by which it is regularly invaded. Its potential for a safe anchorage is obvious, and at its southern end is an artificial channel cut wide enough for birlinns to pass through; this may date from Viking times. On the loch's north shore is a Neolithic chambered cairn, probably the best preserved on Skye (NG39341636). You can crawl through the entrance passage to the central chamber, which was left roofless after an excavation in the 1930s. On a promontory just east of the canal is an Iron Age dun in reasonable condition, with the entrance and galleries within the wall still visible (NG39581597). East from the loch a small, shallow cave in the hillside can be seen (NG39951625). An excavation in 1932 found evidence that the overhang had been used as a 'workshop' for several thousand years. Stone-knappers had been making stone tools at the time of the later stage of the Neolithic chambered cairn; smiths had been smelting iron when the dun was occupied; and other people had been using the cave on a more casual basis up until at least the Middle Ages.

The stream to the left (north) leads to the ruins of Rhundanan House, a substantial eighteenth-century building that was still occupied in the 1860s. This was the home of the MacAskills of Rubha a Dùnain, a family of Norse origin who traditionally had occupied this land for nine centuries. All that came to an end with the nineteenth-century Clearances, and several other fragments of the former township form a melancholy sight. In *The Screaming Skulls and Other Ghost Stories*, Elliott O'Donnell gives an episode of second-sight from Rhundanan. For three nights a shepherd was woken in his cottage by the apparition of Mary, one of the maids from the big house. There was a handkerchief tied around her head, and she was dripping wet. After gazing at the shepherd for a few moments she kissed him on the forehead, went to the door, and vanished before his eyes. Soon after, the lady of the house was helping Mary take linen out of a cupboard when a sound like a gun was heard. 'Oh, ma'am,' said the alarmed maid, 'there will be grave-clothes taken from that chest before this week is over.' Her employer laughed this off, as she did with the shepherd's tale, but the next day Mary drowned in the Rhundunan river, and was found with her handkerchief around her head.

Right: Fairy Pools, Glen Brittle. Notice how the fairies have kindly provided car parking and picnic tables.

Below: One of the Cuillins-fed Fairy Pools, seconds before the author jumped into the icy waters.

In *The Charm of Skye* Seton Gordon tells the tale of Iain Dubh MacAskill, who got the beautiful dairymaid Ciarag pregnant. The great man could not wed such an ordinary lass (or perhaps he was already married?) so he ordered his grieve (farm manager) to marry the girl. The man refused, so his employer threw him into a deep cave or pit. As you do. After three days Iain returned to the cave in a winter blizzard and shouted down. The grieve was still alive but adamantly refused to marry. Iain eventually relented, rescued the man and carried him on his back to Rudha an Dùnain. Ciarag, however, was so upset, the grieve would not marry her that she lost her mind and lived as a hermit in the cave later called Uamha Chiarag or Ciarag's Cave. This is probably the cave on Loch Brittle-side below the path at NG406181, north of the Rubha na Creige Mòire outcrop. The return route is by the Slochd Dubh wall and the same coastal path.

CARBOST

MacGregor's *Over the Sea to Skye* has two stories from this area above Loch Harport. A poor shepherd and wife gave refuge to a little old man. Several times in the night their guest complained of black raindrops falling on him from the roof. The next morning the couple saw that the drops were in fact blood. The old man told them that in his youth he had murdered a man and buried the body near what was now their house; the rain of blood was his supernatural punishment for the crime.

The Beatons were the famous hereditary doctors in the service of the MacLeods. One of their number, known as Fearchar Lighiche ('Farquhar the Physician'), attracted a great deal of folklore – for example, he knew the language of birds, and hence the ravens would come and tell him who was sick. One day Fearchar met a funeral near Carbost. He addressed the coffin, and the corpse came alive.

EYNORT

The lonely minor road from Carbost terminates at this miniscule township at the head of Loch Eynort. Reachable along the beach or by a path from the road-end is the delightful St Mealrubha's churchyard, also known as Borline and Kilmoruy. Coffins were often brought by boat (many people buried here were from the isle of Soay). The larger of the two ruined buildings (NG37572599) is the eighteenth-century church, while its smaller and more complete companion is its medieval predecessor converted into the private burial chapel for the MacLeods of Talisker, with good armorial stones within.

The Revd Macculloch recounts the story of the elaborately-carved medieval font that once stood within the ruins. Some Catholic fishermen from South Uist, sheltering from the weather in Loch Eynort, discovered the font: 'deeming it too sacred for the Protestants of Skye, [they] resolved to carry it to their priest.' Twice they set out, and twice were forced back by a storm. Fearing that St Mealrubha was displeased, they replaced the font, and were instantly granted fair weather. On their next visit the re-emboldened men again lifted the font, and this time were unimpeded by wind or wave. The font made its way through various antiquarian hands and now

Above left: A drawing of the carved medieval font from St Mealrubha's Church, Eynort, portrayed in Joseph Anderson's *Scotland in Early Christian Times* (1881).

Above right: Eynort church. Many coffins were landed on the beach and brought through the sea-gate seen in the background.

resides in the National Museum of Scotland in Edinburgh. The clear carvings are of Christ on the Cross, the Virgin and Child, a mitred bishop holding a crozier (this may be a representation of St Mealrubha) and a sword-wielding St Michael slaying the dragon. An unusual detail of the last image is that the archangel is planting a limb of the Cross in the dragon's mouth. Two stones carved with simple crosses can be found at Tusdale to the west (NG35412484).

In 1927 the Revd Canon R.C. MacLeod of MacLeod published a history of the clan, *The MacLeods of Dunvegan*. In it he gives a legend that clearly relates to the endless enmity between his ancestors and the MacDonalds. Once upon a midnight hour a shepherd was at his task near Eynort church when he saw the graves open and from them emerge a host of winged warrior spirits. They gathered up the terrified man and swooped across all the MacLeod territories of Skye, being joined by further clan-spirits at each graveyard. The ghostly host then flew on to South Uist where they were met by a great army of MacDonald spectres; and among their number was a mortal MacDonald man. Surrounded by their phantom ancestors, the two men were forced to fight. Long and severe was the duel, with neither gaining the advantage over the other (it is not explained how a simple shepherd was skilled in sword-play). At the first light of dawn, with the conflict still unresolved, both forces dispersed, each warrior returning to his grave, and the hapless shepherd being deposited at the exact spot from which he had been abducted.

TALISKER

Note that Talisker Distillery is actually in Carbost, 5 miles (8km) away by moorland road. South of the few buildings at Talisker is Dun Sleadale, a ruined broch still retaining its entrance passage and some galleries (NG32382920). Mary Julia MacCulloch tells the tale of two shepherd lads at Talisker, one of whom seemed to be wasting away. The other discovered that each night the mistress of the house was bewitching the lad with a magic halter and riding him as a horse. He offered to swap sleeping places with his companion, and that night the witch rode him through the air to an inn, where she parked on the roof and went in for a convivial drink. The canny boy removed the halter, hid above the door, and threw the magic item over the witch when she emerged. She was duly transformed into a horse, and the lad had her shod at a smithy. The next day the mistress of the house said she could not leave her bed because she was ill; but soon it was discovered that her hands and feet were nailed with horseshoes, and her witchery was revealed. This tale is told of many other places in Scotland, including ULLINISH, where the details, as given in MacGregor's *Over the Sea to Skye*, are almost exactly the same, the only difference being that the witch-ridden lad is given the advice by the unsuspecting farmer, who then finds his own wife lying in bed with her feet horseshoed.

> An aged island laird dreamed, previous to a visit to Skye, that he should fall over a precipice: he was returning in the evening to Talisker, accompanied by a servant, when the augury was realized; his servant was severely hurt, and he himself crippled for life. This gentleman assured me, that his housekeeper dreamed the self-same dream on the same night.
>
> Lord Teignmouth, *Sketches of the Coasts and Islands of Scotland*

PORTNALONG

Minginish is noted for its association with fairies. *The Charm of Skye* tells of a man who was ordered to build a byre to hold as many cows as there were days in a year (it is not clear who issued this order; presumably it was his clan chief). He constructed the walls but could not put the roof up. In desperation he kidnapped an elf; only when the fairies agreed to roof the byre did he release his hostage.

In 1911 the splendidly-named American anthropologist Walter Yeeling Evans-Wentz published *The Fairy-Faith in Celtic Countries*, a wonderful compendium of current belief about, and stories of, the Little Folk. Two of his tales were given to him by Frances Tolmie, who heard them from a Minginish goat-herd, Mary Macdonald. Two women walking towards Ardtreck Point heard churning going on under a hillock. One said she fancied some buttermilk, and instantly a diminutive woman came out from the fairy knoll with a bowl. The human woman, however, declined the kind offer, and in consequence was imprisoned in the hillock. She was told she would not be set free until she had spun all the wool from an enormous bag and eaten all the meal in a vast chest. The task seemed unending until she was assisted by another captive, an old man who told her to wet her left eye with saliva each morning before commencing work. This ensured the wool and meal were consumed, and eventually the woman was set free. Sad to say the old man's role in her early release was suspected, and he was cursed by the fairy to remain in the knoll for ever. There is a dun, Dun Ardtreck, near the point, in so-so condition (NG33503581); this may have been the fairy knoll.

The second tale, set somewhere in Minginish, concerned an infant who was cursed by three witch-fairies: 'When that peat now burning on the hearth shall be consumed, her life will surely come to an end.' The child's mother immediately put the fire out and carefully wrapped up the half-burnt peat ember, hiding it in a safe place. There it remained until the child grew to be a beautiful woman. Just before getting married, the maiden found the package and, thinking it was just an old worthless fragment of peat, threw it on the fire. By the time it had burnt through, she was dead.

Frances Tolmie had a passion for folklore and collected many songs and tales, with many of the former published in the *Journal of the Folk-Song Society* in 1911. Ethel Bassin's 1977 biography, *The Old Songs of Skye: Frances Tolmie and her Circle*, describes Tolmie learning the 'Lamentation of the Water-Horse' from Kate MacDiarmid, who led the singing at the waulkings (the cleansing of wool during clothmaking). In this lullaby the each uisge is entreating his human wife to return to him and their child. Tolmie's companion on her folklore-collecting trips was often Oighrig (Effie) Ross, who taught Tolmie the song of the gruagach, the guardian spirit of cattle, which killed a girl in Glen MacAskill after she had insulted an intractable cow. When the girl's mother lamented her daughter's death through the night, the invisible gruagach, with his long golden hair and shining white bosom or shirt, stayed up to watch her until daybreak. The song is ambiguous as to whether the gruagach was learning about human behaviour and grief, sorry for what it had done, or guarding the grieving woman. The elderly Effie was apparently eccentric and wild-looking; in previous centuries she would have been the stereotype of the witch. She told Tolmie that one day she had gone down on her knees to pray to a beautiful cloud as it passed overhead; this seemed to her as natural as going to church.

FISKAVAIG

Since 2006 the same team responsible for the excavation at HIGH PASTURE CAVE have been investigating Uamh an Eich Bhric (Cave of the Speckled Horses), in the cliffs south of Geodh' an Eich Bhric, to the south-west of Fiskavaig. Access to this remote site is both arduous and dangerous. The dramatically-sited rock shelter has yielded extensive evidence of use during the Iron Age, with a wide range of pottery, bone, stone and metal finds. The most fascinating piece is a fragment of a human skullcap with a drilled hole. The current speculation is that the skull was suspended, and that it was therefore perhaps a revered ancestor. See www.high-pasture-cave.org for updates. In 1927 a carved Pictish stone was recovered from the shore at Fiskavaig Bay. It is now in the National Museum of Scotland in Edinburgh.

BRACADALE

Dun Taimh, west of the A863 opposite the junction with the minor road to Colliore, is worth the slog and scramble up the hill (NG36303664). This is an Iron Age hill-fort, as distinct from a broch or dun. It has a formidable position, with one side defended by sheer cliffs, and an entrance guarded by two walls. At a date traditionally ascribed to the fourteenth century, MacLeod, laird of Gesto (the house just to the west), remonstrated with his kinsmen who were removing stones from the fort for building purposes. He reasoned that it was such a position of strength that one day they might need it as a refuge. Much to his surprise he found himself at the receiving end of gratitude from the fairies, whose dwelling he had inadvertently saved. At the shore they summoned fifty white cattle from the sea and gave them to MacLeod, and from that day onwards the MacLeods of Gesto were especially favoured by the Sithe. The white cattle were bred for generations but are no longer to be found on Skye. The prohibition on removing stones clearly did not count for much in the nineteenth century. In 1887, at the Golden Jubilee of Queen Victoria, the walls were robbed to build a cairn in the centre of the fort. One of the lintel stones of the 'cupboard' in the cairn is faintly carved with Norse runes. If this stone came from the Iron Age fort, it may mean Dun Taimh was visited much later in its life by a Viking graffiti artist.

Another fairy dwelling was Dun Garsin, in the valley north-east of where the main road crosses the Amar (NG36093878). Its almost complete state of dereliction is ascribed to the work of a greedy man who, when he knew the fairies were absent, helped himself to the stones so he could build a cattle-byre. He acquired two cart-loads, but on the third trip, 'an unearthly light shone forth and mysterious voices were heard, threatening this mortal with dire vengeance.' (*The Misty Isle of Skye.*) The fairies were never seen again, save one greybeard who returned to weep for his despoiled home, before vanishing. The guilty man lost everything to animal disease and crop failure, and eventually was forced to emigrate. Dun Diarmaid, to the south-west, is even more dilapidated (NG35453816). It bears the name of the hero killed by the poisonous hairs of a boar, a connivance engineered by Fingal because his wife, Grainne, had run off with the handsome youth; if there was any folklore attached to the site, it appears to have been lost.

The graveyard in the shadow of the Free Church (NG35583880) contains, one behind the other, the graves of the climbing pioneer Norman Collie (a rubble-covered mound), and his guide John MacKenzie (an eroded cross). For strange stories associated with Collie, see SLIGACHAN. The burial ground is supposed to house the remains of the pre-Reformation St Assind's Chapel, and several carved medieval graveslabs, but the former is now just a tracery of foundations, and the latter appear to have either eroded away or been covered by turf.

In 1893 G.F. Black contributed a paper entitled 'Scottish Charms and Amulets' to the *Proceedings of the Society of Antiquaries of Scotland*. In it he mentioned several holed spindle-whorl charms owned by Dr B. de Brus Trotter of Perth. One had been given to the doctor's brother around 1858 by Hugh MacCaskill of Dunanellerich, Bracadale, Chief of Clan Caskill; it had been in the MacCaskill family for time out of mind. It was dipped in water which was then given to 'elf-shot' cows to drink.

Mary Julia MacCulloch recorded the importance placed on such apotropaic holed stones, which in the Portree area were used to both cure snake-bite and keep snakes away: 'This stone was a most valued possession, and the only one I knew of in the village was hardly allowed to be shown.'

The graves of the 'Edmund Hillary and Sherpa Tensing' of Cuillin mountaineering, Norman Collie (front) and John MacKenzie (middle). Bracadale Free Church is in the background.

GLEN BRACADALE & LOCH DUAGRICH

There are two souterrains in this area. The first, named Glen Bracadale (NG38263896) is easily reached along a path east from the end of the minor road at Amar. It's not really possible to get far inside. As far as I can tell, what appears on the map to be a simple walk to the second souterrain is actually impossible unless you happen to be amphibious and can breathe bog-water. This means that the Tungadale souterrain is the most remote archaeological site on Skye that is worth visiting. The day-long walk involves leaving the Dunvegan-Sligachan road at NG390349, between Bracadale and Drynoch. From here a good track climbs east then north through Bealach Mor and the Tungadale forest. When the track ends follow the firebreak down the hill (tough going) until you come to Loch Duagrich. Then walk right (east) along the forest boundary past the end of the loch. Just before the next firebreak turn right up the steep hill and blunder and crash about in the trees until you finally stumble across it (NG40764006). After all this effort, the souterrain is actually amazing. It is accessed through the wall of a stone-built Iron Age house, only part of which is overground. In other words, the entrance was concealed within the thickness of the wall. The long passage is low, narrow and dark, and can only be crawled along. Bring a powerful torch.

Otta Swire tells the story of an old woman who begged a night's shelter from the nine girls staying at a shieling by Loch Duagrich. One of the girls suffered from toothache. When the pain woke her she saw the crone – now revealed as a water-horse – sucking blood from the girl next to her. The terrified girl ran off, and was only safe once she had crossed running water. The next day all her eight companions were found dead.

STRUAN AND STRUANMORE

The key sight here is Dun Beag, a reasonably-complete ruined broch north-west of the township (NG33953861), almost opposite the road to Ullinish. It is a short uphill walk from the car park and, the site being in the care of Historic Scotland, there is good interpretation. If you only visit one broch or dun on Skye, this is the easiest to visit and understand. The site was built in the Iron Age and reused in medieval times – and possibly later, as a cache of coins was found here, stretching from the reigns of Henry II (1154-1189) through Edward I, James II (VII of Scotland), George II and George III (1760-1820).

The Revd Macculloch, writing in 1905, notes the following: 'When anyone is found dead, a cairn is secretly erected on the spot, nor is it ever known who erects it. There is such a cairn on the road near Struan, where a woman was found dead from exposure to a storm four years ago.' I do not know the location of this cairn.

ULLINISH

The chambered cairn north of Ullinish Lodge Hotel and just west of the road has lost most of its cairn cover, leaving six upright stones clearly showing the location of the central burial chamber (NG32373791). Macculloch tells us the local tradition was that in ancient times the dead were burned here – which wasn't too far from the truth.

BALMEANACH

In former times there was a belief that what pregnant women experienced could 'impress' on the anatomy of the child. A man called Beaton and his new bride were driving their cows home to be milked on the outskirts of Balmeanach when they met a curious group. They kindly offered the strangers some fresh milk, which the handsome 'man of quality' among them appreciated. Later the Beatons learned they had met Bonnie Prince Charlie, escorted by Flora MacDonald and a guide. Months later the wife gave birth to a daughter who, unlike her parents, was very attractive. She was named Mairi a' Phrionnsa, Mary of the Prince, because clearly the encounter with the fugitive Pretender had made a deep impression on the unborn child. The story is in MacGregor's *Over the Sea to Skye*.

FOUR

THE NORTH-EAST: TROTTERNISH PART 1 -THE EAST COAST

PORTREE - THE STORR - STAFFIN - THE QUIRAING - FLODIGARRY

Here is a scene for dark tragedies; here might lurk the fabulous creatures of the Celtic mythology; here might rise the altars of some horrid and ghastly faith propitiating the gloomy powers with human sacrifice.

J.A. Macculloch describing The Storr, in *The Misty Isle of Skye*

PORTREE

If you've been out in the wilds, the few traffic-choked narrow streets of the attractive 'capital' of Skye can seem like the M25. The Bank of Scotland in Somerled Square, at the heart of the town, boasts what may be the loneliest gargoyle in Scotland – certainly the only one of its species on Skye. The ridge that sits south-west of and above the town is Suidh' Fhinn (Fingal's Seat) where the giant would while away the time, not a bad choice given the beauty of the loch.

C.F. Gordon-Cumming recorded that in 1872 an Englishman died by his own hand on THE STORR. Suicides attracted a particular horror, and when his body was brought to Portree for burial, the coffin was carried in head-first and buried with the feet to the west, both being the reverse of usual practice. The young man was interred on the north side of the churchyard, the area also reserved for unbaptised children. Gordon-Cumming noted that fisherfolk in particular were opposed to any burial of a suicide in a churchyard, because it was believed that the herrings would desert any waters within view of such a grave. She had heard of cases where the accursed corpse had been secretly dug up at night and reburied either on the shore at low water mark or on a mountain out of the sight of the sea. Otta Swire noted that 'herring fear blood and fly from it' and that the fish could never be caught by a murderer or a man with a woman's blood on his hands.

In 1885 Alexander Smith noted that a murderer was reputedly buried in a secret spot on a green hill in Portree, and in 1922 Mary Julia MacCulloch mentioned that there was a place where horses shied, this being where the ghost of an alleged murder victim had been seen. These two stories may be related.

The only gargoyle on Skye. The lonely beastie is in Somerled Square, Portree.

Portree Masonic Lodge, Somerled Square, showing the Masonic symbols of the sun, moon and stars, trowel, set-square and compass, and plumbline.

MacCulloch's articles in *Folklore* also mentioned supernatural warnings of forthcoming deaths in Portree. Sometimes these took the form of the noise of chains or horses' hoofs, while on other occasions they manifested as strange lights. One such light was seen at the spot where shortly after a certain man committed suicide (could this be the same unfortunate described by Gordon-Cumming?) More elaborate lights, called dreag, attended the deaths of people of consequence. The lights had the form of a long-tailed comet and were seen either on the house where the person was to die, or hovering between the house and the kirkyard. Some years previously MacCulloch had been one of several witnesses of a light that looked like 'a lantern held near the ground and moving slowly along.' The local belief in Portree was that it was the spirit of a girl who had worked on the Sabbath and was thus abducted by the forces of evil as punishment. A brave youth who approached and questioned the light received this reply: 'I am the girl who broke the Sabbath and disobeyed my mother. From henceforward for ever I am doomed through that mother's curse to wander over moor and hill as a warning light, and from this doom I shall not be free till the end of the world.' The belief-system of a strict Sabbath-keeping Presbyterian culture is evident.

Death-warnings are of course tied up with the belief in the second-sight. The Revd Macculloch mentions an old man of good education at Portree who 'saw' a coffin lying near the house of an aged woman. To all intents and purposes the coffin was solid – he tapped it with his stick, and it sounded hollow. The next day the coffin was gone, and soon after the woman passed away. This man died in 1902.

Alexander MacGregor's *Highland Superstitions* recounted that about 1840 a wise-woman from Kilmuir foresaw on several occasions many people drowning in a storm. Some (unspecified) time later, a boat leaving Portree on a market-day overturned and all aboard were consigned to a watery grave. Neither of these cases are what you might call strong evidence for premonitory powers.

Mitchell and Dickie's *Philosophy of Witchcraft*, published in 1839, was deeply sceptical of second-sight, noting that Highland seers:

> … talk in a mysterious manner of accidents by field and flood, in a country where numbers perish annually, either at their occupation as fishers, or in crossing the lochs and bays … If it should happen that a death takes place after the meaningless ravings of a reputed seer, the circumstance is laid hold on as a convincing proof of his foreknowledge.

The authors also suspected that some people claiming second-sight used underhand means to prop up their visions – or even employed second-sight as an alibi. One case they quoted came from the *Glasgow Argus* on 8 April 1839, and related to an event from 11 January:

> Mr McLeod, gamekeeper to the laird of Raasay, went with his only brother on the morning of that day to Portree. As they were leaving that place to return home, the gamekeeper fell behind, and his brother, dreading no danger, came on without him. The other never returned … After an interval of eight days, a man from Portree came forward, and stated that fourteen years ago, while he was herding cattle in the daylight, he had a vision of a man falling over a certain rock, which he described, dressed in light clothes, and resembling in his general appearance the individual who was missing. It

was agreed to visit this spot, and accordingly a boat was procured, and the 'gifted' seer proceeded with a party of men in the direction of the rock by the sea side. At the precise spot the body of the unfortunate gamekeeper was discovered. It is supposed that, after he had left Portree, he had gone on in his journey as far as the cairn opposite Raasay, and that mistaking his way at this point, (for the evening was dark and stormy) he had fallen over a rock and thus met with his death. The body was carried away amidst the tears and wonder of the people, who were astonished at this wonderful discovery.

The editor of the *Argus* added a comment: 'As the second-sight has long since been abandoned to poets and novelists, it becomes a fair subject of inquiry whether any knowledge of the gamekeeper's death, could not have been obtained at first sight, by the person professing the occult power.' In other words, the suspicion was that the 'seer' was involved in the murder.

In 1905 the Revd Macculloch described how a man from the Outer Hebrides 'healed' some children in Portree. He brought some water from a holy well, but no adults were allowed to view the mysterious ritual, which took place with the children in a darkened room. Macculloch noted: 'They recovered soon after; probably they would have done so in any case. But the healer's reputation is made, and he will have many cases in time to come.'

Mary Julia MacCulloch's articles are rich in dream-lore, with the tales having a clear moral lesson. A poor old woman from Portree dreamed that God and Satan were weighing up her good and bad deeds on a set of scales. The balance was heavy towards the Devil's end but just as he was about the claim the woman's soul, God threw into the scale the peasant's recent sharing of her last meal with a beggar, and so Satan was thwarted. A man at Sluggans in the north of Portree learned in a dream that gold was hidden in DUN BORVE. When he awoke he could still hear the mysterious voice, but eventually recognised it as a wile of Satan, and so refused to go treasure-hunting. MacCulloch also knew two supposed Portree witches, Kate Bess and 'Lexy of the Moors'. The former used her spells to cure cows and other animals, but the latter was reputed to curse those who annoyed her. A man fell from his cart and was killed near her cottage. Another fell from his horse at the same spot but escaped with minor injuries. No doubt Lexy did little to discourage these beliefs, as a fearsome reputation can be of some help to an otherwise poor woman. Witchcraft belief was so widespread that when a young man of good family became insane and committed suicide in 1910, his friends and sisters were convinced he had been the victim of black magic (this may have been the same suicide mentioned above, but the article does not give names).

Writing in the *Celtic Magazine* in 1888, Alexander MacDonald related the tale of the Fairy Snuff-Box, which he had been told by Kenneth MacLeod of Eigg. A man addicted to snuff walked many miles trying to find a travelling pedlar selling the product, eventually tracking him down in Portree. On his way home he met an elderly gent beside a well, and told him of his troubles in getting the snuff. His new companion gave him a snuff-box filled to the brim, saying that as long as he offered it open to others, it would never run out. For months the man did this, and was never short of snuff. One day, however, Lord Macdonald came round collecting rent (as if aristocrats did that in person!) and was insulted when offered the box already open. He insisted on the crofter shutting the lid first, which of course nixed the enchantment and the ever-full box was now empty. In recognition of the loss he had inflicted on the man his lordship gave him the croft rent-free for life, a tale even more unlikely than the original fairy snuff-box itself.

BRAES

These scattered townships garland the cul-de-sac B883 road that leaves the A87 south of Loch Portree. The first part of the road, where it crosses the uninhabited moor, had a bad reputation, no doubt partly fostered by Braes-dwellers who found themselves having to cross it after leaving Portree at night. Campbell's *Witchcraft and Second Sight in the Highlands and Islands of Scotland* states that 'sounds of throttling are heard and dark moving objects are seen.' The moans were from a dying man, and the mysterious apparitions included a dog. It all meant that a murder would be committed at the spot, which is at the top of the rise, at the place known as an Drochaid Mhor, the Big Bridge, close to the car park (NG488403). Somewhere on McQueen's Rock (the hill and cliff to the east) was a Gruagach Stone, where libations of milk were left for the guardian of the cattle (for another gruagach and its stone, see SCORYBRECK).

According to MacGregor's *Over the Sea to Skye*, Camustianavaig, the first township, was the haven of three witches. A fishing skipper, seeking magical revenge on a rival crew, popped round with a bottle of whisky, always a popular move. Only two of the beldames were in, and when the third arrived she was not happy to find that they had emptied the bottle without waiting for her. The trio argued so bitterly the captain thought his wisest move was to exit quietly. The following evening he sailed past Camustianavaig – and a witch-powered squall sent him and his boat to the bottom. Moral: when visiting witches, take more than one bottle of whisky.

MacGregor was told the story by a Camustianavaig man who in his youth knew one of the witches. One day he and some companions set several barrels of nets, but were forced ashore by bad weather. The next day the crew were anxious to haul in the nets, but they could not put to sea because one man was missing. He was staying with the witch, who, it transpired, was not even awake, never mind having fixed breakfast for her paying guest. When the men pleaded with her to hurry up she told them the nets would not be recovered for several days, although they would not be damaged. Despite this they set out, only to be beaten back by the weather. After days of storm the nets were sighted further south, off Braes, and on recovery they were indeed found to be still in good condition.

The Revd Macculloch adds that a witch who lived in the area in the 1860s would place pieces of egg-shell, each representing a boat, into a cup of water. She would then agitate the water, and the pieces that sank caused the corresponding fishing boats to be storm-swept to a watery doom.

West of Gedintailor is an area called Sithean Uaine (Green Fairy Hill, NG507355). This may be where, around 1800, a woman returning from her cattle fold saw her dog run to a hillock and hold its ear to ground. She did the same, and heard a fairy woman singing along to the churning of the milk. The 'Song of the Hillock' became a regular in the Skye fairy-song hit parade (see also DUNVEGAN CASTLE). Achnahanaid, by the road to the north-east, was one of only ten places where the red and speckled fairy sea-cattle of Skye could graze on land. All this fairy-lore is in Campbell's *Superstitions of the Highlands and Islands of Scotland*.

Mary Julia MacCulloch reported another ghost story with an obvious moral. A man living in a remote house in Braes lost his wife. After some time he overcame his grief and neglected his several children to court another woman. Strangely, the children seemed to thrive. One day he returned and casually asked if the children had been lonely in his absence. They were never alone, they said, because as soon as he went away, their mother came and looked after them. Needless to say the man dropped the courtship and thereafter devoted himself to the welfare of his family. I suspect the father was less clever than the offspring.

TORAVAIG & SCORYBRECK

A splendid walk leaves from the slipway at the end of the road in the bay and proceeds east around the point before heading inland past the site of the now-vanished Bile Chapel (NG49724430) to Toravaig. From here the path can be followed back to Portree (via the grounds of the Cuillin Hills Hotel) or the minor road can be taken through Scorybreck to join the main highway north of the campsite.

A giant from the mainland threw a rock at a rival in Portree, and a man from Raasay tried to do the same to his wife. Both throws missed, and the boulders grace the shore here. Deciding which large rocks are the off-course missiles is a challenge, as there are so many candidates. Somewhere high up on Ben Chracaig, the precipice above the path, is MacCoitir's Cave (NG495438). Here lived an evil brigand, whose demon-summoning activities are described under RIGG. Martin Martin wrote about this cave, although so exaggerated is his account that I suspect he never saw the actual location:

> There is a big cave in the rock on the east side of Portree, large enough for eighty persons; there is a well within it, which, together with its situation and narrow entry, renders it an inaccessible fort. One man only can enter it at a time, by the side of a rock, so that with a staff in his hand he is able by the least touch to cast over the rock as many as shall attempt to come into the cave.

I was told the cave is virtually inaccessible, something I wish had known before attempting (and failing) to ascend the steep and dangerously unstable boulder-strewn slope up to the cliff-face.

The summit of the hill bears a pile of rubble, this being Dun Torvaig (NG49374422). A herd boy from Scorybreck fell asleep on the dun and woke to find himself surrounded by fairies. After watching, entranced, their dancing and feasting, he made his way home – to find himself interrupting his own funeral. Despite napping for just a few hours of fairy-time, in the real world he had been missing, presumed dead, for three weeks. It was noted that he was never the same lad thereafter, always pining for the realm of Faery. The tale was told to Mary Julia MacCulloch by one of the boy's relatives. MacCulloch also gave the story of a ghost with a purpose who visited the Nicolson mansion at Scorybreck. The recently-widowed laird was being comforted by a friend when a knock came at the door. The friend answered it and asked the woman standing there for her name. 'I am his dead wife,' she replied. Weirdly, the widower did not recognise her, so he asked her to prove that she was indeed his deceased spouse. She told him two things: firstly, the location of a secret hoard of money, known only to herself. And secondly, that a number of women who had worked for them at clothmaking, still remained unpaid. She carefully enumerated the names and the amounts due. When the laird promised to pay the debts, she rose, satisfied, and disappeared from his sight. The cache of money was duly found hidden in the place she had indicated.

Another, more folkloric, story, told of a spectral woman who was several times seen washing clothes in the Scorybreck burn. She performed this task as a posthumous service for anyone who died but whose friends neglected to wash his clothes before the funeral (Skye ghosts are often concerned with the cleanliness of the corpse at the funeral – see also FLODIGARRY).

The Nicolsons owned a cere-cloth, a cloth dipped in wax in which bodies were wrapped before the funeral. A long-term friendship with the MacLeod chiefs meant that the cloth was sent for every time a death occurred in Dunvegan Castle. The house also held the mort-cloth, the linen draped over a coffin on its way to the grave. A story connected to this mort-cloth is related in Alexander MacGregor's *Highland Superstitions*. Around 1830, a parish minister stayed overnight at Scorybreck as the guest of the widowed Mrs Nicolson. His hostess went up to the upper level to fetch something – and then screamed and fell into a faint. On being revived she said she had seen a bright light on the mort-cloth, containing within it the distinct image of the minister's niece, a daughter of Captain MacLeod. Shortly after the girl became ill and died; her coffin was the first to bear the mort-cloth after Mrs Nicolson's vision.

J.G. Campbell's *Witchcraft and Second Sight in the Highlands and Islands of Scotland* gives the legend of a Norwegian with leprosy or some other incurable skin disease who came to Scorybreck. Here a waterfall, the Easa suc Con, forms a natural trough about the length and breadth of an adult. She had the trough emptied, and lay down in it while the water was allowed to return. In accordance with the prophecy that had brought her here, she was cured.

The cow-byre of Scorybreck once housed a gruagach stone, onto which milk was poured as an offering to the gruagach, the guardian spirit of the cattle. If there was no libation, the cows would not give milk and the butter would not churn. The gruagach was sometimes regarded as male, sometimes as female. Whatever its gender, it was dressed as a person of quality, and had long yellow hair. The Scorybreck gruagach liked to lie on the roof of the byre. Fairy cows came ashore from the sea at Creag Mhor, MacNicol's Big Rock, to the east of Scorybreck. They were highly desirable to Skye pastoralists as they were of better quality than the island stock. On one occasion the cattle were prevented from returning to their watery home by a wily farmer, who threw earth from a churchyard between them and the sea. Another fairy cattle-herder lived on Dun Gerashader, the fort to the north-west (NG48924527). Each day she sent the animals to pasture at BRAES some 8 miles (13km) away, and stood on Dun Gerashader at twilight calling the cows home by name. The fort is badly damaged but some of the massive walls can still be seen, and its defensive position can be easily appreciated. Sadly no fairy cattle are now in evidence. Access is via a short but boggy walk from the main road. Away to the north-east is a stream called Lon an t-Sithein, the Fairy Pool or Meadow, which comes down from Sithean a' Bhealaich Chumhaing (Fairy Hill of the Narrow Pass, NG508464).

LOCH FADA

This, the first loch passed on the A855 as it winds its way up the east coast, once had two supernatural denizens, a water-bull and a water-horse. The latter had to be dispatched after it killed a man, the chosen implement being an iron knife. The beasts are mentioned in Macculloch's *The Misty Isle of Skye*. Prince Charles's Cave, shown on the map at NG51804819, can only be approached from the sea. The fugitive prince did not sleep here, using it only as a shelter while en route to Raasay. Flint arrowheads and stone tools were found here in the nineteenth century.

BEARRERAIG BAY

A public access road leaves the A855 at the north end of Loch Leathan, crosses the Storr Lochs Dam and ends at a car park, from which a spectacular descent of 674 concrete steps follows the water pipes and funicular railway of the hydro-electric power station down to Bearreraig Bay (NG518527). Note that you will, of course, have to climb 674 steps on your return. Pottering around the bay for some hours may turn up fossils such as ammonites. In 1891 a rabbit hole revealed a Scandinavian treasure hoard – 111 coins of Anglo-Saxon and Arabic origin, some originating from as far away as Samarkand. There were also several pieces of hack silver, fragments of the valuable metal cut from brooches and other worked items. The best guess for the date of deposition is AD 935, making it the earliest of the many Norse hoards found in Scotland. The standard explanation for these caches is that they were buried during times of violence, with the owner hoping to return when the coast was clear. An alternative story is considered by Ian Armit in *The Archaeology of Skye and the Western Isles*. In his view, the sheer amount of treasure that was never recovered suggests the hoards were not buried for safekeeping but were intended as offerings for the gods.

From here there are good views of Holm Island, opposite which once stood the farm of Holm. One night the tenant went to bed leaving a large pot of indigo dye on the floor. Later his wife was woken by a strange noise, and screamed out at the sight of a green snout poking out of the pot. Her husband sat on the pot lid until the monster beneath eventually stopped breathing. He lifted the lid expecting to find that he had drowned the Devil – only to discover his only pig, which had blundered into the pot. The episode can be found in Campbell's *Superstitions of the Highlands and Islands of Scotland*.

THE STORR

In every direction are heaped confused piles of rock, tossed about in forms gigantic and terrible, like the colossal ruins of some stupendous city, or the burial-place of some race of giants; a place utterly desolate and silent, where the spirits of the past may dwell undisturbed, in unbroken solitude, and where the floating vapour-wreaths that cling to the weird rock figures, seem like the ghostly winding-sheets of an army of mighty dead.

C.F. Gordon-Cumming, *In the Hebrides*

Unless the cloud is down, it is impossible to miss The Storr; it is the Martian landscape of shattered rocks and eldritch upthrusts west of the road, part of the longest chain of inland cliffs in Britain. Here geology has been transformed into a Wagnerian opera. The Old Man of Storr, so familiar from photographs as to be almost an icon of Skye, is a 140ft (43m) high pillar whose shape and name do not refer to an elderly gent but to an active part of the male anatomy. A path leads up from the Storr car park. Do not ascend without proper equipment; despite its popularity, this is still a dangerous place that regularly attracts the wrath of the weather gods.

A typical nineteenth-century view of the Old Man of Storr, as portayed by Lt-Col. Murray in D. Morison's *Sketches of Scenes in Scotland* (1834).

The Revd Macculloch notes that a gruagach from Storr killed a woman who had cursed him for his pranks, and also sets a tale here that combines diabolism with not-so-subtle criticism of the Church of Rome. A Skye clergyman wished to know exactly when to celebrate Easter, a question that preoccupied medieval minds (even today Easter, the occasion of the Crucifixion and Resurrection, and hence the keystone event of the Christian religion, is a mobile date calculated with reference to the phases of the Moon). This cleric was skilled in black magic. Standing on the storm-swept edge of The Storr, he summoned the Devil and transformed him into the swiftest horse ever known. The pair set off for Rome, all the while the Satanic steed subtly asking questions about Christianity; if the priest once uttered the name of God, the Devil would vanish, and the mission aborted. The man, however, was too clever for this trick, and early the next morning horse and rider arrived at Rome. The Pope hurried in – wearing a lady's slipper on one foot, a clear hint that the supposedly celibate Holy Father had been enjoying a bit of nocturnal company. The proper date of Shrove Tuesday and Easter was communicated, and the priest agreed to ignore the slipper if the Pope overlooked the black magic. Both parties satisfied, the Skye man returned home safely astride the now-impressed Satan. John Gregorson Campbell adds in *Witchcraft and Second Sight* that the priest was sometimes identified as Parson Sir Andro of Rigg. Similar stories from elsewhere in Scotland are told of the supposed medieval master-wizard Michael Scott.

There is something about The Storr that suggests the demonic. In an 1891 paper for *The Gaelic Society of Inverness*, Norman Matheson related the tale of the Revd Espol, minister of Snizort and Scorribreck. Having previously cheated the Devil out of the soul of a maid who had carelessly bargained it away, the minister was marked for special attention by the denizens of Hell. One moonlit night he was crossing the pass at The Storr (probably Bealach Beag) when he heard 'shouting and clanking of chains sufficient to rend the very rocks, and as if all the demons together were let loose in a crowd, and were jostling each other in their eagerness to catch him.' Being an athletic gentleman, Espol took to his heels and managed to outpace the hellspawn by crossing to safety over the running water of the Rigg burn.

In the summer of 2005 NVA, the Glasgow-based environmental art organization, transformed The Storr into a strange and ghostly night-time wonderland, with multiple lighting effects and a soundscape that included eerie music, the poems of Sorley MacLean, and haunting songs by the Gaelic singer Anne Martin. Visitors were guided up and down the mountain in groups, the ascent beginning at 11 p.m. Reactions were mixed. Some people didn't care for the constant need to keep moving, wishing for more time to pause and appreciate the atmosphere, and on bad nights nothing was visible but rain and cloud. Many others, however, found it a powerful, even spiritual experience. The work is catalogued in *The Storr: Unfolding Landscape*, a book compiled by NVA's Angus Farquhar, with many excellent contributions ruminating on Scottish and Gaelic culture, and our changing relationships with mountains and wilderness. Recommended.

The Storr appears briefly in both the dinosaurs-still-live-in-the-Antarctic! fantasy film *The Land That Time Forgot* (1975), based on a novel by Edgar Rice Burroughs, and the greatest British horror film ever made, *The Wicker Man* (1973).

As the road proceeds north it skirts an area of broken rocks and cliffs just to the west, a place called Carn Nam Bodach, the Old Man's Cairn (NG512552). Somewhere in this area a probable Iron Age souterrain was uncovered in 1913. The underground section was around 70ft (21m) long, and contained pottery and stone tools, along with the bones of horse, ox, pig and red deer. Sadly all trace of the souterrain has vanished.

RIGG

J.G. Campbell's *Superstitions of the Highlands and Islands of Scotland* notes that on one Hallowe'en the sixteen small farmers of Rigg found all their horses being ridden by fairies, who were gleefully sitting backwards on the animals, controlling them by pulling on the tails.

Sure-footed investigators can proceed from the Rigg car park (NG520777) to the cliffs to view a natural arch, a rock stack, and a set of offshore rocks called Na Famhairean (The Giants).

TOTE

[They] took a live cat and put him on a spit; one of the number was employed to turn the spit, and one of his consorts inquired of him, 'What are you doing?' He answered, 'I roast this cat until his friends answer the question' ... And afterwards a very big cat comes, attended by a number of lesser cats, desiring to relieve the cat turned upon the spit, and then answers the question.

Martin Martin, *A Description of the Western Islands of Scotland Circa 1695*

Martin is describing the Taghairm, one of the more gruesome methods used to see into the future. This particular rite was supposed to have taken place at an isolated rock on the shore south of Tote, which from the great arch that pierces it is known as the Eaglais Bhreagach, or the False Church (NG522590). John Gregorson Campbell (*Superstitions of the Highlands and Islands of Scotland*) identified the perpetrators as the McQuithens, apparently a very bad lot if the rhyme giving the various versions of their name is a guide:

The McCuthan, expert in lies,
The McQuithens, expert in base flattery,
The McVannins, expert as thieves.

Between them, J.A. Macculloch and Otta Swire elaborated the full details of the rite. Several cats were roasted alive, their screams attracting first a host of other wailing cats, and then a bigger, scarier, animal. The leader of the clan, the infamous brigand MacCoitir (see TORAVAIG) knocked down this creature with the cross of his sword-hilt, which compelled it to appear in its true guise – the King of Hell himself. MacCoitir and his band asked for wealth and long life; these the Devil granted, but later reneged on his promise and soon all but MacCoitir were suffering in Hell. When his time came, MacCoitir was unrepentant, even threatening the Devil with a *coup d'état*: if he could arm his erstwhile companions with 'three short swords that would neither break nor bend they would vanquish all the devils in Hell and make prisoners of them.' Satan seems to have taken this threat seriously as, despite MacCoitir's long catalogue of appalling crimes, he was refused access to Hell on the grounds that the robber had once done a good deed. Shut out from both Heaven and Hell, MacCoitir to this day walks the moors of Trotternish.

Getting to the False Church is easier said than done. From the large Inver Tote lay-by (NG516604) walk south over the bridge then left through a gate and right onto the old road. Just before the sheep-pens turn left (east) along a track and then north to the Lealt Gorge and down to the shore, with views of the ruins of the works where diatomite stone was once processed. The route is then south along the shore but only at low tide. Check the tide tables or you chance getting trapped. The going is very tough and slow. The arch is, however, impressive, with a second, smaller passageway next to it and, nearby, an isolated stack called the Cubaid (the Pulpit). The Pulpit of Satan, that is. For an easier and tide-free visit, simply head south along the clifftop from the initial path to the utterly wasted ruins of Dun Grianan fort (NG52225982), part of which has fallen into the sea. From here and further south there are views of the Eaglais Bhreagach.

LEALT & BACA RUADH

Part of the track that runs west from Lealt to Loch Cuithir follows the line of the dismantled railway that served the diatomite works. From here, well-equipped hill-walkers can tackle the mighty buttress of Sgurr a' Mhadaidh Ruaidh and its companion to the south, Baca Ruadh. Otta Swire notes that two experienced mountaineers had separately told her that they had felt a sense of 'potent, living evil' on Baca Ruadh. In the foreword to Swire's book, Sir William Tarn wrote that he could 'confirm by experience', but not explain, the sensation. This sounds like another example of 'mountain panic'.

CULNACNOC

The enigmatic and completely ruined Dun Hasan (NG52626262) occupies part of the delightful peninsula called Rubha Nan Brathairean (Brothers Point). It was not a dun or fort, and may have been a defended settlement, possibly even a monastery. By tradition the most recent inhabitants were Donald Mac Dubh Ruaraidh and his brothers, who during clan battles cleverly threw their lot in with the MacLeods or MacDonalds depending on which side was already winning. Their subsequent booty was hidden in a cleft on the shore called Preas Dhomhnuill Dhuibh, Black Donald's Cupboard. To the south is a tall rock pinnacle and the Sgeir Dubh skerry, which wrecked a boat from Portree in 1812, killing sixteen people. Access is either all the way along the beach north from Inver Tote, or via a track from the main road opposite the turn-off to Grealin (NG516625).

ELLISHADDER

Every now and then the storms of Skye expose and erode a thin layer of Jurassic Era rocks, sometimes throwing up dinosaur fossils. In fact the first dinosaur remains in Scotland were found on Skye, and the island still holds the record for the number of Scottish dinosaur finds. Many of these have ended up in Staffin Museum (which, confusingly, is not in Staffin but in Ellishadder to the south). This fine single-roomed collection also holds other finds from this fossil-rich coast, geological curiosities, and archaeological and social history items. Highlights include:

- Several dinosaur footprints, notably those of the carnivore *Coelophysis* and an enormous print of a hadrosaur.
- Bones from a stegosaur and the sauropod dinosaur *Cetiosaurus*.
- The imprint of the skull and teeth of an *Ichthyosaurus*.
- Fossils such as nautilus, shark fin spines and belemnites (extinct relatives of squids, some of them huge). Belemnites were regarded as having magical powers. Macfarlane's *Geographical Collections*, written about 1750, noted that on Skye they were called bots- or bats-stones because they were used to cure worms in horses, known as 'bots'. The process involved steeping the bots-stones in water, which was then given to the animals to drink. There are also many ammonites, also known as snakestones, of which Martin Martin wrote in 1695: 'These Stones are by the Natives called Crampstones, because as they say they cure the Cramp in Cows, by washing the part affected with Water in which this Stone has been steep'd for some Hours.'
- Big chunks of fossil wood.
- Very attractive geological formations called septarian nodules, also known as turtle stones.
- Neolithic items such as quern stones, arrowheads and axe heads.
- An eagle's talon, a fox skull, and the skull of a blackface ram with a great spread of horns.

Opening hours are a little haphazard, being more-or-less 10 a.m.-ish to 3 or 4 p.m.-ish, Monday to Saturday in the summer, and possibly also in May, September and October. Modest admission charge. (http://borve.net/staffin-museum.co.uk.)

The outline of a broch, Dun Grianan, can be seen on a promontory poking out into the north of Loch Mealt (NG50556529). Almost opposite, a signposted car park gives excellent views of the spectacular Mealt Waterfall and Kilt Rock, the latter being where 300ft (91m) high columns of dolerite form 'pleated' cliffs resembling the folds of a kilt. Perched above the next layby to the south is the bare trace of Dun Dearg (NG51376430), a fort now chiefly notable for being a beacon site, where fires were lit to summon the clans. The tradition is that the last time this occurred was during the 1745 Jacobite Rebellion.

CLACHAN

Here is found the old graveyard of Kilmartin, although there is little of interest to see these days (NG48726682, easy access from the road). In 1695 Martin Martin recorded that sixty-two years earlier 'a wicked and mischievous race of people' from Kilmartin had engaged in an attempt to foretell the future using occult practices. A man was selected by lot and taken to the river-boundary between two villages, a very liminal place:

> Four of the company laid hold on him, and having shut his eyes, they took him by the legs and arms, and then tossing him to and again, struck his hips with force against the bank. One of them cried out, 'What is it you have got here?' Another answered, 'A log of birchwood.' The other cried again, 'Let his invisible friends appear from all quarters, and let them relieve him by giving an answer to our present demands': and a few minutes after a number of little creatures came from the sea, who answered the question and disappeared suddenly.

STAFFIN

An interpretation panel by the shore at An Corran indicates where on the beach large dinosaur footprints were found in 2002. Unfortunately, even with the directions I failed to find them, probably because they are among seaweed-covered rocks. The panel also indicates where evidence of a Mesolithic hunter-gatherer camp was found by a cliff-face nearby. There is nothing to see now of the 8,500-year-old site, the earliest known human occupation on Skye.

A replica of the dinosaur footprint found on the beach at An Corran, Staffin.

Celtic cross, at the Columba 1400 Centre, Staffin. The cross is just a few strips of metal.

In her collection of anecdotes and fictional stories, *The Light Fantastic: Skye Folk Tales and Fantasies* (2005), Rhona Rauszer claims that Staffin was the last place on Skye to wholly convert to Christianity. Apparently, for a period of five years the minister of Bracadale and Snizort refused to christen a child from Staffin because its parents were pagan. This minister was Roderick MacLeod, known as Maighstir Ruairidh, who led many Skye Protestants out of the Church of Scotland and into the Free Church during the Disruption of 1843.

On 31 October 2008 the *Daily Express* reported that two days earlier an off-duty police officer and a member of the public saw flashing lights in the sea off Staffin. Fearing it was a boat or sailor in distress, they called the coastguard. After an hour's search with powerful searchlights, the source of the flashes was finally discovered – a toy boat, 8in. (20cm) long, bearing the message 'Happy 42nd Birthday Ollie xxx.'

The website of the Staffin Community Trust tells the story of a local man who could not find the key to his car. He therefore tried every key first in his shed, and then in his neighbour's house. None of them fitted. As a joke, someone suggested the key of a corned beef tin. Ha-ha, they went. But lo, the key worked, and the man achieved his errand in a car started with the key from a can of convenience food. One suspects this was in the days before electronic keylocks.

MARISHADER

This hamlet is on the cul-de-sac west from Garafad. Skye's first author, Martin Martin, hailed from here. Otta Swire states that there are two stones on the moor near Garros which mark the site where two brothers killed each other over an inheritance. I have been unable to locate said stones, although it is possible they are around the poor remains of Dun Connavern (NG50856284).

STENSCHOLL

Swire tells the weird tale of Airidh Mhic Iain Ghill, who one morning set his dogs on a strange beast he found sheltering among his cows. The creature, whatever it was, spoke to Iain in Gaelic, begging him to call the pack off. Iain refused, the creature fled, and the next day all the dogs were found dead.

BROGAIG

The Staffin Community Trust website (www.staffin.net) tells the fascinating story of Tommy Elder of Brogaig, who served in the Merchant Navy during the Second World War. One day he was at the Glasgow centre where sailings were assigned. He was about to sign up for one vessel when an anonymous man spoke to him in Gaelic, telling him to refuse the job. Later that night the ship was torpedoed off the west coast of Ireland, killing the other men who had been in the queue around Tommy.

THE QUIRAING

> The Quiraing is a nightmare of nature ... it might be the scene of a Walpurgis night; on it might be held a Norway witch's Sabbath. Architecture is frozen music, it is said; the Quiraing is frozen terror and superstition.
>
> Alexander Smith, *A Summer in Skye*

Here humans walk amongst the land of the gods. This popular exploration is, however, fraught with danger and unstable ground. Proceed with caution. A still-ongoing landslip has created an awe-scape of Tolkienesque pillars and defiles. It appears in *The Land that Time Forgot* (see THE STORR) and the 2007 fantasy film *Stardust*. The easiest jumping-off

The Quiraing, from D.
Morison's *Sketches of Scenes in
Scotland* (1834).

point is the car park at the very top of the single-track road that winds up and up from
Brogaig. Paths lead north to the 120ft (36m) pinnacle of The Needle and the castellated
mass of The Prison, the latter of which Seton Gordon claimed to have once been
haunted by the ghost of a cleric who was eventually banished by some saintly man. This
may be the same spectre which Swire describes as being dispatched by having a knife
thrown through it. Gordon's *The Charm of Skye* also named other features: Creag a'
Bhatail (Battle Rock), so-named because when a sudden gust of wind strikes it fires two
cannon-like reports in quick succession; two pillars called na Bodachan (the Old Men)
and Creag an t-Sabhail (Barn Rock) where hay was kept to feed the cattle sequestered
on The Table, a 120ft (36m) by 60ft (18m) piece of level ground ringed by tortured
rocks. This sward has also been used for games of shinty. And in a car advertisement.

In the summer of 1993 David Furlong ran a week's inner development course on
Skye. This coincided with a major planetary conjunction of Neptune and Uranus, so
the group decided to honour the event by holding a meditation up on the Quiraing.
The day was wet and when they arrived at The Table visibility was zero. During the
meditation, Furlong felt he had made a connection with the 'spirit of the mountain'.
When he opened his eyes the mist had vanished, and the scene was bathed in brilliant
sunshine. His impression was that the communication with the forces of nature had
improved the weather. The episode is in Furlong's *Working With Earth Energies*.

In contrast to Furlong's benign experience, several people have reported feelings of terror on Bioda Buidhe, the mountain south of the road. Possibly connected to this, and possibly not, is a long-noted haunting at Lon Airigh an Easdain, the stream at the waterfall beside the roadside west of the summit car park (NG432674). In 1891, in 'The Apparitions and Ghosts of the Isle of Skye', Norman Matheson reported that the figure of a murdered pedlar had been seen by dozens of reliable witnesses when crossing the pass. One crofter told how, no matter what he did or what direction he faced, the red-faced one-armed ghost was always in front of him, desperately attempting to convey some vital information. Eventually, one traveller spoke to the spirit, which gave a partial description of the man who had murdered him, but this did not bring the villain to justice.

Another weird tale is in 'Old New Year's Day', one of the autobiographical pieces in Rhona Rauszer's collection *The Light Fantastic*. One snowy January day she was walking over the mountain road between Uig and Staffin when she saw a man behaving suspiciously. She followed him to a lonely cottage where, through the window, she glimpsed a bizarre scene. A pair of old women were moaning horribly while two men were burning things and splashing some kind of liquid over everything, including what appeared to be a corpse. Rauszer thought it was a magical rite of human sacrifice, a fear confirmed when soon after one of the men came out with a large white bundle – obviously the wrapped-up body! – and threw it into the river. Rauszer, fearful of discovery, legged it from her hiding place. When she telephoned the key figure of authority in the area – the doctor – she found him greatly amused. A man called Andrew Stalker had recently died of diptheria in the remote dwelling, and so the GP had told the family to burn all the dead man's clothes and fumigate the house. This action against contagion had clearly been performed using illegal whisky – the liquid that Rauszer had seen splashed everywhere – and the 'murdered' man she had seen was simply drunk. The 'wrapped corpse' was the mattress on which Stalker died – they should have burned it but just dumped it, a fact confirmed when a fisherman later found the mattress in the bay.

On the way up to the top of the road you pass a cemetery and car park, from which an alternative path proceeds to the Quiraing. Otta Swire describes the founding legend of this graveyard, a variant of a tale widespread throughout the British Isles (although it usually applies to a church). Long ago it was decided to construct a burial ground near Garafad, south of Staffin. However, each morning the workmen found their previous day's digging covered over and their tools missing. After several days of these supernatural hints, the graveyard was relocated to where the tools kept being left, and no problems were thereafter encountered. It is possible that Swire mixed up her graveyards and the story actually applies to the Kilmartin graveyard in CLACHAN, which is much closer to Garafad.

DIGG

A new path with interpretation panels winds down from the car park north of Digg to the clear waters of petite Loch Sheanta (NG471699). Here, as recorded by everyone from Martin Martin onwards, was a holy well much used for healing. Martin describes it as effective for 'Stitches, Head-aches, Stone, Consumptions, Megrim [Migraine].' His account from 1695 continues:

> They move thrice round the Well, proceeding Sun-ways, from East to West, and so on. This is done after drinking of the water; and when one goes away from the Well, it is a never-failing custom to leave some small Offering on the Stone which covers the Well. There is a small Coppice near it, of which none of the natives dare venture to cut the least branch, for fear of some signal judgement to follow upon it.

In 1792 the *Old Statistical Account* described the well as a stone-lined bath with offerings of rags, pins and coloured threads left on a shelf. Statements vary as to the exact location of the well. Sadly, after thirty minutes of blundering through a close-set phalanx of thorn trees, briars in full summer effulgence, and ankle-deep mud on a steep slope, I am none the wiser.

Seton Gordon's *The Charm of Skye* tells of how two men at Digg were working hard on the land. When one expressed a wish for buttermilk, a young woman appeared and he drank gratefully, although his companion declined. The first man then saw a small army of fairies throwing their darts at the human who had spurned their hospitality.

Loch Sheanta near Digg; the holy well is apparently somewhere in the trees.

'Elvis has left the building.' Bed and breakfast sign, Digg.

FLODIGARRY

Fairies were abundant in this area. Shortly after assisting at a delivery, a midwife was imprisoned in a fairy hill. After two weeks she was released, to find herself at a house celebrating the wedding of the child whose birth she had attended. In the real world twenty years had passed. One man got rid of his troublesome fairies by giving them a sieve, and telling them to scoop up the sea with it. Another had the happiest moment of his life the one time he heard fairy music. And a third joined in a fairy reel for a day – but when the dance ended he found he had been away for a year. The first story is given by Mary Julia MacCulloch, while all the others come from the Revd Macculloch. The fairy residence was probably the ruin of Dun Flodigarry (NG46397196) close to Flodigarry Hotel.

Immediately east of the battlemented hotel, in the grounds, is the spring called Tobar Kiltavie (NG46457185). According to Otta Swire, the Christians and pagans of the area argued over the use of the well and both appealed to St Turog, a hermit on Eilean Flodigarry. So disgusted was he by their conflict that he wielded his staff and the well instantly dried up. Some days later the penitent inhabitants begged for forgiveness. The saint then either caused two springs to gush forth – one for each faith – or had each side dig a well, with water appearing in both after three days' of hard labour. At this point pagan and Christian practices become interlaced, as the holy man warned the people that the wells would only flow if, on the first day of each month, they walked sunwise round each well before taking the water, and left an offering each time. Swire claimed that (even in the 1950s?) one well was filled with small carved crosses and other Christian items, while the second yielded beads, shells and curios. These days some moss-covered boulders mark the site of a well, which is often dry; it drains into a reedy pool. Is this one of the wells brought forth by Turog's magic? Or are they lost or elsewhere?

John Gregorson Campbell's *Witchcraft and Second Sight in the Highlands and Islands of Scotland* tells of a Flodigarry man who had been killed by witchcraft. One day his widow saw him sitting by the fireside. Why, the ghost asked, had they had not shaved him before putting him in the coffin?

EILEAN FLODIGARRY

Each night Allan swam out from Flodigarry to meet his sweetheart Mhairi on the island, despite their love having been forbidden by their respective fathers. One night Allan saw a terrible creature in the water and swam away until he was exhausted. He knew it must have been the Tarbh-Uisge, the supernatural water-bull that was at the time terrorising Flodigarry. Rather than risk another encounter the couple agreed to elope. The next night Allan was rowing out in a boat to pick up Mhairi when he saw something in the water ... Which on closer inspection proved to be Mhairi's father's black bull, which was simply heading to Skye each night for a feed. It was only many years later when Allan and Mhairi returned from Australia that they revealed the real identity of the water-bull. The story is told by Otta Swire. Meanwhile, www. staffin.net tells how a First World War conscript called Duncan deserted – an action punishable by execution – and travelled back to Skye where he hid in a cave on the south-east of Eilean Flodigarry, sustained only by a couple of people who secretly supplied him with food at dead of night. After the war ended he made his way to Glasgow where he assumed a new identity, and finally became safe again when an amnesty was granted to deserters after George V died in 1936.

KILMALUAG

In 1910 Mary Julia MacCulloch was told by a middle-aged woman named Mrs Macdougall that the Kilmaluag fairies reaped all her grandmother's corn in one night. MacCulloch also heard of a Kilmaluag midwife who was brought into a fairy hill to attend to a birth. After a few hours with the mother and child, she was allowed to leave, to find she had been absent from the real world for eight days, and in that time her cows had been carefully tended by a fairy herdsman.

Norman Matheson told of an old woman at death's door who, as requested by her daughter, agreed to come and visit from the afterlife. The spirit duly appeared, but each night beat the poor young woman. The elders of the Presbyterian Church held a vigil to lay the ghost, and when it appeared they posed a question in the name of God. The ghost replied that her daughter's request had upset the natural balance of things, and hence it was compelled to beat her. The men addressed the spirit in robust terms and it troubled the living no more.

EILEAN TRODDAY

This uninhabited island lies north of The Aird. Dr Johnson recorded that in 1740, and possibly later, the dairymaids who attended a herd of cattle on Trodday put a libation of milk out for the gruagach every Saturday. The practice was apparently stamped out by the Revd Dr Macqueen, minister of Kilmuir. Johnson gave the meaning of gruagach as 'the Old Man with the Long Beard' but the Trodday cattle-guardian, as with others of its kind, was more usually thought of as being a blond long-haired maiden or youth. Perhaps Johnson was confusing Gruguach with Bodach, the Old Man of Trodday, a rock stack at the west end of the island.

In 1929 Seton Gordon reported the experiences a few years earlier of a shepherd who spent a night on the island during the lambing season. After dark, Trodday was beset with terrifying noises that persisted until dawn, at which time the shepherd lit a fire to attract a boat. He swore he would not spend another night on the cursed isle.

FIVE

THE NORTH-EAST: TROTTERNISH PART 2 – THE WEST COAST

DUNTULM – KILMUIR – UIG – KENSALEYRE – SKEABOST

> The blight of Fate had descended upon Duntulm, which was to involve in one universal doom wide keep, strong walls, black dungeons and sun-kissed towers … Duntulm, from that time forward, was deserted by the Macdonalds, and its lonely halls echoed no more to the pomp of the Chief or the sound of human life.
>
> A.M.W. Stirling, *Macdonald of the Isles*

DUNTULM CASTLE

Mrs Stirling's highly-coloured account from her 1913 book (subtitled *A Romance of the Past and Present*) serves as an appropriate introduction to what Otta Swire calls 'A place of ghosts and bloodshed and unhappy memories.' The grim ruin sits not far from the car park on a headland (NG400074359). A sign advises you not to enter; most people ignore this, but take great care as the site is unstable and rockfalls are not unknown. Do not go down any of the holes in the ground. The origins of the site are lost in prehistory. It was probably a broch, then might have been a Viking stronghold. In the Middle Ages it swapped between the MacLeods and the MacDonalds until the latter consolidated their power base here in the sixteenth century. This is the best-recorded period of the castle, with the MacDonalds acting as near-kings of their own domain – although the castle was still occasionally changing hands a hundred years later. Around 1732 the upwardly-mobile clan chiefs decamped to a more refined house at Monkstadt – most definitely not a primitive draughty castle – and the site fell into decay, being mostly quarried for the new mansion. At a time of Georgian sophistication and (relative) peace Duntulm had outlived its medieval usefulness; it was also semi-derelict by the 1720s. However, the apparent sudden abandonment of what, in Skye terms, had been both fortress and palace, led to the creation of a panoply of legends about the 'doom of Duntulm'; they are still being added to today.

Option one for the source of the 'doom' is that the inhabitants were driven out by the ghost of Donald Gorm Mor, Big Blue Donald. There are variations of this story. Alexander Smith was told that while Donald lay sick in Edinburgh, Duntulm was filled with apparitions, horrible noises, the sound of weeping and the slamming of doors. A young man from Kilmuir, armed with sword and Bible, sat up to

Duntulm Castle, 'a place of ghosts and bloodshed and unhappy memories.'

Looking through the 'cursed window' of Duntulm Castle at Fladaigh Chuain. The larger island to the left is Lord MacDonald's Table; that to the far right is the lonely hermitage.

confront the spirit – which turned out to be Donald Gorm Mor himself, resplendent in tartan finery. Donald affirmed that he did not have enough strength to harm the man, exchanged some platitudes about his nephew and successor Donald Gorm Og (Young Blue Donald), and then wailed, 'Woe's me! Woe's me! I have spoken to a mortal, and must leave the castle tonight.' Donald died in Edinburgh soon after, but his ghost continued to haunt the castle; eventually things got so bad that the family had to quit.

The second version, as outlined in J.G. Campbell's *Witchcraft and Second Sight in the Highlands and Islands of Scotland* was that Donald's ghost, along with two phantom companions, kept helping himself to the bottles in the castle cellars. An important family document went missing, and someone had the bright idea of consulting the ghost of the old chief. Seven brave men, including Donald Gorm Og, entered the haunted room armed with pine stakes 'with fire at their points', a precaution insisted on by a wise-man. Within, they found the three spectres dead drunk. Donald Gorm Mor indicated where the missing documents were to be found, then fixed his eye on his nephew and growled menacingly, 'If it were not for the slender lances of pine, this would be thy hurt, young Donald Gorm.' Some time after the ghostly roistering proved too much and the castle was abandoned. The curious thing about these traditions is that they place the desertion of the castle at the time of Donald Gorm Og, who died in 1643, ninety years before the MacDonalds actually left.

The second 'doom of Duntulm' story is that a nursemaid accidentally dropped a MacDonald child out of one of the windows onto the jagged rocks below. Depending on the variant told, the woman was, as a punishment, sent to drown in a boat filled with holes, or her friends substituted a dummy onto the boat and smuggled her out of the castle. Whatever her fate, however, the death of an infant of the house cast a dark fate over Duntulm, and it was soon left to the owls and foxes. Otta Swire's mother's great-aunt Jessie swore that a few months before the incident a feast had been held. As Jessie's grandmother watched, an old man came in to propose the health of the newborn heir – and then collapsed, apparently under the weight of a vision. He did not say what he had 'seen', but when the baby died everyone made the connection. The 'dropping a baby out of a clifftop castle' story is told about at least six other locations in Scotland, including GLENELG; either nursemaids to the elite were a thoroughly clumsy lot, or this is simply a travelling folktale, called up to explain any ruined castle in a dramatic setting. In 2009 I listened in amusement as a kilted guide told his tourbus group that the great window in the ruins was 'cursed' because it was where the baby fell to its death, and any woman who looked through the arch would become unable to bear children. And so the legends continue to grow and mutate.

As to alleged contemporary ghosts, you have a bagful to rummage amongst. There are of course the cries of the nurse and baby. Kilted warriors march past. The weeping is heard of Margaret MacLeod, wife of Donald Gorm Mor (she was sent back to Dunvegan when Donald fell for a younger model; Margaret had lost an eye, so Donald compounded the insult to the MacLeods by despatching her on a one-eyed grey horse, led by a one-eyed boy, and followed by a one-eyed dog. Given the chief's reputation for violence, it is unlikely either humans or animals were originally monocular) and screams and groans issue from the dungeons, where Hugh

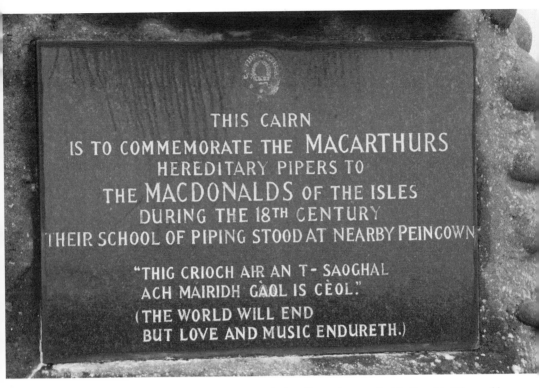

A memorial at Duntulm to the MacArthurs, the hereditary pipers to the MacDonalds. 'The world will end, but love and music endureth.' How true.

MacDonald, Uisdean MacGillespie Chleirich, expired. Hugh plotted to usurp his cousin Donald Gorm Mor and become chief. As part of the conspiracy he wrote two letters – one assured his cousin of his loyalty, while the other told a friend about his plans to assassinate Donald. Unfortunately for Hugh he got the letters mixed up … Tradition insists Donald imprisoned the traitor with a platter of salted beef and a water-jug. Hugh devoured the meat – and then found the jug empty. In the madness of his raging thirst he chewed the pewter dish to pieces.

Duntulm and its legends also dominate the surrounding landscape. So thickly do these tales fall that it is now impossible to discern which, if any, contain a glimmer of real historical events. Ru Meanish, at the very tip of the headland, has usually been translated as the Hill of Pleas, and so a number of tales are told here of the MacDonalds dispensing justice. One chief ordered an incestuous brother and sister to be buried alive. A condemned man, Black John of Garrafad, was given magical powers by the Devil for a year and a day and so simply carried off the gallows that were meant to hang him. When the debt-collector came for his soul John fobbed him off with his shadow, and so never cast a shadow for the rest of his life. Whatever the status of these tales, the Gaelic scholar Ronald Black, in his introduction to the 2006 edition of Otta Swire's book, insists that Ru Meanish does not mean 'the Hill of Pleas' (and there appears to be no obvious translation).

Cnoc Roll, to the south-west of Duntulm, is supposedly the place where (a) a fake army of domestics and peasants endlessly circled both hill and castle as a ruse to fool the attacking MacLeods, who withdrew thinking the castle was strongly garrisoned; and (b) where accused criminals were subject to trial by ordeal, placed in a nail-studded barrel and rolled down the hill. If they survived they were innocent.

Duntulm was built by 5,000 fairies in one night. Treasure from a wrecked French ship lies buried under the great beach boulders of Lùb an Sgòir. I have heard two tour guides set the story of the land-grabbing severed hand at Duntulm, probably because the castle is easier to take tourists to than the tale's traditional location in BORNESKETAIG.

A jovial tale entitled 'The Government Factor and the Widow's Cow' was recited by Alexander Macgregor in the *Celtic Magazine* in 1880. The Government had placed a man named Domhnull Mac Euairidh Mhic Uilleim as factor over Trotternish, and he was so diligent in collecting rents that he became much disliked. One day he called upon a woman at Erisko, north of Duntulm. Her husband and two sons had all recently died, but because she was behind with her rent the factor heartlessly took her only cow to pay off the arrears. He penned the animal up along with his own pony and went off to dinner. Immediately a group of lads acquired a boat and spirited both cow and pony off to the island of Fladaigh Chuain (see below). When the factor found both animals missing he was astonished – and also gullible, because the same lads persuaded him to consult the local seer, in reality a harmless peasant swiftly decked out in the guise of a witch. This woman played her part well, declaiming that she had earlier that evening seen a host of angry green-garbed fairies in the sky:

> I beheld the transformed figures of a cow and a horse rising up from the earth into the clouds until hidden from my view amid flaming fire and murky elements. The scene lasted but for about five minutes of time, so rest assured, cruel man, that the fairies, who are the good friends of the fatherless and widow, have snatched away, and justly so, your horse and the widow's cow into the secret chambers of their lovely dwelling-place, therein to keep them in safety.

The factor, now terrified, left the district, and soon the poor widow was not only reunited with her cow but had gained a fine pony for her trouble.

In *Over the Sea to Skye* Alasdair Alpin MacGregor gives the factor's name as Coinneach MacUilleim or Kenneth Williamson, and notes he was mentioned in a legal document of 1508, two centuries earlier than the period given by Alexander Macgregor. (*Over the Sea to Skye* also names the widow as MacRuari and the 'witch' as Ishbel, a speawife who lived by the shore at Duntulm.) Williamson was probably greatly disliked, and the tale was simply brought into contemporary times by later generations of storytellers.

FLADAIGH CHUAIN

Along with its smaller neighbours, this island (usually known as Fladda-Chuain) is visible from all along the north coast. In some traditions it is Tir na h' Oige, the Celtic land of youth and eternal summer, although it would take an oceanful of fairy glamour to make a paradise of these storm-tossed rocks. Here was once a chapel dedicated to St Columba (or perhaps St Colm), founded at a date unknown, by persons unknown, and supposedly inhabited by a monk or hermit called O'Gorgon, about whom nothing is known (although his skull allegedly turned up in a rabbit hole – how did the finder know it was O'Gorgon's?).

The name Cladh a' Mhanaich (NG36388091) translates as The Monks' Burying Place, and it is overlooked by Creag na Croise (Rock of the Cross). When the altar of the chapel was still extant, fishermen would visit to obtain favourable winds. The ritual involved walking round the chapel three times sunwise and pouring water over a 'Weeping Stone'. This stone also possessed the usual curative properties, and was employed for swearing solemn oaths. It is variously described as round or straight, and black or blue. The practice is first mentioned by Martin Martin in 1695. By the time the *New Statistical Account* was published in 1845, druids were all the rage, and the rather unlikely claim was made that the pagan priests would gather on the island once a year and conduct ceremonies with nine smooth stones 1ft (30cm) in length. These stones, whatever they were, had recently been stolen.

Martin mentioned that very big whales were seen in the area (these were probably basking sharks). He added:

> ... the natives distinguish one whale for its bigness above all others, and told me that it had many big limpets growing upon its back, and that the eyes of it were of such a prodigious bigness as struck no small terror into the beholders.

Otta Swire tells the tale of a fisherman who suffered from bad luck. He went to Fladda to seek favourable winds and good catches, but on the way back was overturned by a whale. Clinging to the upturned boat he prayed to St Columba, who appeared on the water all in white and ticked off the whale. As penance the creature had to push both man and boat back to the islands. The *New Statistical Account* noted that no toads, frogs, mice, rats, or snails could live on Fladda, and even mice taken to the island as an experiment had died. This is reminiscent of the belief that St Patrick banished snakes from Ireland – had Columba of Fladda banished amphibians and vermin?

Some stormbound fishermen were boiling potatoes in a deserted bothy on Fladda when they heard voices outside – but no one was around. Twice more this happened, so that they were thoroughly spooked. Some time later a boat en route to the Western Isles took refuge with them. The voices of the crew were the exact duplicates of those heard several days earlier. The episode is in J.G. Campbell's *Witchcraft and Second Sight*.

One of the other islands in the group, Am Bord, The Table, has the alternative name of Lord MacDonald's Table, for here in 1715 Sir Donald MacDonald of the Isles buried the title-deeds to the MacDonald estates before heading off the fight for the Jacobites. This was a canny hiding-place; Martin describes Am Bord as, 'surrounded with a steep rock and has only one place that is accessible by climbing, and that only by one man at a time: there is a violent current of a tide on each side of it, which contributes to render it an impregnable fort.'

KILMUIR

More of an area than a discrete settlement, Kilmuir occupies several miles of the main road. If you want to find out how islanders lived in previous times, the best place to visit is the Skye Museum of Island Life (open Easter to October, 9.30 a.m. to 5 p.m. Monday to Saturday, admission charge, some wheelchair access). Here several thatched cottages have been preserved, and they are stuffed to the rafters with tools, implements, furniture, domestic items and other aspects of the material culture of nineteenth-century Hebridean life. The cottage called the Ceilidh House contains two ancient stone church fonts. One of these has a story to tell. Two murderers made a lad who had accidentally witnessed the act swear on pain of death that he would not tell a living soul. The troubled boy tried to open up to the minister, but said he was on oath 'not to tell a living soul'. The canny minister pointed the lad to the font and had him speak into it, all the while listening in from a distance. The lad therefore did not break his oath, and the murderers were still apprehended.

A modern standing stone on the roadside at the Skye Museum of Island Life.

The memorial to Seton Gordon, with the Skye Museum of Island Life behind. Gordon lived for more than fifty years in the area. In the background to the right is An t-Iasgair, the island bombarded by the Royal Navy.

Kilmuir Cemetery. The medieval graveslab stolen from Iona by Angus Martin.

Along the minor road up from the museum is a memorial to Seton Gordon (1886–1977), who lived at Upper Duntulm nearby. The museum has Gordon's typewriter, on which the great author bashed out his many works on Skye, much-quoted in this book. One of the local traditions he recorded was of a sad and lonely fairy called An Teoagan, who entered houses late at night to sit at the fireside and croon:

> I will do my warming
> And my heating
> While others shall be in their
> Sound sleep.

A little further on the minor road is the well-cared-for Kilmuir cemetery (NG39907187), with the tall, dignified memorial to Flora Macdonald. The graveslab carved with an armoured warrior is supposed to be that of Angus Martin, a semi-legendary heroic figure who married a Danish princess and had seven sons. Angus nicked it on one his voyages to Iona, where it once covered the sepulchre of a king or chief. Angus (a mighty man was he) carried the stone on his back up from the shore at Kilmuir. Another gravestone has a curious inscription:

Above left: The memorial to the Jacobite heroine Flora Macdonald in Kilmuir Cemetery. The cross-head in the foreground is from the previous monument, storm-smashed in 1871.

Above right: The tombstone left unfinished by an out-of-pocket mason. Although his craftsmanship must already be in doubt, as he carved the word 'the' twice in succession. Kilmuir Cemetery.

HERE LY
THE REMAINS OF
CHARLES MAC
KARTER WHOSE
FAME AS AN HON
EST MAN AND
REMARKABLE PIP
ER WILL SURVIVE
THIS GENERATION
FOR HIS MANNERS
WERE EASY & RE
GULAR AS HIS
MUSIC AND THE
THE MELODY OF
HIS FINGERS WILL

Charles MacArthur was a famous hereditary piper to the MacDonalds. We can never know what 'his fingers will' do because his son, who commissioned the stone, drowned, and the mason, lacking a pay-day, left the job unfinished.

Both Seton Gordon and Otta Swire state that the skull and leg-bones of the ill-fated Hugh MacDonald (see DUNTULM) were displayed on the window ledges of the old church until the early nineteenth century, after which both church and bones vanished. The area has a legacy of lost monuments, many of them now untraceable even as to their location. In 1845 the *New Statistical Account* stated:

> Old men remark that there were many Druidical circles and places of worship in Kilmuir parish, the remnants of which have been destroyed by the progress of agriculture and other causes; there were many erect stones and cairns piled up in the form of a cone, with flat stones on the top, on which, it is said, sacrificing fires were kindled; but most of these relics have been destroyed.

One such site was called Pein-Na-Cille, where stood two standing stones, possibly part of a stone circle; when they were taken down human bones were discovered. The Revd Macculloch describes 'Fingal's Graves', burial mounds as 14ft (4.25m) long. All these sites are lost. Not lost, although badly damaged, is the souterrain of Tigh Talamhain (NG41467124), on the moors east of the large sheep-pen of Lachasay. Sadly the interior is no longer accessible.

KILVAXTER

In contrast, the Kilvaxter souterrain is one of the best archaeological sites on Skye (NG38996960, by the side of the main road, with small car park). Accidentally discovered in 2000 and now fully excavated and restored, the entire 55ft (17m) underground passage can be investigated, although potential explorers should note that it is pitch dark, low, claustrophobic and dirty. The curving shape is more easily followed overground, and the remains of an adjacent Iron Age farmstead are pointed

Above left: The underground entrance to the cramped Iron Age souterrain at Kilvaxter.

Above right: Inside the souterrain. The author's visit was curtailed by heavy rain that flooded the passage.

out. The interpretation panels suggest the souterrain was used for the storage of barrels of perishable food, collected or produced in the summer and needed in the winter.

Away to the east is Loch Sneosdal, home of a water-horse with a penchant for drowning travellers (NG413692). Seton Gordon states the pass from the loch to the hill above is called Bealach na Beiste, the Monster's Pass, this being the route it took to high ground in search of prey. 'Ghost Lights of the West Highlands,' an article by R.C. Maclagan from 1897, notes: 'There are several fresh-water lochs in the parish of Kilmuir [where] ghost lights are said to have been frequently seen before funerals passed, and after the funerals had passed the lights disappeared.'

BORNESKETAIG

This scattered township, spreading across several minor roads west of Kilmuir and Kilvaxter, is home to two of Skye's more unusual sights. The first is easily reached on the road to the shore at Camas Mor. Here, beside the campsite, a one-room barn houses … something surreally strange. To say Macurdie's Barn of Laughs is eccentric is too mild: bizarre and bonkers is more accurate. The 'exhibits' consist of a series of visual and verbal puns and bad jokes (for example, two drawn bugs, one marked 'The Lesser of Two Weevils'). Call it quirky, or off-beat, or an indulgent in-joke, even Outsider Art if you will; it is an essential visit. The unstaffed 'gallery' has good disabled access and seems to be open most days; honesty box.

The second sight is more of a challenge to head, hands and feet: Uamh Oir (Cave of Gold). Here a dread beast guarded a pot of treasure; here a MacArthur piper entered, bravely playing his pipes – his friends followed the music for a mile above ground, but then it ceased, and the piper was seen no more. Here, too, are basalt columns and hexagonal pavements to rival the Giants' Causeway in Northern Ireland or Fingal's Cave on Staffa, but the difficulty of reaching them means they are little visited. To reach the cave, take the more northerly of the two roads, passing the ruined church (NG39927186).

Shortly after this turn right and walk from the end of the road to the coast, turning left to follow with care the fence line along the cliffs. Pass through a kissing gate and continue along the broken-down fenceposts until they veer left. The descent from here is steep and often wet and dangerous – as I can testify. Scramble over the basalt blocks to the right until the vertical rectangle of the cave entrance is reached. It is not possible to enter the cave or cross over to the other side of the entrance gully, and the platform in front of the cave can be tricky in strong wind or when the tide is in. In other words, this is a risky place where caution is advised. Return the same way. Note that many other routes in the area are blocked off with signs forbidding walkers.

The headland, Ru Bornesketaig, is the traditional site of the 'race of the severed hand'. The MacLeods and MacDonalds, competing for the right to the land, engaged in a boat race. Whoever placed a hand first on the shore gained the ownership of Trotternish. The MacLeods were winning, so a MacDonald cut off his hand and threw it ashore. There are numerous versions of this tale, set in dozens of different locations. The origin of this obviously fictional tale is in Irish mythology: the Milesians were supposedly the first Celtic conquerors of Ireland; as the seven sons of Miledh of Esbain approached the shore, one of them cast his severed hand onto the beach, thus becoming the first king of Ireland. The O'Reillys and O'Neills of Ireland have the bloody hand on their coat of arms.

On the headland sits the few scattered stones of Dun Bornaskitaig (NG37267161), a fairy dwelling of note in the old days. A local widow was too frail to complete her harvest, so the fairies came out of the broch by moonlight and cut and bound all her crops for her. Nearby was a spot called Totagan nan Druinich. The Druineach were a diminutive quasi-human race – a kind of Caledonian Hobbit – who lived in small round stone houses. Their diminutive stature brought them favour with St Columba, who employed them to embroider the minutely detailed vestments of the early church fathers. These tales can be found in Seton Gordon's *The Charm of Skye*; some of them may possibly not be true.

Above left: A typical pun-tastic exhibit at Macurdie's Barn of Laughs, Bornesketaig.

Above right: The sandpiper (a common bird around Skye) according to Macurdie.

Above left: Uamh Oir, the Cave of Gold at Bornesketaig, one of Skye's most famous gateways to Hell.

Above right: Some of the weird basalt columns near the Cave of Gold.

The gauntly prominent ruin of Kilmuir church above Bornesketaig, which was built in 1811.

AN T-IASGAIR

We are once again beholden to Gordon, who tells us that on a day sometime before the First World War the pride of the British Navy was sailing past – and decided to use this offshore rock for target practice. As a consequence, it is much smaller than once it was.

BALGOWN/LINICRO

Looking on the Ordnance Survey map you see something called Eilean Chaluim Chille (St Columba's Island), marked with a ruined church and a 'cashel', an ancient monastic settlement (NG37706879). It is possibly one of the earliest Christian sites on Skye. That, you might think, is a place worth exploring, a focus of ancient mysteries and intriguing ruins. Well, think again. Eilean Chaluim Chille does indeed have stories to tell; but the route, initially along a track south of Kilmuir Manse, is boggy and dreary; the former Loch Chaluim Chille, through which you must pass, is a treacherous swamp; and the ecclesiastical remains are little more than an amorphous scatter of stones. Nothing is known of the early history of the site. Before the loch was drained – a process which after three false starts in 1715, 1763 and 1824 was finally completed in 1829 – the settlement stood on low-lying slivers of solid land. This watery isolation has inevitably generated folklore that takes advantage of the narrative possibilities of an island hideout. Otta Swire tells us that after the Vikings were defeated at the Battle of Blar-na-Buailte in the bay of Lùb an Sgòir, one of their leaders, Arco, holed up on Eilean Chaluim Chille with his war-band. All attempts to winkle them out having failed, the Gaels resorted to subterfuge. A man called MacSween disguised himself as a bard and rowed out to the island where he entertained Arco with songs and stories – and a certain amount of wine. As soon as Arco drifted off to sleep, MacSween cut off the Viking's head and escaped, to receive a reward of the land of Braes from the Lord of the Isles.

Seton Gordon's version is similar in content but different in context. For some reason MacDonald of the Isles had fallen out with the abbot of the monastery. He offered MacLeod of Raasay the whole of Trotternish if he cut off the abbot's head. MacLeod disguised himself as a beggar and hitched a boat to the monastery, agreeing to pay his board by telling tales. After the evening's entertainment the abbot started snoring away, until MacLeod separated his head from his body with a sword. The assassin took the boat across the loch and met up with his six confederates. Unfortunately for them, the treacherous MacDonald – who had no intention of paying the reward – had them ambushed on a hill near CUIDRACH. Gordon also mentioned other folklore associated with the site. The loch possessed a miraculous spring but one day it was abused – we are not told the details – and it took the huff, moving a ¼ mile (400m) away. The story of the stone thrown by a giant at a milk-stealing witch near KYLEAKIN also occurred here, although in Gordon's version the stone-chucker is Fingal. And the Brahan Seer (Coinneach Odhar) allegedly pronounced a triple prophecy: 'The loch on which Callum the monk lived will be drained to the sea' (this has evidently come true). 'A thunderbolt will fall to the west between the loch and the sea' (Gordon claimed a furrow was cut by lightning at Knockhoe, south of Bornesketaig). 'A church will be built to the east of the loch, and on a day when there will be present 'nine nines of name' (notable persons) and 'nine without name', with the voice of the preacher in their ears, the church will fall over their heads.' (This appears not to have been fulfilled, although Kilmuir Church, built in 1811, is a ruin.)

UIG

Witches were apparently still active here in 1880, for in that year the elders of the Free Church of Uig sent a letter to the local landowner complaining about a woman and her five daughters who by their devilish arts were transferring the milk from their neighbours' cows. When the proprietor mentioned this to an employee he trusted, the man said he himself had recently employed a wise woman to unwitch his cow – the charm involved red thread tied to the animal's tail. The following year a Free Church elder took things further. As Gordon-Cumming recorded, he 'went to a

Justice of the Peace to make affirmation on oath, that everything he had on his lands was bewitched by a woman who was his neighbour, and should be sharply dealt with at once. The JP, however, refused to interfere.'

Shapeshifting was also in vogue in Uig. One of Mary Julia MacCulloch's inform-ants told her of his great-grandfather, who saw six cats transform into women, one of whom he knew. In contrast to the usual form of punishment wreaked on those who witnessed cat-women at work, he found himself blessed with an abundance of milk from his cows – far, far too much, in fact (is this because the witches were cats?). Scared by the endless flow of milk, he appealed to his witch-neighbour and the spell ceased.

Otta Swire described how a large whale destroyed the nets of three fishermen in Loch Snizort. One of the men managed to stick it with a three-pronged pitchfork. The next day an old woman in Uig was found dying with a triplet of wounds in her side. (J.A. Macculloch sets this story in Waternish, on the opposite coast of Loch Snizort.)

Writing for the Gaelic Society of Inverness in 1891, Norman Matheson told how a finely dressed gentleman joined a party playing at cards in Uig Inn. It was late on Saturday night when they started and the game continued well into Sunday – a day on which gambling was forbidden. When one of the cards fell to the floor, a player bent down to retrieve it – and found himself staring at a hairy goat's-foot. His disguise rumbled, the 'gentleman' revealed himself as His Satanic Majesty and disappeared through the roof in a burst of fire. This particular tale is found worldwide.

The Making of Religion by Andrew Lang, published in 1898, included examples of second-sight recorded by Dr Alastair Macgregor, the son of a minister in Trotternish. Macgregor's father was a sceptic but a good listener; his parishioners told him of their visions, and he jotted down the details – partly to have a record to compare against anything said to have fulfilled the vision. So many 'future-seen' events came to pass that he eventually concluded that second-sight was genuine, and noted that it was 'neither voluntary nor constant, and was considered rather annoying than agreeable to the possessors of it. The gift was possessed by individuals of both sexes, and its fits came on within doors and without, sitting and standing, at night and by day, and at whatever employment the votary might chance to be engaged.' In one example, a mother 'saw' her fisherman son engaged in the unlikely activity of chasing a lamb. He then fell off a high rock at Uig, crying out in Gaelic. One month later the man took a day off from fishing, walked to Uig, was temporarily engaged by a sheep farmer, and pursued an errant lamb to a precarious point. Just as the clifftop gave way the farmer heard him cry out the exact phrase the seer had heard: 'This is a fatal lamb for me.' On another occasion Christy MacLeod, a known seer, had fainted after experiencing a vision. She revealed to the minister that she had seen the mangled body of a lad called Macdonald lying on the plank next to the fire. Six weeks later the young man fell over a precipice. When his body was found it was so damaged it could not easily be transported, and so a makeshift stretcher was pressed into service – the very plank on which the seer had seen the shattered remains.

There is little of interest at the old burial ground on the road to Glen Conon (NG399638) because in October 1877 a storm washed most of it away. Gordon-Cumming has the Gothic scene:

Clach Ard, a standing stone above Uig Bay.

The bodies lay tossed about in hideous confusion, partly embedded in mud and gravel. Broken coffins, and corpses whom the waves had robbed of their shrouds, lay scattered round ... Many bodies were actually carried away by the current and thrown ashore at Grieshemish – a distance of fourteen miles.

The river Conon was supposedly the home of a water-horse. Folklorist Margaret Bennett was told by her mother, Peigi, that when she was a child belief in the monster was waning, and that as she grew up she realised the story was designed to frighten children from playing near the dangerous water. The castellated tower overlooking Uig Bay opposite the road to the Fairy Glen is known as Captain Fraser's Folly. Clach Ard, known to Martin Martin as the High Stone of Uig, is a fine standing stone recently re-erected within a denuded cairn on a prominent knoll south-west of the youth hostel (NG39436284). A sort-of gate at the bottom of the steep slope gives access.

FAIRY GLEN (SHEADER)

Grass-covered cones, weird crags, rocks that resemble pyramids or castles, strange curvilinear hillocks – it's easy to see why this cul-de-sac is known as the Fairy Glen. Landslips have created an otherworldly landscape that has found its way into fantasy films such as *Stardust*. The highest, most prominent crag is known as Castle Ewan and does indeed look like the last gable of a ruined fortress (access only for the sure of foot).

This area deserves several hours of your time – find a quiet spot and just absorb the subtle but tangible atmosphere. One of the miniature glens contains a modern spiral of stones on one of the slopes. At the centre I found a cache of 'offerings' – not just the usual coins, stones, shells and feathers, but lapel pins, earrings, buttons, even hairclips and a pencil(?!). Another cache was placed in a 'heart' of stones nearby. Interesting although such practices are – why are the offerings left, and for whom? – I should point out that leaving non-biodegradable artefacts is not to be encouraged. Metal items rust and stain the ground, plastic rots and looks unsightly, and the offerings ultimately become litter and pollution. Please respect this unique place and leave nothing behind.

Fairy Glen. The prominent outcrop is 'Castle Ewan'.

Fairy Glen from Castle Ewan.

A spiral constructed in stones in one of the valleys of Fairy Glen.

One of the many weird natural rock formations caused by landslips in Fairy Glen.

BEINN EDRA

This summit on the Trotternish ridge is best reached from the road-end of either Glen Conon (walk up to Bealach Uige then south along the ridge) or the Fairy Glen (follow a track and then a wall). Of the two routes, the latter has better views of the waterfalls en route. Seton Gordon's *Highways and Byways in the West Highlands* tells of Colann gun Chean, a headless female spectre which killed travellers in Morar on the mainland. Eventually it was tackled by Macgillichallum (Iain Garbh, 'Mighty John' MacLeod – see RAASAY), who struggled with the demon from midnight until dawn. As the sun rose Colann's power waned, and Iain Garbh made it swear by the Book and by the Candles (a mighty Catholic oath) to leave the area. Colann was as good as its word, and moved to Trotternish, where it haunts Beinn Edra and the pass of Bealach a' Mhòramhain (NG456626 and NG455622 respectively). There is a hint here that MacLeod of Raasay deliberately banished the spectre to the lands of his MacDonald enemies. (And as a matter of interest, how does a headless spirit manage to speak?)

Gordon also describes how one day a shepherd and his wife were amusing themselves by rolling great stones down from the ridge into Loch Dobhar-sgoth or Loch Corcasgil north of Beinn Edra. There came a great commotion in the water, and a fierce black horse swam to the shore, where it furiously searched for the culprits. Failing to find the pair – who were now quaking in fear behind a rock – it stormed back into the water.

EARLISH

Around 1850 a neighbour told a new mother that she had seen a vision of the infant's body mangled and bleeding. At the time the statement was dismissed as being both ridiculous and insensitive, but a month or two later, when the mother was briefly out of the house collecting water, a pig came in and partially devoured the child. As a result, a local man named Farquhar Beaton never ate pork again. When Beaton paid his regular weekly visit to the manse, the servants there, knowing his disgust for pigmeat, always passed off the pork as mutton. Before Beaton died in 1848 aged 100, he came to know Alexander Macgregor, who in *Highland Superstitions* recorded the 'grace' the old man said before a meal, which included the words, 'Preserve the aged and the young, our wives and our children, our sheep and our cattle, from the power and dominion of the fairies, and from the malicious effects of every Evil Eye.'

CUIDRACH

The stark, even sinister, block of Caisteal Uisdein (Hugh's Castle, NG38045824) can be reached by a rough track from South Cuidrach (ask permission at the farm). The doorway is around 9ft (3m) above the ground, a hopeless means of entry unless you happen to have a ladder upon you (which is how the original defence-minded residents got in, pulling the steps up behind them). The agile can squeeze through a narrow window on the ground floor into the rubble-strewn roofless interior. This was the home of the violent and treacherous Uisdean MacGhilleasbuig Chlerich, the Hugh MacDonald who plotted against his chief and died of thirst in the dungeons of DUNTULM CASTLE. An aged woman told Seton Gordon a story handed down to her by her fisherman father. Around 1829 he and his companions had a hard day at the nets and so, the afternoon being warm, they came ashore to rest. All fell asleep except the teller of the tale, who said he saw a weasel emerge from a hole in the castle with a small bright object in its mouth. It played with this item for a while, then placed it on a stone and went inside, returning with another. Soon there was a small heap of shining coins. The man woke the others, whose approach caused the weasel to try and hide the money, to no avail. When the animal saw that its treasure trove had been taken, it 'began to lament, and then tore at the fur of its throat, biting into the flesh until it fell dead.' This somewhat unlikely tale is in *The Charm of Skye*. Martin Martin, perhaps being more credulous than usual, claims that the island contained two kinds of weasel, one of which, the larger species, had poisonous breath that killed calves and lambs.

The prehistoric remains in the area are all extensively damaged but retain elements of interest. Dun Borve (NG38015976) is the easiest to visit, being next to the road leading to Cuidrach. Dun Maraig is more intriguing, a fort occupying the whole of a tiny tidal islet in the bay (NG37695915). A causeway to the shore is now destroyed, so dodgy access is only possible at very low tide. The fort at Peinduin (NG38825770) contains the remains of what might be a souterrain – or might not. According to Seton Gordon, the assassins of the abbot of EILEAN CHALUIM CHILLE were themselves murdered on Cnoc Theab by Cuidrach. As each man's head rolled down the hill it cried, 'Theab! Theab!' The severed heads also gave the name to the loch into which they rolled, Lochan nan Ceann, the Lochan of the Heads. Norman Matheson's version is different: a man called Taog Mor MacQuinn was decapitated here by a piper from Duntulm, and the rolling head repeated the words 'Ab, ab, ab.' Tobar-nan-Ceann (Well of the Head) was haunted either by the victim or the murderer, who was hanged for his crime. I have not been able to identify the lochan, the well or Cnoc Theab.

KINGSBURGH

Mary Julia MacCulloch gleaned two stories from this area. The first concerned four cave-dwelling giants, all brothers. One day they found a cow bogged down in the moss, so they tore it into four pieces with their bare hands, and had a feast in the cave. The second told of many suspicious deaths that had occurred at the Red Burn. A herd-boy suspected a local woman was the cause and so ostentatiously displayed to her the money he was carrying. Shortly afterwards he was set upon by a pig or wild boar. He stabbed it, but could not withdraw the dagger. The iron weapon transformed the pig into the woman, who was now so severely wounded she could only crawl home. There, the woman's husband told the lad the best thing to do would be to allow her to bleed to death.

Otta Swire was staying at Kingsburgh during the long illness of George V (this would have been around 1928-30). Up on the hill lived a man of over eighty years, who had been a stalker when the prince had shot his first stag. As such, he was deeply attached to the popular monarch and every night, even in the worst of weather, he would trek down and ask for the latest news – which was always bad. Then came the greatest storm in living memory. That night the old man came and asked not his usual question – 'How is my King?', but 'Is my King still alive?' When this was confirmed, he asserted that worst was over. For the next few days no sign was seen of the man, so a party went up the hill to check on him. He was fine, and after they told him the King's health was improved, they asked why he had ceased visiting. He told them he was no longer worried, as the Royal storm had come for George V, but had returned without him. 'When a Royal storm is sent back empty ... the one for whom it came would live and do well ... It is seldom that a Royal storm is sent back. But my King is a very great man.' He stated that Royal storms did not come for every king, only the great ones, and that they also arrived to claim other notable men, such as Lord Kitchener.

The walls of the large clifftop fort Dun Santavaig (NG382572) are almost entirely lacking but the setting is spectacular. A ruined broch sits above the track to the shore at NG38915688. East of Kingsburgh is Creag nam Meann, where the magical cow of the Fingalians sheltered (see KENSALEYRE).

KENSALEYRE

The pair of standing stones west of the road, on the very edge of the loch, are Sornaichean Coir' Fhinn (Fingal's Cauldron, NG41425251). Martin Martin stated there was a third stone here, so it is easy to see how they could be imagined as the tripodal support for the giant's pot of venison stew. Access is by a gate unless there is livestock in the field. South-west of Kensaleyre, Carn Liath (NG42015138) is an 18ft (5.4m) high chambered cairn with no obvious entrance (access via gate and wet feet). This, or one of the other more damaged cairns in the area, is by tradition the sepulchre of those slain in a battle nearby. Further south, just past the junction to Tote, the main road slices through a cairn (NG42565065), while the rough ground to the east contains another cairn (NG42605059) and two low and bulky standing stones (NG42615076 and NG42625048, boggy access).

When she was sixteen, Rhona Rauszer went with her mother and the local doctor to inspect an old manse near Kensaleyre – Rhona's mother was thinking about buying it. When she arrived Rhona already knew every detail of the internal layout – including how to get in through the scullery window – because although she had never been there in person, she had visited the house many times in her dreams. In fact she had drawn a fully-accurate sketch of the manse the day before the visit. Her mother found Rhona painting a half-completed daisy-chain pattern round the edge of the kitchen floor. The house was too run-down so Rhona's mother returned the key to the solicitor in Portree. Some months later she revealed what he had told her. A scullery-maid had been murdered during a botched burglary – the thieves had interrupted her as she was making patterns round the kitchen floor with pipe clay – and her ghost was often seen. Shortly after the visit the building was pulled down. 'They should have done it years ago,' said Rhona's mother. The teenager's reply was: 'Well they couldn't till I had finished the daisy chain, could they?' The episode is in the short story 'The Broken Daisy Chain' from Rhona's collection *The Light Fantastic*.

The Sornaichean Coir' Fhinn standing stones at Kensaleyre, where the Fingalian giants boiled up their meals.

A wedding party was returning from Kensaleyre to Portree when the bridegroom dropped down dead. One man went for assistance – and promptly expired as he crossed the burn where the first death had occurred. It was recalled that on the way to Kensaleyre they had met the groom's former girlfriend, her head muffled in a shawl. That night the dead bridegroom appeared to his mother; on his instructions she found the black spot which the jilted witch had placed on his shirt to kill him. The widowed bride re-married, and died around 1900. On another occasion a couple saw a strange-looking beast near Kensaleyre. The woman asked it, 'God bless you. What are you?' The holy name caused the creature to change into a woman who they knew. Both of these tales were collected by Mary Julia MacCulloch.

BORVE

MacCulloch also identified Dun Borve, prominently situated to the east (NG45914772), as a fairy stronghold. The inhabitants once harvested a man's crops for him overnight, but thereafter kept plaguing him with multiple requests for payment – no one fee was over-grand, but the persistent fairy presence became an intolerable nuisance. Eventually, the man called out 'Dun Borve is on fire with all in it, dog or man.' The fairies rushed off to quench the fictitious flames, and were never seen again – except, that is, one who met the farmer at Portree Market. Realising he was not invisible to this man, the fairy put spittle in the farmer's eye and the human lost his magical sight. (In the usual telling of this tale, of which there are many variants around Scotland, the fairy blinds the unfortunate mortal.) Three remaining stones of the Clachan Erisco stone circle form a shallow arc by the roadside in the village (NG45194801).

The three remaining stones of the Clachan Erisco stone circle in Borve. Stones scavenged from the circle may be built into the nearby dykes.

A cheery carving on a gate at Borve.

SKEABOST

This scattered settlement appears to be little more than a series of road junctions, but it hides some special secrets, foremost among which is Skeabost Island, also known as St Columba's Isle (NG41824850). From the A850/B8036 junction (signposted Tote) take the disused road west to the river, then walk right (north) to a footbridge. The green island is surrounded by two burbling arms of the river Snizort and in sunshine is one of the loveliest places on Skye. It contains the ruins of several religious buildings, as well as numerous gravestones. The remains are difficult to interpret but basically the first rectangular building you come to (now mostly reduced to grass-grown foundations) is the late-medieval cathedral church of the Bishops of the Isles. The Catholic bishops based here administered a scattered diocese that included most of the Hebrides; neither the bishops nor the building survived the Reformation. The church's shape is distorted by several later burial enclosures. Further on to the west is the earlier but more complete 'Teampull' or Chapel of St Columba, also known as Nicolson's Aisle. Tradition states that twenty-eight Nicolson chiefs are buried here, and it contains a slab carved with the effigy of a knight. Nineteenth-century descriptions mention the ruins of several other chapels, and earlier reports claim the site was originally a Celtic monastery, although this cannot be proved without further investigation.

An episode in Adomnán's *Life of Columba* has been traditionally associated with Skeabost, although there is nothing in the original text that suggests this. Columba was standing somewhere on Skye near the sea:

> He struck a spot of ground near the sea with his staff, and said to his companions: 'Strange to say, my children, this day, an aged heathen, whose natural goodness has been preserved through all his life, will receive baptism, die, and be buried on this very spot.' And lo! about an hour after, a boat came into the harbour, on whose prow sat a decrepit old man [Artbrannan], the chief of the Geona cohort. Two young men took him out of the boat and laid him at the feet of the blessed man. After being instructed in the word of God by the saint through an interpreter, the old man believed, and was baptized at once by him, and when the baptism was duly administered, he instantly died on the same spot, according to the saint's prediction, and was buried there by his companions, who raised a heap of stones over his grave.

It is very unlikely Skeabost was actually founded by St Columba; perhaps the instigator was St Colm (see INTRODUCTION: SAINTS). Whatever the real history of the island, it has clearly been a place of sanctity for centuries, and such places inevitably attract traditions. Otta Swire states it was the disputed boundary between the properties of the MacLeods of Dunvegan and the MacDonalds of Duntulm. During their ethnic cleansing of Trotternish in 1539 the MacDonalds defeated a MacLeod force here, with the severed heads of the losers floating down the river. Seton Gordon (*Highways and Byways in the West Highlands*) claims the island became a burial ground after a battle between the two clans in which ten on each side died. The island was chosen as the place to bury the dead, and so became neutral territory. A large (probably prehistoric) cairn nearby was said to have marked the mass grave; when the cairn was removed for agriculture in the nineteenth century, the legend became transferred to other cairns. The Revd MacCulloch reports that an isolated boulder by the road was used by Columba (or whichever saint it was) as a preaching platform.

Swire notes that when a French privateer was spotted off the coast it was thought to be the harbinger of Napoleon's invasion fleet, so the local landowners buried their valuables in the graveyard. Some fifty years later a flood uncovered jewellery and silver spoons and forks.

Mary Julia MacCulloch related the episode of a servant girl who, on her way to the well, was menaced by a strange shape that moved so fast it seemed to teleport. As she fled in fear she saw it enter one of the old tombs on the island.

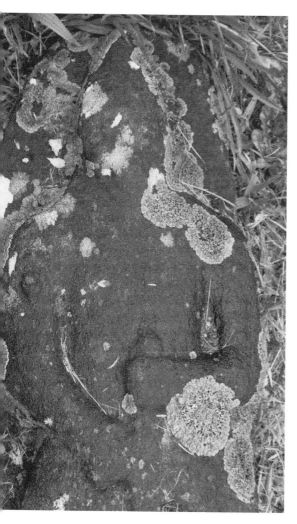 

Above left: A sword-wielding warrior on a graveslab at Skeabost.

Above right: A gravestone at Skeabost carved with symbols of mortality – hourglass, skull and bones, coffin, and the gravedigger's tools.

A track north-east from the disused road leads to the large overgrown mound of a chambered cairn (NG41404905). The cairn is in a garden but can be easily viewed from the track. It is yet another of the locations tradition fingers as the burial place of those slain in the 1539 Battle of Trotternish. South of the main road are Sithean Gorm (the Blue Fairy Hillock, NG411481) and Cnoc Sithean (the Fairy Hill, NG428475). Between them is the shattered broch of Dun a' Cheitechin (NG41754785), standing on Carolina Hill, named by a former emigrant who had returned from America. A stone-lined well sits next to the track leading south of Skeabost (NG421476). Its faded inscription reads 'Tobar Iain Bhain 1841'. Iain Bhain was the father of Mary MacPherson, the Skye poet. The sign for the Snizort Free Church on the main road (NG406490) states that prayer meetings are held on Wednesdays and 'Alternative Saturdays'. Either this should have read 'Alternate Saturdays' or weekends in Snizort are more way out than hitherto suspected.

TOTE

Clach Ard, one of the few Skye examples still standing of stones carved with Pictish symbols, is in a small enclosure beside the cul-de-sac into Tote (NG42104908). In 1880 the eighth-century stone was found being used as the door jamb of a neighbouring house – the story went that it could never be kept in the actual house itself. The symbols are badly damaged but include a crescent and V-rod and double-disc. Despite extensive academic and popular theorising, nobody really knows what Pictish symbols mean. In 1922 a now rather dull-looking cairn on the shore west of Tote House (NG40974975) was excavated by archaeologist T.C. Lethbridge, who in later life went on to develop an interest in what today are known as 'earth mysteries' – ley-lines, earth energies and the like. The most interesting feature of the Bronze Age cairn was a secondary burial that had been inserted during the Iron Age or more probably the Viking period. Grave-goods included an iron axe, a bronze brooch, a bone bead, and many iron and wood fragments, the remains of either a shield or a boat burial. Whoever was interred here was a person of status.

The second cul-de-sac off the B8036 leads to Skerinish, from where a track takes the walker to the sizeable Iron Age fort of Dun Cruinn (NG41085185). This is a puzzling site, the puzzles arising from its probable re-use over many periods, with extensive rebuilding. The surrounding wall is almost gone, but there is a line of what look like standing stones but are more likely part of a wall (maybe). A smaller dun has been built over part of the fort, and below the ramparts are the obvious remains of a settlement, possibly Iron Age but more realistically medieval or later. Mooch around and see how many lumps and bumps you can find to speculate about.

Martin Martin had in interest in 'sports' or freaks of nature. He heard of a calf from Skerinish that had 'all its legs double, but the bones had but one skin to cover both.' After it lived for nine months the owner had it killed because he thought it was an omen of disaster. Martin also recorded similar prodigies – a cow from Waternish that gave birth to five calves at a time, of which three died, and a calf from Vaterness that was born without legs: 'It leaped very far, bellowed louder than any other calf, and drank much more milk. At last the owner killed it.'

The Pictish stone at Tote. The double-disc can clearly be seen. Above it is the crescent symbol.

GLENGRASCO (WOODEND)

All the following stories are from Mary Julia MacCulloch's articles published in *Folklore* in 1922. Several of her informants came from this area, including Mrs Mackinnon, Mrs Beaton and Mrs Morag Buchanan. Mrs Buchanan's grandfather was frequently visited by fairies when he was working with the sheep and cows at the shieling in the high country. They crept under his overcoat and told him that a soldier going to war would be unharmed if he drank the fairy women's milk; refusal would mean death in battle.

A woman treated her delicate stepdaughter badly until she was 'buzzed' by a little bird. That night the bird revealed itself to the stepmother – it was the angry spirit of the child's birth-mother, long dead, and it warned her to improve her behaviour. Unfortunately, the warning came too late and the abused girl died soon after. On another occasion, a flight of souls was seen rising in the air in the form of birds.

An old woman walking the lonely hill road south to Glenmore met a monstrous shape which ran across her path. She thought it was the spirit of a local woman who had recently died and been buried not on her home turf but in a distant churchyard. A group making their way home late were startled when one of them pushed the others aside, telling them to make way for the funeral. As there was nothing in sight one or two paid no attention to the warning – and were shoved to the ground as the spirits rushed past. Soon afterwards someone known to all the group died, and the funeral proceeded along this route.

SULEDALE

Dun Suladale (NG37445255) is the best-preserved Iron Age broch on Skye, with stairways and a chamber still visible in the thickness of the walls. Access is along a track south from Suledale, and then west over the boggy moors. You will be the only visitor.

SIX

THE NORTH: WATERNISH AND GRESHORNISH

EDINBANE – FAIRY BRIDGE – STEIN – TRUMPAN

Then we were told many wild legends of the coast, and can bear witness how marvellously these gain in interest when the narrator can point out the very spot where the weird spirit appeared, or the miserable victim perished. And if diverse caves will claim the same history, well, you must try and believe it to be true of each in turn.

C.F. Gordon-Cumming, *In the Hebrides*

EDINBANE

The ghosts of the Lodge at Edinbane got an outing in *The Sunday Times* on 14 January 2007. Owners Peter Jones and Hazel Abenscheim reported hearing footsteps emanating from empty rooms and seeing several apparitions such as a man dressed in a sixteenth-century frock coat going up the stairs and a woman wearing a long lace gown entering the ladies' toilet. These two ghosts had also been seen by guests. The hotel's website talks of 'a few harmless hauntings' which include a gentleman in black seen at the entrance, an elderly lady in a night-dress behind the bar, and a grandmotherly figure knitting by the fire, accompanied by a spaniel. *The Sunday Times* article mentioned rumours of dark deeds on the premises, such as a man who hanged himself on the first floor, and a fatal fight between a crofter and a fisherman.

An Edinbane woman whose infant had been replaced by an unpleasant fairy changeling went to the fairy hill and slapped the child hard. Immediately a voice was heard from within, 'Throw her out her own ugly brat,' and the fairy and human children were instantly exchanged. The story was collected by Mary Julia MacCulloch.

GRESHORNISH

The quiet minor road stops at Greshornish House hotel, the former home of the popular laird Kenneth MacLeod, who died in 1869. Kenneth encountered an engrained fairy belief which initially seemed to be backed up by empirical observation. Shepherds refused to put their sheep onto the best grass on the Aird, on the way to the Point, because the greenery was bewitched by fairies who caused the sheep to run around in circles and die. The laird himself saw this happen to his sheep, and was determined to find a root cause that did not involve fairies. After extensive tests on the sheep corpses, the plants, and the snails found on the plants – and several more cases of livestock running in circles and expiring – the mad sheep disease was identified as coming from a microscopic brain parasite passed on to the sheep by the snails. This episode is given by Mrs Swire, who also notes that the house was allegedly inhabited by a kilted apparition and an invisible spirit that pulled the bedclothes off at midnight in the 'haunted room'. By the 1950s neither of these ghosts had been encountered for many decades.

Treatises on the Second-Sight by 'Theophilus Insulanus' (The Revd MacLeod) included the testimony of Margaret MacLeod, who described how a dairymaid at Greshornish saw what appeared to be her doppelganger. The figure looked like her, was dressed in the same manner, and walked a short distance from her as she went to attend the cows. To check the nature of the apparition, the girl went out with part of her dress reversed – and saw that her double was identically arrayed. The maid interpreted the phantom as an omen of death, and indeed she soon succumbed to a fever that brought her to the grave.

A splendid circular walk can be made from the hotel around the peninsula. A good track runs west to Loch Diubaig, passing a knoll crowned by the small fort of Meall an Dùna (NG33685408). At the very head of the loch are the ruins of abandoned houses – guarded by apotropaic rowan trees – and three overgrown twentieth-century graves (NG327541), with the names of those interred now obscured. Otta Swire tells of an old man fishing off the rocks at Diubaig who saw a terrible black monster with long whiskers, horrible eyes and terrifying tusks. The next day a group went out to seek the dread beast – and captured a walrus, which presumably had floated here on an ice-floe calved off during the hot summer. Sillar and Meyler's book *Skye* states that walruses have also been seen between Scalpay and Raasay, and off Sleat, Waternish and the tip of Trotternish. In 1883 C.F. Gordon-Cumming stated that a walrus' head had been preserved, 'as that of so rare a guest deserved to be', but I can find no record of anyone having such an odobenine trophy in their cupboard.

From Diubaig take the rough clifftop paths north-east, passing rock stacks and caves, including Uamh an Oir, the Cave of Gold, one of several said in legend to penetrate the entire breadth of Skye and emerge at HARLOSH. After passing Greshornish Point, the next item of interest is Dun na h-Airde, a mostly-destroyed but still enjoyable Iron Age fort strategically situated on a cliff-girt promontory (NG35075577). From here, progress down the western shore of Loch Greshornish, scene of a First World War incident when an aircraft bombed the waters in search of a suspected U-Boat.

In 1772 Thomas Pennant, visiting the area, was presented with a denarius of the Emperor Trajan which had been found on near the shore. How, one wonders, did this Roman coin get here?

FAIRY BRIDGE

'What bridge is this?' I asked of Malcolm, who was still trudging alongside with the reins in his hand. 'The Fairy Bridge' – and then I was told that the fairy sits at sunset on the green knolls and platforms of pasture chirming and singing songs to the cows; and that when a traveller crosses the bridge, and toils up the hill, she is sure to accompany him. As this was our own course, I asked, 'Is the fairy often seen now?' 'Not often. It's the old people who know about her. The shepherds sometimes hear her singing when they are coming down the hill; and years ago, a pedlar was found lying across the road up there dead; and it was thought that the fairy had walked along with him. But, indeed, I never saw or heard her myself – only that is what the old people say.' And so in a modern dog-cart you are slowly passing through one of the haunted places in Skye!

Alexander Smith, A Summer in Skye (1885)

Fairy Bridge – not The Fairy Bridge – was, and perhaps still is, long thought to be 'an unchancy place', as Jim Crumley put it in his 1994 masterwork *The Heart of Skye*. Alexander Smith's guide, Malcolm, knew the story of the dead pedlar; other tales circulate about a murder – or three – having occurred here. Otta Swire's grandfather, John Robertson of Orbost, was puzzled by the fact – attested by common experience – that every horse coming this way shied when passing over the bridge. He thought the fear of the superstitious rider or driver was somehow picked up by the horse. One day, by way of experiment, he arranged for a horse and rider – both of them just arrived on Skye, so without fore-knowledge of the area – to follow a route that passed Fairy Bridge twice, and he made sure not to tell his guest the name of the bridge. That evening on his return the visitor pronounced himself happy with the horse – except that twice it had refused to cross a certain bridge …

Remember to wave to the Little People as you pass Fairy Bridge. Just in case.

Jim Crumley noted that some Skye folk still waved to the fairies when they crossed, not because they were saying a glad hello, but because it was wise not to offend the Little Folk. Perhaps this practice has fallen into desuetude now that the old bridge has been replaced by a new version that carries the B886 road to Waternish, and the nineteenth-century arch is now only visited by those stopping at the car park just north of the road junction with the A850 (NG27825135). As long ago as 1905 J.A. Macculloch suggested the fairies had abandoned the spot after it was used as a preaching place by Revd Roderick MacLeod, who led many islanders out of the Church of Scotland into the Free Church during the Disruption of 1843. In *Highways and Byways in the West Highlands*, Seton Gordon rejected the name Fairy Bridge, calling it instead Drochaid nan tri Allt, the Bridge of the Three Brooks.

BAY

Around 1 mile (1.4km) north of Fairy Bridge, along the sole single-track road that penetrates the Waternish peninsula, is one of the most intriguing – and frustrating – sites on Skye (NG272527). A triangle of land thrusts out high above the Bay River and a tributary, creating a semi-island set apart by two gorges. Here on this highly defensible spot are numerous overgrown scattered remains of what has been interpreted as an early Christian monastery built over a prehistoric fort. The fragments include a boundary wall, ramparts, oval chambers (or domed beehive cells?), the outline of a probable church, and what are possibly relatively modern shieling huts. Bodies of unchristened children were buried within the 'church' enclosure up to the very start of the twentieth century.

The actual history of the site, however, is completely lost. It is called Annait, a name which in early Christian Ireland and Scotland usually indicates the mother church of a community, or a primitive monastic community, or a place where the relics of the founding holy man were venerated. But we know nothing of whatever monastery, church or saint was here. Thomas Pennant visited in 1772, and Boswell came a year later. Both were guided by Dr MacQueen, the minister of Bracadale, who had some enthusiastic but eccentric antiquarian opinions. MacQueen had interpreted 'Annait' as 'Anaitis', the name of a female Persian deity widely worshipped in the Ancient Near East. He was convinced the Celts had erected a temple to the pagan goddess here, and declared to Boswell that, 'the ruin of a small building, standing east and west, was actually the temple of the goddess Anaitis, where her statue was kept, and from whence processions were made to wash it in one of the brooks.' Boswell made copious notes on MacQueen's theories, but after due reflection decided against inflicting them on his readers. This may have come about because of Dr Johnson's robust dismissal of MacQueen's belief in an exotic Mediterranean religious import: 'We have no occasion to go to a distance for what we can pick up under our feet.' As Johnson divined, the entire Anaitis farrago is a house of cards constructed solely out of the similarity between two words from entirely separate cultures and periods.

Getting to the enigmatic (and in truth, not particularly visually interesting) site is not easy. Yomp across the bogs west of the road, aiming for the patch of flat land in front of the right angle in the treeline of the forestry plantation. Carefully descend into the gorge and get wet crossing the Bay River before ascending the steep slope up to the triangle; if the river is in spate do not attempt to cross. Mud and midges await you.

South-west of Annait a small cairn lies in the plantation (NG27115258). This prehistoric burial mound appears to be the structure known as the Lad's Cairn or Cats' Cairn. Alasdair Alpin MacGregor, Otta Swire and Mary Julia MacCulloch all relate the associated legend, which tells of a boy who was lying in bed when he saw three black cats transform into women. The witches then discussed their evil plans until they noticed the apparently sleeping boy. The witches warned the interloper he would be killed if he revealed what he had seen and heard. Eventually, the lad confessed to his mother, who inadvertently let the story out. The details vary between the versions as to what happened next. MacCulloch says the unfortunate boy was set running about the country with his tongue hanging out, and could not stop till he died. Swire states his body was found raked by long sharp claws. All agree the cairn was raised over his grave, which MacGregor says was haunted. Swire places the site east of the road, not west. So this may not be the spot after all.

STEIN

Martin Martin described 'the King of the Herring', a fish double the size of any normal herring that compelled the other herring to follow it as it moved through Loch Bay. If caught it was returned to the sea, for the fishermen 'judge it petty treason to destroy a fish of that name'. According to Robert Watt's *Glossary of Scottish Dialect Fish and Trade Names* the 'King' was probably a ratfish, *Chimaera monstrosa*.

Mary Julia MacCulloch gives the tale of a woman who was so harassed by witches wanting her to join them on their cantrips that she asked her husband to impersonate her. The witches set sail in a sieve, while the disguised man stayed on the shore holding a string as a kind of anchor. He let the string go and the witches drowned. It's possible there is something missing from this story, which seems curiously incomplete.

HALLIN

Dun Hallin (NG25665927) is another broch worth visiting, with a reasonable amount of walling still upright and good views from its prominent knoll. There were once rectangular pits used as wolf traps in the area, but these have vanished along with the wolves. The wolf was enticed in by a piece of flesh at the upper end of the hollow, and then trapped by a closing door. A story is told that either here, or at other wolf traps near Trumpan, a hunter fell into a pit – and found himself face-to-face with a wolf. He only managed to escape because his friend grabbed hold of the tail of the enraged animal. As I said, it's a story that is told.

TRUMPAN

Trumpan is a place of massacres, evil deeds, secret funerals and ongoing folk beliefs. The focus is the ruined church opposite the car park (NG22496121). Here, in one of the most infamous atrocities of the clan wars, a raiding party of MacDonalds burned alive all the MacLeod inhabitants. Only one woman escaped, and although mortally wounded, raised the alarm. The MacLeods proceeded from Dunvegan and engaged the enemy, utterly defeating them. It is frequently asserted that the MacLeod forces were actually quite small, so the Fairy Flag was unfurled (see DUNVEGAN CASTLE), thus magically appearing to increase their number by three-fold. A few MacDonalds managed to escape in a galley but the others were slaughtered to a man on the beach at Ardmore Bay and their bodies contemptuously covered by the tumbling down of a dyke, thus denying them a Christian burial. Apparently the MacLeods regretted this hasty action, as the turf and stone dyke on the shore was designed to keep the sea at bay, and they feared their crops might be swamped. The fight was known as Blar Milleadh Garaidh (the Battle of the Destruction of the Wall or the Spoiling of the Dyke).

As with all such dramatic and bloody events, the story of the battle is a mix of fact, fable, fiction and folklore, and from this distance in time it is almost impossible to distinguish which is which. The raid was in revenge for an equivalent MacLeod atrocity the previous year, when the entire MacDonald population of the isle of Eigg were all suffocated by smoke from a fire set in front of the cave in which they were hiding. These two events have commonly been set in 1577 and 1578, but there is now a thought that they took place between 1530 and 1540. The woman who escaped was

The view from Trumpan church (where the MacDonalds killed the worshipping MacLeods) onto Ardmore Bay, site of the MacLeods' revenge at the Battle of the Spoiling of the Dyke.

said to have lost a breast squeezing through a window in the burning church – for her to make it as far as Dunvegan, and for the MacLeods to reach Ardmore Bay before the raiders left, is a remarkable feat of logistics. The MacDonalds could not escape because their galleys had been beached by the low tide, an error one would have thought unlikely for experienced seafarers to make. The *New Statistical Account* reported that in the 1840s human bones were still being found when stones were overturned on the beach at Ardmore, in the bay east of the church.

Once the church was the centre of a medieval village, but this has been obliterated by time. The graveyard is full of intriguing items. There are two fine carved graveslabs, one inside the church depicting a sword with interlace and a pair of opposed beasts, and the other showing a cleric with hands in the attitude of prayer. Numerous coins can be seen deposited in the water-filled hollow of the old font or holy water stoup; the water is said to never run dry, no matter how often it is emptied. Many more coins have been inserted into every crack and niche of the 'Priest's Stone', a prehistoric standing stone in the churchyard. (Although both coin-deposits are what might be regarded as examples of modern 'wishing well' practice, the question arises – who or what is being propitiated here? Which supernatural force do twenty-first century people think is granting wishes in exchange for these coins? Fairies? The spirits of the earth or water? The 'Priest' after whom the stone is supposedly named? The Christian God? A pagan deity?) The stone is also known as Clach Deuchainn (the Trial Stone). Near the top is a small hole, to which people were led blindfolded. If they succeeded in putting their index finger in the hole, they were, depending on the version told, either guaranteed a place in heaven, or innocent of a crime of which they had been accused. I attempted this feat myself while blindfolded and utterly failed to find the hole. Oh well.

In 1745, the year that Bonnie Prince Charlie attempted the last hurrah of Jacobitism, a secret funeral took place at Trumpan, bringing to a close one of the more unpleasant episodes in the Jacobite farrago. In the coffin was the body of Lady Grange, once a noted beauty and a radiant jewel of Edinburgh society. She had the misfortune to marry Lord Grange, James Erskine, who was oxter-deep in Jacobite plots. When his wife discovered his plans in 1732 she threatened to expose him – and hence he had her abducted. The moving spirit in the abduction was Lord Grange's brother, the notorious Simon, Lord Lovat (who originally proposed a simple murder rather than the complications of a kidnapping).

Lord Grange put about the story that his wife had been 'sequestered' on grounds of insanity. In reality she was first taken to the remote island of Heiskar on the west coast of North Uist, a property of Sir Alexander MacDonald, one of the conspirators. After two years she was transferred to St Kilda, the tiny archipelago at the most distant western reach of the Scottish islands. Here she languished for seven years, in a culture where only one person spoke English and communication with the world beyond was limited to the annual visit of the factor. And the factor, like all the islanders, was beholden to Norman, the MacLeod of MacLeod, another of the conspirators. Nevertheless, Lady Grange managed to smuggle a message out, but before her friends could rescue her she was whisked off to Assynt, and then Skye, where she lived for a time in a cave on IDRIGILL POINT. Unfortunately, by now her mind had given way, and so she was allowed to wander about the island, sustained by the charity of the clanspeople.

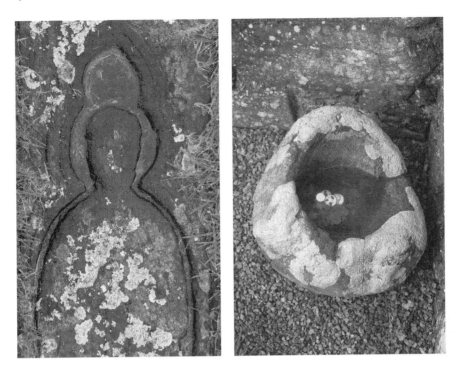

Above left: Medieval gravestone of a praying cleric at Trumpan.

Above right: The old font at Trumpan, still used as a 'wishing well' today.

The Priest's Stone at Trumpan. The hole at the top determined guilt or innocence. Coins have been inserted into every nook and cranny of the prehistoric standing stone.

The memorial to Roderick MacLeod, hero of the Battle of Waternish near Trumpan. The story goes that he had his legs cut off at the knees, yet continued to fight standing on his bloody stumps until he was killed.

She finally died of misery and disease in May 1745, having spent over thirteen years in exile. Even in death she was subject to bizarre secrecy – for some reason an 'official' funeral took place at Dunvegan, the coffin there being filled with turf and stones. It is not clear why the actual interment at Trumpan was carried out secretly. The sad tale was lightly fictionalised by Harriet Martineau in her 1847 novel *The Billow and the Rock*.

A stone bearing the marks of arrows sharpened by women at the Battle or the Spoiling of the Dyke supposedly sits beside the burn near the church. Somewhere nearby is Cnoc a' Chrochaidh, the Hanging Knoll. The name is supposed to come from an incident of the early seventeenth century. According to J.A. Macculloch, a Morrison and his men had killed some MacLeods on the isle of ISAY. The perpetrators were caught at Ardmore and Morrison was hanged from a gallows constructed from three of his own oars. Before he died he asked to kneel and pray, and many years later silver coins dated 1604 were found in a crevice in the rocks; presumably the murderer had sequestered the cache while praying, so as to keep it from the pockets of his executioners.

The long walk north from Trumpan to Waternish Point is flat most of the way and passes several points of interest. This area was the location of the second Battle of Waternish, which took place within a few years of the Battle of the Spoiling of the Dyke. Once again it was a contest between raiding MacDonalds and defending

MacLeods, and once again the carnage was awful. To the right of the path is a prominent modern cairn on the hill known as Beinn a' Ghobhainn (Hill of the Blacksmith, NG24856130) Here the tradition is that a blacksmith, John MacLeod of Unish, was losing to his opposite number. His wife ran up to the MacDonald warrior and struck him with her distaff (spindle), crying, 'Turn to me!' The MacDonald momentarily turned his head, allowing John MacLeod to run him through with a sword.

Further along the path, on the left, is a second pillar, this one in memory of John MacLeod's son Roderick (NG23006320). Then to the west of the path comes Dun Borrafiach (NG23556371), a broch well worth visiting, with a gallery still visible between the two walls, and another broch, Dun Gearymore (NG23676490), in a more dilapidated state.

ISAY

Here another 'happy families' episode was played out, when Rory Nimhneach MacLeod, greedy for land and titles, set up a great feast for his relatives and then murdered his nephews and the entire male line of the MacLeods of Raasay. Only a boy of nine survived, because he had been away from home at the time of the invitation.

SEVEN

THE NORTH-WEST: DUIRINISH

DUNVEGAN – GLENDALE – MILOVAIG – HERIBOST

The Free Kirk minister of Bracadale ordered the people to deliver up all the elf-shot, adder-beads, and charms they had in their possession, as he was determined to root out the devil and all his superstitious rites from among them. It was said that he got two creels full of them (another account said half a boat-load), which he took into the middle of Dunvegan Loch and threw overboard.

G.F. Black, quoting Dr R. de Brus Trotter, 'Scottish charms and amulets' (1893)

DUNVEGAN

This long one-street village is the capital of western Skye. The unmissable sight here is the Giant Angus MacAskill Museum (open daily, 10 a.m. to 6 p.m., good disabled access, modest admission charge). At 7ft 8in. (2.36m) tall, Angus MacAskill was the tallest recorded 'true giant' (that is, he was simply an unusually tall normal man, not someone suffering from a pathological condition). He died in 1863. The highlight of the exhibition is a life-size figure of Angus standing next to General Tom Thumb, the midget with who he often performed in stage shows. Angus could hold Tom in his hand. Other exhibits include recreations of Angus' super-sized clothes, chair, bed, drinking mug, eating utensils – and coffin.

Real human giants always become associated with feats of strength, whether genuine or fictional, and it is now difficult to disentangle one from the other in Angus' life. Among other things, he is said to have carried a 300lb (136kg) barrel of pork under each arm, pulled a fishing boat in two, hefted an adult horse over a fence, and picked up an anchor weighing between 2,200-2,700lb (1,000-1,225kg). Part of the amiable eccentricity of this single-subject collection is that Angus MacAskill had absolutely no connection with Skye – he was born in the Outer Hebrides and emigrated with his family to Canada when he was four years old. The fascinating museum is the obsession of local man Peter MacAskill, who founded it in 1989.

Moving from giants to the Little People, J.A. Macculloch reported that shortly before 1905 a boy saw people of various sizes dancing near the manse at Kinlochfollart. They vanished before his eyes. The manse is on the minor road past the campsite (NG252466).

There is a depleted mound on the lawn which may have been taken as a fairy hillock. In 1860 Alexander MacLeod of Kinlochfollart owned a charm for curing cattle that had been elf-shot, that is, attacked by fairy arrows. It was a spindle-whorl from a weaving loom and had been in his family for generations. The requirements of the charm were quite complicated: 'a red woollen thread was put through the hole, and it was dipped three times in water taken from a well on which the sun did not shine, by a young girl with red or yellow hair. A rhyme, in what was supposed to be Gaelic, was said over the water, which was then given to the cow to drink.' Forty years later the charm was in the possession of Dr R. de Brus Trotter, who wrote this description, quoted in an 1893 article for the *Society of Antiquaries of Scotland* by G.F. Black.

Sometime in the early twentieth century a group of boys from a crofting township went bathing in the loch on a Sunday. One saw a swimmer approaching at speed – which turned out to be a fish-tailed female-breasted mermaid. They watched it for some time and then vowed never to swim on Sunday again. This moralistic tale (doing things on Sunday! Bad!) is in Seton Gordon's *The Charm of Skye*.

Somewhere in the loch is the Rocabarra, 'stone of the sea-tangle top', which according to Otta Swire has only appeared above the waves twice, once to an unnamed person, and again to salute St Columba. When it rises for a third time the end of the world is nigh.

J.A. Macculloch tells of John MacLeod, who dreamed of the death of George II the night before the news arrived by the post, and 'saw' a former minister shrink to the size of a child, and then return to his natural form. Shortly after, the minister sickened and died. MacCulloch was not impressed by either of these cases, suggesting prior knowledge in the first, and coincidence or invention in the second. Another shrinking vision was given in Theophilus Insulanus' *Treatises on the Second-Sight*, in which Donald MacLeod of Feorlig saw Lieutenant Keith dwindle to the size of a boy. The same Keith was 'seen' as a corpse three hours before he actually died. This vision was experienced by the keeper of the inn north of the castle, and took place before 1763.

Above left: The 7ft 8in (2.36m) Angus MacAskill next to his performing partner, General Tom Thumb, in the Giant Angus MacAskill Museum.

Above right: A replica of Angus MacAskill's giant-sized coffin.

Above left: St Mary's Church, Dunvegan. In the foreground is a graveslab carved with symbols of mortality. On the hill behind is the modern Duirinish Stone.

Above right: A memorial stone at St Mary's commemorating the MacLeods. Note the bull killed by the MacLeod chief, and the clan motto 'Hold Fast!'

Right: The massive Duirinish Stone, brought here and erected by hand as a project to mark the millennium.

St Mary's Church, on the road to Portree (NG25504781) is another of Skye's roofless post-Reformation ruins. The graveyard is dominated by the obelisk erected by the infamous Simon, Lord Lovat, in memory of his father Thomas, who died at Dunvegan in 1699. A short but steep walk up the Druim Na Creige knoll behind the church brings you to the Duirinish Stone, a massive standing stone erected by hand in 2000 to mark the millennium (NG25304797).

DUNVEGAN CASTLE

(Open daily April to October 10 a.m. to 5.30 p.m. Admission charge, guidebook. Disabled access to the gardens but none to the castle.)

This is Skye's most popular paying attraction, and is almost always busy. Dunvegan is the ancestral and present home of the MacLeod Clan Chiefs, and may be the oldest still-inhabited castle in Scotland (although much of the present architecture is nineteenth-century fake Gothic superimposed on genuine medieval grimness). The fortress lowers threateningly from an impressive promontory formerly occupied by a

Viking stronghold, and is as replete with legends, dark deeds and folklore as anywhere on Skye. The guidebook and in-room information boards are full of detail; here are given only the elements relevant to the theme of this book.

Exterior

Today visitors enter the castle over a bridge thrown across a ravine. Up until 1748, however, this was an uncrossable moat, and the only entrance was via a sea gate, which can still be seen piercing the rampart at what is now the back of the castle. The worn set of narrow steps leading up from the loch lead to a barred door and passage where the groove of the portcullis can still be seen. Wandering up this little-visited and precipitous route it is easy to appreciate how formidable the castle must have once been.

Dining Room

The massive sideboard is a masterpiece of the woodcarver's art, being decorated with an entire menagerie of grotesque and Classical figures. There are winged heads, foliaceous creatures, sea monsters, lion masks, horn-blowing Tritons astride fish, a pair of small dragons, wild men, beasts spewing vegetation, and more ordinary birds, animals and humans. The sides are decorated with further sea monsters, plus foliaceous birds, Athena holding her staff and owl of wisdom, and Samson pulling down a pillar. Some of the human figures have perfectly ordinary feet; others have legs that end in snakes.

Above left: Dunvegan Castle holding fast on its rock. The original seaward entrance can be seen in the lower left.

Above right: Once this was the only way into the castle, up a narrow flight of stairs and through this gate, then a portcullis, then along a passage used as a killing zone. Maybe they expected some unwelcome visitors.

Drawing Room

Here, placed on a linen background within a plain case, is a scrappy piece of torn and faded yellow silk. Yet this unprepossessing rag is the most legend-rich artefact in the castle, if not the whole of Skye. For this is the Bratach Shi, or Fairy Flag. In *Letters on Demonology and Witchcraft* Sir Walter Scott described it as, 'The fairy banner given to MacLeod by the Queen of Fairies; that magic flag which has been victorious in two pitched fields, and will still float in the third, the bloodiest and the last, when the Elfin Sovereign shall, after the fight is ended, recall her banner, and carry off the standard-bearer.' It has been in the possession of the Clan MacLeod since the time beyond memory, and its magical powers are intertwined with the Clan's fortunes.

In 1927 the Clan MacLeod Society published *The MacLeods of Dunvegan*, written by R.C. MacLeod of MacLeod, who delved through the family documents and manuscripts to construct a detailed history of the clan. He identified three origin stories for the flag. In the first, one of the chiefs married a fairy, but she had to return to Fairyland after twenty years. On parting from her husband at FAIRY BRIDGE she gave him the flag as a keepsake, telling him it could be waved during a crisis, and the fairies would keep their pledge of assistance to the MacLeods; but the offer was only good for three occasions. According to the second tradition, a MacLeod on Crusade in the Holy Land was crossing a river when he was set upon by a water fairy. A fierce fight ensued, with the MacLeod the victor. In recognition of his prowess the spirit gifted him a box of scented wood containing several smaller containers, fitted like a Russian doll. The inmost box held a magic banner which could summon a host of armed men. As with all such items of supernatural power it came with a warning – if it was opened within a year and a day of the gift, 'for another year and a day no crops will grow in your land, no sheep or cattle will produce their young, no children will be born.' Back on Skye the MacLeod warrior presented the box to his chief, who gave it to his wife, who immediately opened the box, with the terrible results as foretold – plus the appearance of a fairy army. In the third version, a newborn MacLeod heir was visited by the fairies, who wrapped it in the flag, and then sang to the assembled clansmen a song of the three-times power of the banner.

A related story has a fairy singing a lullaby over the baby in its cradle. The words and tune were memorised by the child's nurse and for generations the qualification for any nursemaid to the chiefs was that they could sing what had now become an apotropaic spell. The author of *The MacLeods of Dunvegan* noted it had been sung to his grandson. The Gaelic lullaby was written down in the nineteenth century, and an English version published by Frances Tolmie:

> Behold my child, limbed liked the roe or fawn,
> Smiting the horses,
> Seizing the accoutrements of the shod horses,
> Of the spirited steeds,
> Behold my child.
> Oh, that I could see thy cattle folds,
> High up upon the mountain side,
> A green shaggy jacket about thy white shoulders,
> And a linen shirt,
> My little child.

Oh, that I could behold thy team of horses,
Men following them,
Serving women returning home.
And the Catanaich sowing the corn.
Oh, tender hero, whom my womb did bring forth,
Who didst swallow from my breast, who on my knee wast reared.
My child it is, my armful of yew [bow and arrows],
Merry and plump, my bullrush, my flesh and eggs, that will soon be speaking.
Last year thou wast beneath my girdle,
Plant of fertility, and this year fair and playful on my shoulder, thou wilt be going round
the homestead,
My little child.
Oh, let me not hear of thy being wounded.
Grey do thou become duly;
May thy nose grow sharp [with advancing years],
Ere the close of thy day.
Oh, not of Clan Kenneth [MacKenzie],
Oh, not of Clan Conn [MacDonald],
Descendant of a race more esteemed.
That of the Clan Leod of swords and armour,
Whose father's native land was Scandinavia [Lochlann].

Inevitably, there are variations even on this clutch of traditions. C.F. Gordon-Cumming records a belief that the flag was a consecrated banner of the Knights Templar, while both she and Alexander Smith gave a version in which the chief wooed a Skye fairy, and was given the flag as a love token. When the perfidious man instead married a human wife, his rejected lover cast a curse causing all children and calves in MacLeod country to be born dead. The chief was forced to wave the flag to remove the spell.

The silk material of the banner actually originated from Syria or Rhodes, and has an approximate date of between the fourth and eighth century AD. No one knows how this ancient artefact arrived at Dunvegan. The guess – unsupported by any evidence, for there is a complete absence of evidence in this case – is that it was some kind of high-status object that was looted during the Crusades.

In *The Chiefs of Clan MacLeod* (1993) Alick Morrison puts forward the alternative notion that the banner is the Landöda or 'Land Ravager' of Harald Hardrada, King of Norway, a flag that always guaranteed victory in battle. In his youth Hardrada had commanded the Varangian Guard of the Emperor of Constantinople. In 1066, when Hardrada was defeated by the Anglo-Saxon King Harold Godwineson at the Battle of Stamford Bridge, he had within his army one Godred Crovan, an Icelander who later helped found a dynasty in the Kingdom of Man and the Hebrides. So if the Landöda is the banner from Rhodes (which was under the dominion of Constantinople), it might have passed from Hardrada to Crovan to Leod, the first MacLeod chief, who died around 1280. That's a lot of maybes, but it's as good a notion as any other.

How, exactly, was this precious palladium used? MacLeod of MacLeod tells us it was frequently taken into battle but not unfurled, its very presence acting as a talisman of victory. The staff was born by a standard-bearer, protected by twelve of the bravest warriors of the clan, and fronted by the chief, who was sworn to lay down his life in defence of the flag. The office of standard-bearer was hereditary, and remained in one family for nearly three centuries. One bearer, Murcha Breac, was killed at the Battle of the Bloody Bay in 1480, and given the highest honour possible – burial in the same grave as his chief on Iona.

There are conflicting traditions as to how many times the Fairy Flag has been unfurled, and on which occasions. Candidates include the aforementioned Battle of the Bloody Bay (when the MacLeods lost), and the Battles of Glen Sligachan (1395-ish), Glendale (about 1490), Trumpan (1530s) and Waternish (1530s/40s), and during a time when a cattle plague was raging. Most authorities plump for the Battles of Glendale and TRUMPAN; at the latter the flag created the illusion that the meagre MacLeod forces were several times their actual size. Many later writers wondered why the flag was not waved when the clan was ruined by the potato famine, or when the MacDonalds were militarily ascendant around 1600, but perhaps there was a belief, based on some of the legends, that the third unfurling would herald an even greater disaster.

It is possible that the third unfurling, and its attendant horrors, have already happened. In 1799 Dr Norman MacLeod was present at a secret conclave when the chest containing the flag was forced open by a smith at the behest of Hector MacDonald Buchanan, the factor of the absent chief. The inner case was made of strongly-scented wood, and within was the flag, which was unfurled and inspected. Norman MacLeod was sworn to secrecy not to reveal the illicit act, and only admitted it in his old age ('I am the only person now living who can attest the truth of it'). He linked the unfurling to a well-known prophecy supposedly uttered by Coinneach Odhar, the Brahan Seer. Here is the doctor's version of the prophecy:

> When Norman, the fourth Norman, the son of the hard, slender English lady would perish by an accidental death; that when the Maidens of MacLeod became the property of a Campbell; when a fox had young ones in one of the turrets of the castle, and particularly when the fairy enchanted banner should be for the last time exhibited, then the glory of the MacLeod family should depart — a great part of the estate should be sold to others; so that a small curragh [a boat] would carry all gentlemen of the name of MacLeod across Loch Dunvegan; but that in times far distant a chief named Ian Breac should arise, who should redeem those estates, and raise the powers and honour of the house to a higher pitch than ever.

During the week following the opening of the chest, several uncanny events occurred. Norman, the MacLeod heir, a lieutenant on HMS *Queen Charlotte*, was blown up at sea. His father, the twentieth chief, was named Norman, as were the eighteenth and nineteenth chiefs. Lieutenant MacLeod was therefore the fourth Norman. Then MacLeod's Maidens [see IDRIGILL] were sold to Angus Campbell of Ensay. And a Lieutenant MacLean, who was staying in the west turret of the castle, owned a fox which gave birth to a litter in his room. During the nineteenth century, the 'gentlemen' among the tenants departed, and much of the estate was sold off. Dr MacLeod's reminiscences, along with the prophecy and its apparent fulfilment, were quoted in the *Celtic Magazine* (1877) and in *The MacLeods of Dunvegan*.

As a source of potent power, the flag attracted other folklore. It could bring herrings to the loch and increase fertility. In *Superstitions of the Highlands and Islands of Scotland*, John Gregorson Campbell claimed that when the flag was out and about every cow that was carrying a calf instantly gave birth, while pregnant women who saw it went into premature labour. There has been no notice of this happening since the castle was opened to visitors. MacLeod airmen who served in the Second World War carried photographs of the Fairy Flag as apotropaic protection against sudden death.

The Drawing Room was probably the scene of a massacre in the 1550s when Ian Dubh, who had already murdered several of his relatives on the way to becoming chief, had a party of visiting Campbells killed at a feast. The signal for the slaughter was the serving of cups filled with blood. Ian Dubh came to a bad end, having been deposed, forced to flee to Ireland, and dispatched by a red-hot iron thrust through his bowels.

Dungeon

Off the passage from the Drawing Room is a hole in the floor, the only access to the miserable 6ft by 4ft (1.8m x 1.2m) pit that formed the castle dungeon. The last 4ft (1.2m) of the 13ft (4m) deep hole is cut out of the very rock on which the castle stands. The only source of light was a narrow loophole high up on the wall. Beside the hole are the cover of the trapdoor and two large iron weights that were used to shackle prisoners. Sometime before 1930 Ratcliffe Barnett was conducted round the castle by the chief, who lit a candle and let it down into the chamber on a string, saying, 'it was down there that my ancestor put his first wife and starved her to death.'

North Room

Here there are more relics with strange stories. The Dunvegan Cup is a wooden vessel richly decorated with silverwork, standing on four legs, and with sockets for precious stones, most of which have now vanished. Its origin is uncertain, but it seems to be made of alder or bog-oak, and was owned by Niall Glen Dubh, the tenth-century High King of Ireland and ancestor of the powerful O'Neills. A passage in *The MacLeods of Dunvegan* suggests it was a gift from Shane O'Neill, who in 1595 rebelled against Elizabeth I with the assistance of 500 men supplied by Rory Mor, the MacLeod chief. Alternatively, it could be plunder or part of a dowry. The cup is inscribed with the legend *Katharina IngenY Neill Uxor Johannis Meguigir Principis De Firmanae me Fieri Fecit, Anno Domini, 1493. Oculi omnium in te sperant Domine et tu das escam illorum in tempore opportune*, which may be translated as 'Katharina, daughter of King Neil, wife of John, grandson of Macguire, prince of Firmanagh, had me made in the year of the Lord 1493. The eyes of all wait on Thee; and Thou givest them their meat in due season.' The second sentence is the fifteenth verse of the 144th Psalm. This, combined with the four versions of the sacred monogram IHS, the abbreviation for the name of Jesus, suggests the cup was probably used as a chalice, the vessel from which the wine was drunk during Mass.

Almost inevitably, there is an alternative origin for the cup which involves the fairies. Lurran, the fastest runner in the Hebrides, entered a fairy hill and stole the cup, outpacing the angry fairies and reaching running water, which they could not cross. There are variants about what happened next: either Lurran was killed and his property seized by his jealous brother, who was then hanged by the MacLeod chief, who confiscated the murderer's property, or the chief murdered Lurran directly so he could get his hands on the fairy cup. In an alternative version Lurran does not feature at all and a quarrelsome clansman called Neil Glendubh – which is, of course, the name of the tenth-century Irish king – is said to have murdered a relative of the MacLeod chief. For this crime he was flayed alive, his family executed, and all his property confiscated – including the precious cup, although the tale does not relate how he acquired it. *The MacLeods of Dunvegan* places these stories on Harris. *Superstitions of the Highlands and Islands of Scotland* states they were also known in Ardnamurchan, Lochaber, Craignish, Mull and Tiree. There is of course also a Skye-based version, with the fairy hill Lurran entered being identified as DUN OSDALE.

Next to the cup is Rory Mor's Horn, a long bull- or ox-horn decorated with Celtic monsters and animals in silver. It holds around five pints and in tradition was quaffed in one draft by the chief as he came of age. This heroic act was referred to in 'The Whistle', a ballad by Robert Burns:

> 'By the gods of the ancients!' Glenriddel replies,
> 'Before I surrender so glorious a prize,
> I'll conjure the ghost of the great Rorie More,
> And bumper his horn with him twenty times o'er.'

As with the other Dunvegan treasures, the origin of the horn is a matter of legend rather than fact. In version one, the MacLeod chief, returning from a clandestine visit to the wife of the chief of Clan Fraser, met a terrible bull in the woods of GLENELG and dispatched it armed with only a knife. In the struggle one of the bull's horns was broken off, which became the chief's drinking trophy (so impressive was this feat that he also gained Mrs Fraser as a permanent companion). In the second variant, the MacLeod chief visited Inveraray in Argyll, where he found one of his clansmen condemned to be gored to death by a bull. MacLeod leaped into the arena and, with the crowd crying 'Hold Fast!' – now the motto of the clan – he subdued the fierce animal, tearing off one of its horns. Neither of these tales ascribes the feat to Rory Mor, the chief after whom the horn is named. The third telling, as given by Otta Swire, remedies this. Rory Mor was some distance from Dunvegan when he saw the beacons blazing, the sign that the MacDonalds were attacking. He immediately mounted a bull, put his men on a herd of cows, told them to 'hold fast' – and stampeded the herd to Dunvegan. There the MacDonalds were routed and the saviour bull was looked after for the rest of its life, and only in death did it provide Rory Mor's Horn.

The final treasure is no longer to be found. In 1926 Alasdair Alpin MacGregor recorded a pendant made of the rock labradorite. It had been sent to Sir Reginald MacLeod of MacLeod in January 1914, accompanied by an anonymous letter bearing a Whitby postmark. The letter read:

Mrs — thinks this has belonged to a very old lady. It brings to her mind some ancestral history and a very old building, somewhat dilapidated but rebuilt. In the family there seem to have been many vicissitudes – attachments, changes of circumstances, political interference, and persecutions. The family is Scotch – a distinguished line of aristocrats – their position and power are not now what it was, but there will be an ascent again. A child will be born more dark than fair and very intelligent, who will be the means of lifting up this family – the father thin and intelligent, the mother dark and psychic. The child will grow into a God-fearing man and will be enterprising and psychic. This pendant should not be worn but put in a case, and it should be sent back to the family it came from. Mrs — felt a very proud tall lady had once worn it who had carried on some clandestine correspondence, and who had been no good in some political crisis and had pushed someone out of some place, and believed to have caused the beheading of this person. Let the thing lie in a case: don't wear it.

MacGregor published the letter in *Over the Sea to Skye* 'in the hope that some imaginative or psychic person may be able to throw some light upon it.' It appears no one ever did, and other than this one mention I can find no other published source that describes the pendant. The present custodian of the MacLeod papers has never heard of it, and the previous chief, who died in 2007, never mentioned it to anyone. Perhaps both letter and pendant perished in the fire that destroyed the south wing of the castle in 1938. Is there anyone now who can tell us why someone in pre-First World War Whitby thought this cursed stone had belonged to the MacLeods, and why it needed to be returned? And how did they get it?

Kitchen

The former kitchen, with its muscular walls, houses a mighty claymore, the Great Sword of Dunvegan, and a Pictish symbol stone carved with a crescent and V-rod and a pair of concentric circles. It once partly covered the well of Tobar Na Maor, beside DUN OSDALE, and was brought here in 1910. There is also a flat-topped figure called the 'Sundial' – a woman in early seventeenth-century costume, possibly meant to represent Isobel, the wife of Rory Mor. It once stood in the Gun Court, and before that may have been one of a pair of fireplace surrounds.

The Gun Court at Dunvegan Castle. When the water in the well developed a strange taste, the body of a man was found in it; he had gone missing at a drink-fuelled christening celebration some three weeks earlier.

The temporal power of the MacLeod chiefs found an echo in the supernatural realm. Balls of light about the castle or loch portended evil for the family. In 1897 R.C. Maclagan recorded a sighting of one of these 'dreag' lights. It appeared in the April gloaming with 'tails, tassels, and serpentine wreaths attached to the dragon-shaped head, moving slowly but steadily westward, about half-way from Portree to Dunvegan.' Shortly afterwards the funeral cortège of the MacLeod matriarch followed the same route. Otta Swire noted that every five years a flock of supernatural swans passed over the castle and the MacLeod lands, bringing good fortune to anyone who saw them. There is a persistent Celtic belief in swans being the souls of the dead, so these birds were probably thought of as MacLeod ancestors checking on how the present generation were faring. Swire tells us that herring would vanish from the loch if any woman other than a MacLeod crossed from Dunvegan to the nearest island, while both J.A. Macculloch and Dr Johnson were told that if the chief was in residence at the castle, this meant herring shoals would be plentiful. Macculloch also described a belief among the inhabitants of St Kilda, a MacLeod property: in May 1895, when the factor came for his annual visit, he came bearing news that the chief had died in February. But the islanders already knew – because they had heard the cuckoo, which only landed on their remote islands when a MacLeod chief had passed on.

FIADHAIRT

The single-track road continues past the castle, finishing at the car park for the popular walk to the 'coral beaches' at Lampay. Along the way it passes Fiadhairt, a little-visited peninsula. Dun Fiadhairt is a fine broch, with chambers, stairs and a gallery still visible between its two walls (NG23115042). Finds from the excavation included an amber necklace and a Roman terracotta model of a bale of wool, showing there were trade links with Roman Britain in the second century AD. Although the promontory is rough, a good path leaves the road at the south end of Loch Suardal. Less easy to get to is a large cairn at Camalaig Bay to the north (NG235511).

CLAIGAN

If, instead of heading north from the parking space to the Coral Beaches, you go east, you soon arrive at Claigan souterrain (NG238539). It is possible to explore this Iron Age underground structure, which, like all souterrains, is dark, low and torch-worthy.

OSDALE

Because the broch of Dun Osdale (NG24124641) is so prominently placed next to the road from Dunvegan to Glendale, it has attracted several legends. First and foremost it is a fairy dwelling. In 1911 the American anthropologist W.Y. Evans-Wentz talked to an old woman from Ebost, in Bracadale, who remembered her father recounting that as a boy he was lying on the grassy slope of the broch when he heard the fairies singing a waulking-song (a chant sung to accompany the working of wool for cloth).

One voice took the verse and then the fairy host joined in the chorus: 'Ho! fir-e! fair-e, foirm! Ho! Fair-eag-an an clò!' (Ho! well done! Grand! Ho! bravo the web [of homespun]!) Evans-Wentz's informant expressed her sorrow that no one heard or saw fairies any more. Otta Swire places the story of Lurran and the stolen cup here (see DUNVEGAN CASTLE), adding the detail that the man's mother was a witch who placed protection spells on her son, but forgot to similarly protect the cup. The fairies therefore enchanted the vessel, making it the most desirable object ever seen. Lurran was consequently murdered by one of his spellbound friends, who in turn was hanged by the MacLeod chief, which is how the cup ended up in the castle. Another tale says the fairy who married the MacLeod chief came from Dun Osdale.

Somewhere opposite Dun Osdale, on the north side of the road, is the site of Tobar Na Maor (Well of the Steward, NG24084648 – I failed to find it). It seems that the Pictish stone now at Dunvegan Castle once partly covered the well. The standard story is that the stone was removed in 1910. Malcolm Ferguson's 1885 book *Rambles in Skye* states that in recent times a stranger had found a 'peculiarly-shaped stone ... maybe left there by the fairies' at the well and had it embedded into the rock with cement. Presumably this was the Pictish stone. This same stranger placed a stick beside the well and nailed to it a rather bad poem:

> This is the Dunvegan Fairies' favourite verdant knoll,
> And at its base their famous magic purling well;
> Here the weary traveller may sit doon and tak' a rest,
> And drink from the pure fountain spring to quench his thirst.

Nearby was a large stone used as a coffin rest, where mourners rested and drank from the well.

In the 1880s Skye's exploited crofters made headlines protesting for land reform. Most of the press were sympathetic, the one exception being *The Scotsman*, whose correspondent stayed as a guest of the landed families and consistently took an insulting tone to the crofters. In *Highways and Byways in the West Highlands* Seton Gordon states that some crofters made an effigy representing the paper and buried it somewhere near Dun Osdale in a place later called Uamh or Uaigh a t-Albannaich, the Cave or Grave of the Scotsman. I have been unable to locate this site.

Dun Osdale, prehistoric broch and fairy dwelling.

The fairy mound of Cnoc an t-Sithean, Colbost. Its inhabitants were fond of music and dancing. In the foreground is the memorial to the protesting Glendale crofters.

Here, too, a water-horse is allegedly buried. The site is actually a fallen standing stone at NG24234597. Take the track south-west of Dun Osdale towards Osdale farm. Where the track passes through a broken-down dyke follow the bank to the right, keeping on the left (west) side of the mossy stones. The stone lies horizontally under the dyke.

COLBOST

The prominent natural knoll of Cnoc an t-Sithean by the roadside was a well-known fairy dwelling (NG199498). Close to it is a memorial to the land reform protesters.

BORRERAIG

Borreraig Park Museum and Croft Shop (open daily, summer 10 a.m. to 6 p.m., winter 10 a.m. to 4 p.m., admission charge, some disabled access) has a fine collection of agricultural, domestic and weaving items, as well as a display on the MacCrimmon pipers, the hereditary pipers to the MacLeods. A memorial cairn to the pipers sits on Borreraig Hoe (NG19085384). The Gaelic inscription translates as 'Near this spot stood the Macrimmon School of Music 1500–1800'.

The MacCrimmon dynasty provided the soundtrack for many generations of MacLeod exploits, and their history and its attendant folklore dominate the area. Ian Og MacCrimmon was having a blast in the Piper's Hollow (Slochd nam Piobairean) when the Queen of Faery appeared, declaiming:

> Thy manly beauty and the sweetness of thy pipe music
> Have brought thee a fairy sweetheart;
> Now I give thee this silver chanter,
> Which, touched by thy finger, will never lack sweetest music.

Ian Og thereafter played all his music on 'the silver chanter of the fairy woman', although we are not told how his relationship with the poetry-spouting smitten sylph progressed. (Source: J.A. Macculloch, *The Misty Isle of Skye*.)

Iain Dall MacKay, the blind piper of Gairloch, was pursued by fellow pupils jealous of his skill, so he leaped from the top of a grassy knoll – to land 20ft (6m) below, completely unharmed. The marks of his heels in the soft grass at Leum an Doill (Blind Man's Leap) were still visible until the early twentieth century. Close to Slochd nam Piobairean was Clach Mhor Mhic Cruimein, the Great Stone of MacCrimmon, a huge boulder said to have been used by Padruig Mor MacCrimmon to drive his horse's tether peg into the earth. (Source: Seton Gordon, *The Charm of Skye*.) The MacCrimmons discovered that a girl had learned a certain combination of notes and passed them on to her sweetheart, who was not of the dynasty. There was only one way of preventing the knowledge leaking in the future – so the pipers cut the girl's fingers off. (Source: Ratcliffe Barnett, *Autumns in Skye, Ross and Sutherland*.)

GALTRIGILL

Here the road ends. Follow the track to the very end and turn right along a fence for about 140 paces, and you're at a large flat square boulder, the Manners Stone (NG182547). The story is that either sitting on the stone magically improved your manners, or the judge sat on it to administer justice, and crofters had to demonstrate good manners by making a bow or curtsey. Follow the burn and then a rocky path down to Galtrigill Bay. At the south end of the beach is Uamh nan Piobairean (the Pipers' Cave). Here pipers practiced, a soundproofing technique doubtless much appreciated by their long-suffering neighbours. In *Nether Lochaber* (1883), Alexander Stewart claims this cave as one of many across Skye and Scotland where a brave piper entered intent on dealing with a terrible danger – in this case, a wolf-pack. The tune he composed before succumbing to the wolfish jaws was later known as 'MacCrimmon's Lament'. Composing a brilliant piece of music is obviously what you do when exploring a terror-filled cave while holding a burning torch in one hand.

According to Seton Gordon in *The Charm of Skye*, some pupils took a vow to fast in the cave until they had received the inspiration for a great composition. One night a MacCrimmon was visited in dreams by an ancestor who played a wonderful tune. In the morning the piper tried it out but could not remember all the notes. That night he was visited again, and got most of the tune, and after the third night he was note-perfect on what was later called 'MacCrimmon's Sweetheart'. This story combines a traditional fairy- and folktale motif – the 'get it right on the third attempt' theme – with the universal story of the shaman or magic-worker seeking initiation and contact with the ancestors through fasting, sensory deprivation and dreamworking. I had never previously thought of a piper as a shamanic figure, but in this case it makes perfect sense.

GLENDALE

This grouping of crofting townships strung along a wide valley is the traditional site of a battle of 1490, when the MacLeods trounced the MacDonalds. Sometime in the

1840s two young women in one of these townships fell out with their father and his new wife, so they imitated a poltergeist, making strange noises and throwing clods at the house. As they did this each time the newly-married couple got into bed, they hoped the polt would be identified as their disapproving dead mother. The elders of the church failed to dislodge the 'ghost' but a group of Glendale lads caught the girls red-handed. The story was recorded in 1891 by Norman Matheson.

The old graveyard of St Comgan, Cille Chomgain or Kilchoan (NG17714976) is along a track west from the road by the bridge. Sadly, the medieval chapel is now lost, and I failed to find the gravestone famous for being carved with a harpist (as well as a chalice, cleric and sword).

In *Over the Sea to Skye* Alasdair Alpin MacGregor summed up the site's most common story. One Hallowe'en an old woman saw a number of spirits rise from their coffins and fly off. She paid particular attention to a tall powerful warrior. Hours later, when the warrior returned, he found he could not return to his rest because the woman had placed her distaff (wool-spinning bar) across the grave. This was a powerful magical act and it compelled the ghost to answer three questions. The first question was, 'Where hast thou been?' The warrior replied he had been to Norway, as spirits were permitted an annual visit to their homeland each Hallowe'en. 'Who art thou and what is thy name?' The ghost gave his name as Til, a son of the king of Norway (in other versions he is called Chiel). He had been drowned in a storm off the coast of Skye, washed ashore, and buried here, the first person interred on the site. He was therefore the guardian of the graveyard, and the elder tree that grew over his grave was taboo, bringing supernatural vengeance on anyone who damaged the tree or collected its branches (this tree has now vanished). The third question the woman asked was, 'What is my fate?' (This is quite a leap from the more factual direction of the first two questions, but comes from a longstanding Gaelic belief that ghosts could foretell the future.) Til predicted that the crone would have a son called Kenneth, and he would be a seer. The woman dismissed this as unlikely but in her old age she gave birth to a boy named Kenneth the Sallow, Coinneach Odhar, who became the famous Brahan Seer. It is only fair to point out that the tale of the woman questioning a ghost disbarred from its grave by her distaff is widely told throughout Scotland and the origin story of the Brahan Seer is usually set in the Western Isles.

Another widely-told tale with multiple locations is also set in Glendale – the departure of the last fairies from Scotland. A boat left from Glendale for Ireland, but for some reason it was much lower in the water that it should have been. It was as if it was leaking, or overloaded, yet both causes were investigated and found to be groundless. Eventually, a sailor with the second-sight had the captain stand on his foot and look over his shoulder – this temporarily transferred the sight to the second man, who could then see that the every inch of the boat was taken up with little people. They were leaving because of the inroads of Presbyterianism and the clearing of the people from the land. With belief in fairies eroded and no one left to leave gifts of milk or oatmeal, there was now nothing worth staying for on Skye, and so they were emigrating to Ireland. As I say, this is a widespread story.

In the 1880s the grievances of the crofters were addressed by the Crofting Commission, which set up mobile hearings at which crofters were questioned and encouraged to describe their problems (when the Commission's report was published it shocked Victorian society with its depiction of British citizens kept in near-feudal servitude by the chiefs or their agents). Alexander Ross, a crofter and fisherman from Glendale, was asked, 'Was there not a rule on the estate which the factor could enforce for keeping down dogs?' Ross' reply was, 'He enforced the rule on my dog by shooting him in a well, and the well has been dry since, although it was formerly one of the best wells in the country.' Wells in folklore, particularly holy wells, frequently run dry or move to another location if they have been abused; this is the only example I can think of where the cruel killing of a dog cursed the well into non-existence. The case was noted by Walter Gregor in 1883.

MILOVAIG

Alasdair Alpin Macgregor was told about Clach na Banachaig, the Dairymaids' Stone, where an offering of warm milk placated the spirits (possibly a gruagach). He failed to find it, as did I.

WATERSTEIN

This beautiful area with its spectacular coastal scenery is chock-full of fairy place names. There is Camas nan Sìdhean (the Bay of the Fairies) Sgeir nan Sìdhean (the Fairies' Rock or Skerry), Bruach na Sithean (Brae of the Fairies), and a ruined building called Bathach na Sithean (the Fairies' Byre). Here an old woman keeping watch over her dead daughter in the dark night was assisted by a water-horse, who magically kept the single peat burning bright until dawn. Fairies lived in the cave behind the waterfall of the Allt na-h-Uamha (NG140476, access only at low tide). Close by is another Uamh an Oir (Cave of Gold) where another piper disappeared (the attrition rate for pipers venturing into caves is abnormally high; someone really needs to do a risk analysis before embarking on similar future ventures). Near Loch Mor Vaterstein was Tobar an Fhiona (the Well of Wine), which was once visited for cures.

NEIST POINT

Noted for scenery, cliffs and shipwrecks, here the wizard MacVurich of the Talents raised a south-west gale that took an enemy galley to the bottom, while an old woman from Glendale, grieving for her murdered son, conjured up wind, fog and rain to annihilate the escaping MacDonalds. (Source: MacGregor's *Over the Sea to Skye*.) Peter MacAskill (see DUNVEGAN) told me that phantom ships had been seen here a week or two in advance of a real vessel hitting the rocks.

RAMASAIG/LORGILL

An appealing walk leaves from the end of the road at Ramasaig to the remote and deserted settlement of Lorgill (NG177419). Peter MacAskill related the tale of a place near here called the Priest's Stone, which traditionally covered a cache of gold. It may have been a prehistoric burial site, or a more recent grave, or something else entirely. Sometime in the late 1960s a shepherd, known for his wild ways, decided to find the treasure. He dislodged the stone, dug down for several feet – and then just packed the task in and hurriedly filled in the hole. Other shepherds who were in the area were convinced he had seen something that had spooked him, but the man never spoke about the experience.

MACLEOD'S TABLES

It is a rule universally acknowledged in human cultures that any unusual or dominating landscape feature inevitably attracts stories, whether they be grandly mythological (such as the home of the gods) or simply folkloric (treasure, fairies, secret passages and so on). And so it is with the two hills known as MacLeod's Tables, which can be seen for miles all around Duirinish. Their flat table-tops are explained as a tribute to Columba – when the saint was refused hospitality by a churlish pagan chief, the mountains truncated their own tops so as to provide a bed and table for the holy man. The rather more prosaic explanation is that basalt lava sometimes forms horizontal layers. As for the name, a MacLeod chief in Edinburgh was fed up with his fellow nobles constantly comparing the grandeur of the capital to the poverty of his homeland, and so stated he had a grander dining table and hall than anywhere in Scotland. When the Lowland toffs turned up to call his bluff, he showed them his table (the flat mountain), the hall (the vault of stars) and his candelabra (flaming torches held by serried ranks of clansmen). Score one to the MacLeod, although none of the several tellings of this tale mention if the midges were biting.

Healabhal Mhor, the northernmost hill, looks to be the larger from below, although it is actually less high than its neighbour. On the north-west edge of the plateau is a badly damaged prehistoric burial cairn (NG22244439) which may have been the home of the fairies of the hill. Seton Gordon gives two tales connected with this sithean. In the first, a

MacLeod's Tables, Healabhal Bheag and Healabhal Mhor, created in honour of St Columba, and home to fairies, Fingal and Valkyries.

man from Osdale made love to a beautiful woman on the plateau. Sadly, however, he may have been speciesist or sizeist (she was a fairy only 3ft (90cm) tall) and after he had had his pleasure he decided to take a human partner. When his wife was about to have a child he climbed the hill and sneakily asked the fairy for advice about helping a cow to calf. The fairy, who obviously did not hold a grudge, told him to rub his hand over the belly. This he did and his wife bore a son. Shortly after he met the fairy again, who, realizing she had been deceived, told him she must take his son. That night the boy disappeared, and the fairy was not seen for another decade, at which time she invited the Osdale man into the sithean to see his son. The man was introduced to the fairy's 1,000-year-old parents (one wonders how that conversation went: 'Mother, Father, this is the human who seduced and abandoned me, so in revenge I stole his child by another woman.' Ah, fairy soap operas.) Another ten years passed, and the man received an invitation to the wedding of the fairy and his now-grown son. The palace within the sithean was filled with handsome men and women tucking into a great feast. The fairy must have retained an affection for the man, because each time they parted she gave him a bag of gold so heavy she had to carry it for him. And after the wedding she gave him two bags.

The second tale concerns Fingal and his 900 warriors, who took refuge from a storm within the sithean. After they had settled in, the Kings of Greece, Spain and another place, each with 900 men, arrived. Space and food were limited so the warbands fell to fighting, with the Fingalians of course victorious. Fingal also obtained his famous magic sword from a one-legged fairy blacksmith here. The sword had to be tempered with blood by slaying the first person who came through the smithy door, which in this case was the smith's mother (this tragic ending is a well-known folklore motif stretching back to the Greek myths).

In the year 1014 Good Friday fell on 23 April. On that day the tribes of Ireland clashed in the Battle of Clontarf, which resulted in the defeat of Máel Mórda mac Murchada, the King of Leinster, by the forces of Brian Boru, the King of Munster; Boru was also killed. Viking forces from Dublin and Orkney were prominent in the affray, and many were killed. Also present were warriors from all the Norse lands of western Scotland, including Lewis, Argyll, Kintyre – and Skye. Some historians see the event as marking the point at which Viking influence in Ireland began to wane, and it certainly changed the balance of power in both Orkney and the Hebrides. Otta Swire tells how, on the eve of the battle, a farmer on Healabhal Mhor saw the twelve Valkyries hovering in the suddenly darkened sky. These Viking guides of the dead traditionally wove the web of fate before a battle, and then chose the bravest of the slain to live in the heroes' afterlife in Valhalla. This time, however, as they wove the web of death, they sang:

> Horror covers all the heath
> Clouds of carnage block the sun;
> Sisters, weave the web of death,
> Sisters, cease, the work is done.

They then tore the web into two halves and flew off in opposite directions. This was taken to mean that the old pagan faith of the Vikings was spent, to be replaced by Christianity. In these terms Clontarff was the last hurrah for both Norse religion and the Valkyries, who were never again seen on Skye.

IDRIGILL POINT AND MACLEOD'S MAIDENS

Here are scenic wonders in excelsis, not to mention more Valkyries. The most striking sight from the land is MacLeod's Maidens, three pillars of rock sculpted by geology and weather, standing in wave-swept isolation off Rubha na Maighdeanan. The largest stack, nearest to the mighty cliffs, is 207ft (63m) high, the tallest in Skye, and is known as the mother, Nic Cleosgeir Mhor; from some angles there is a distinct resemblance to Queen Victoria. In *The Lord of the Isles*, Sir Walter Scott called the trio the Choosers of the Slain and Riders of the Storm, titles redolent of the Valkyries, although he did not say if a local had given him these names or whether he had simply invented them himself. I suspect the latter. The stacks could be identified with the Norns, the Norse Fates. One weaves the thread of life, the second fulls or thickens it, and the third, who is blind, cuts it. This is an apt metaphor, for on An Dubh Sgeir (The Black Skerry) to the west, Campbell of Ensor placed false lights to lead ships onto the rocks; with the crews drowned the wreckers would then plunder the cargos.

The Maidens are reached by a long but excellent walk starting from the parking space at the end of the Orbost road. Care is needed near the windy clifftops on the headland, and walkers must be prepared for serious weather. Idrigill Point is home to mighty sea-caves, including Uamh a' Choinnleir (the Cave of the Candlestick), which is apparently named because candles were needed to explore it, although it may also refer to a vaguely candlestick-shaped rock. One of the caves – it is not clear which one – was home to the ill-fated Lady Grange (see TRUMPAN). These caves cannot be visited by land and are only visible from the sea.

Near Brandarsaig Bay at NG249392 is Rebel's Wood, a carbon-offset plantation by Future Forests, with a sign reading, 'These Trees Have Been Planted in the Living Memory of Joe Strummer 1952-2002.' Strummer was the leader of The Clash; for more on the punk firebrand, see DUN CAAN on Raasay.

No dramatic sea-coast is complete without sightings of mermaids. Otta Swire tells of a man atop the cliff above the Maidens, who spotted a mermaid and three seals on the rocks below. Quietly he sneaked down and managed to catch a baby seal. Immediately the water was filled with a host of angry mermaids. One offered him a reward in exchange for the pup. He asked for her gold comb but she refused this and instead offered three wishes. We are not told what he wished for but, as is traditional, the wishes did not do him any good. J.A. Macculloch has a complementary tale. A MacLeod retainer, resting on the cliff, saw a mermaid sitting on a reef combing her hair. 'I lifted my gun, meaning to shoot her, for I thought if I got her I could carry her round the country, and myself would be a rich man. And then I put down the gun, for I thought she's so humanlike that if I shoot her I will be hanged. And so I kept lifting it and putting it down, until, plop, the merry-maid took one dive and disappeared into the sea.' Hooray for second thoughts about slaughtering innocent mer-creatures.

A small mound within an enclosure on the east bank of the River Ollisdal in remote Glen Ossidal (NG21904080) bears a slab inscribed with the words 'ANGUS MacDERMIT found dead in this ravine 1905.' A coastal path from Idrigill Point passes this way, and gives access to the best clifftop walking on Skye, with tremendous caves, stacks, pillars and natural arches. This long route is so far from a road or any dwelling that pre-planning is crucial, and extreme care employed on the edges.

ORBOST

Otta Swire lived here and so obtained a rich collection of local episodes, some very close to home. When her father's setter was bitten by an adder, the keeper cured it by bathing the wound in hot water containing a snake-stone – a holed stone through which vipers supposedly passed to shed their skin. Her mother, as a child, believed that if horse-hairs floated in water they became eels, and the eels later transformed into land snakes. Otta and two other people were in a room at Orbost House when they heard a coach approach the house. The sound of the horses' hooves was clearly heard as the vehicle approached the front door, but no coach actually appeared. Strangely, two other people in the same room heard nothing. By 1950 the invisible coach had become a powerful car or lorry, the sounds of gear-changing, brakes and acceleration all being clearly heard. I have not encountered another example of an audio phantom updating its technology.

A long-vanished graveyard at the top of the hill on the road to Roag was still haunted in the 1950s. Nearby was once a hollow stone into which milk was poured for the gruagach. In 1920 two men walking nearby at night saw two luminous white figures walking in the heather. The witnesses knew they were not ghosts, and in another context, and at a later date, these shining and ice-clear figures would have been identified as aliens. About ten years later a man was found dead at the very spot, and another individual expired in the same place in the late 1940s. Were these same-site deaths mere coincidence? Were the shining figures harbingers of doom? Or had both victims seen something that contributed to their demise?

One stormy night a handsome man arrived at a dwelling, but the maiden and her mother found sand and seashells in his hair, a sure sign of a water-horse. As they fled he changed into a great stallion, but the mother threw down an iron knife which blocked his path. While he was at bay she threatened to tell the world his true name. Magical traditions the world over recognise that anyone who possesses the true name of a wizard, witch or supernatural being has power over them (largely because they can be named in binding spells). The alarmed water-horse leaped into the deep pool by the bridge and vanished.

HERIBOST AND ROSKILL

A couple were reaping corn at moonlight when the man found he had a wound on his hand. He came to the reasonable conclusion that the fairies were displeased at the moonlit work, and so packed in for the night. The next morning he found an elf-arrow in the field where he had been hurt, which proved he had been a victim of fairy assault. The story is in Seton Gordon's *The Charm of Skye*.

HARLOSH

Harlosh Point, beyond the road-end at Ardmore, has a ruined chapel (Cnoc A' Cladh, NG28354082) and a dun overlying a prehistoric fort (Dun Nèill, NG28144075). The former is only a rectangle of turf, and while the latter is fragmentary at best, it has a splendid setting on an isolated plug of coastal rock. The coastline has wall-like natural basalt dykes and excellent rock stacks. Close to the most spectacular stack on the east coast by the Point (NG281401, not shown on the OS map), and only accessible at low tide, is yet another Piper's Cave. In a variant of the story told at BORRERAIG, Otta Swire states that it was here that the MacCrimmon piper joined in the flesh with the beautiful Fairy Queen. As a post-coital gift she gave him the silver chanter, on the condition that he would be compelled to return to her one day. He returned to Borreraig and, being now the greatest piper in the Isles, founded a dynasty of hereditary pipers to the MacLeods. Finally the dreaded day arrived, and with his terrier, and his pipes powered by the fairy chanter, he entered the cave. His family and friends traced the sound of the underground bagpipes and barking as far as FAIRY BRIDGE, where the music ceased (presumably because the piper had met either his fairy love, or a less pleasant fate). The subterranean barking, however, continued, and eventually the dog ran out of the Cave of Gold at GRESHORNISH. During its trans-Skye journey the terrier had had every hair singed off, thus confirming the notion that the various caves had some interconnectivity with Hell.

FEORLIG

South of the main road, between the road junctions to Upper Feorlig and Harlosh/Balmore, are two enormous piles of stones (NG29794408 and NG29844398). These are the Barpannan chambered cairns, amongst the largest remaining of Skye's prehistoric funereal structures. The northernmost mound is around 20ft (6m) high and 90ft (27m) in diameter, its partner being lower – through having been robbed for building stone – but even larger. The scale of the labour involved in building these cemeteries is impressive. In folklore, one cairn covers MacDonalds, and the other MacLeods, warriors who died in the supposed last battle between the clans (there are an awful lot of 'last clan battles' – this one, if it did happen here, was almost certainly not the final conflict). According to legend the body-count was so high because thick mist descended during the battle; with no sense of who was winning or losing, individual clansmen fought on until they dropped. In the end only women, children and the aged were left to make the grave mounds.

J.A. Macculloch stated that in the nineteenth century the MacLeod chief began to excavate one of the cairns, but found 'the feeling of the countryside was against all such meddling with the dead,' possibly because the mounds were haunted by the vengeful 'Barrow-Dweller'. Otta Swire identified this ghost with the spirit of a Viking leader, who is also supposedly buried here. The spirits of those slain in the battle apparently still walk the moors. Swire's mother had been inside one of the tombs sometime between 1880 and 1890, and had seen several small rooms off a passage, all too low to stand up in. Barpa, another chambered cairn, stands west of the Harlosh Road (NG29844357), but it is very badly damaged. Further west, beside the path from the main road to Vatten, is another large stony pile, which may be a chambered cairn, or just a pile of field clearance stones (NG292442).

The tree-filled graveyard of the roofless St John's Episcopal Chapel at the head of the loch (NG30504374) is one of the loveliest sites on Skye. The church's unusually short life (1838–1855) may have contributed to the notion that it is haunted. J.A. Macculloch thought the 'things' allegedly seen in the burial ground may have originated in the local prejudice against Episcopalianism. As one of his informants stated, 'Well, there was no good man ever buried there.' Otta Swire says the tradition is that the church was built on a prehistoric burial mound and/or a fairy hill.

EIGHT

THE ISLANDS: RAASAY, RONA, SCALPAY & PABAY

All such solitary places in Skye – the cliffs seldom trodden by mortal foot and against which the sea is always dashing, and the ruins of long ago which crown so many of them, inspire some minds with a fearful joy – the joy at so much wild beauty, the catching mysterious fear of the unseen forms which must (you feel it) haunt these windswept heights.

J.A. Macculloch, *The Misty Isle of Skye*

This chapter deals with the four large islands off the north coast of Skye. Raasay is easily visited by ferry from Sconser and has an abundance of items of interest. It is also large, and deserves time to explore, especially via the splendid walks. It is possible to visit Rona by boat trip from Portree. Scalpay is privately owned and neither it nor Pabay have any regular public access.

RAASAY

Much of Raasay's history and folklore – and here they are often the same thing – is bound up with the political, financial and military dominance of the MacLeod chiefs of the island. The key chief is Iain Garbh (Mighty John), a heroic figure who is credited with many great feats, including the defeat and exile of the evil spirit Colann gun Cheann (see BEINN EDRA). Iain, who became chief in 1648, was a self-confessed enemy of evil witches, and, according to legend, this brought about his doom. His boat, returning from Lewis, was beset by a terrible storm raised by the Staffin witch Gorm-Shuil Crotach on the instructions of MacDonald of Duntulm. All seemed lost until the chief took the tiller and through his skill and example inspired the crew. What happened next is described in the purple prose of William Grant Stewart's *The Popular Superstitions and Festive Amusements of the Highlanders of Scotland* from 1851:

Lo! to their great astonishment, a large cat was seen to climb the rigging. This cat was soon followed by another of equal size, and the last by a successor, until at length the shrouds, masts, and whole tackle, were actually covered with them. Nor did the sight of all those cats, although he knew well enough their real character, intimidate the resolute Raasay, until a large black cat, larger than any of the rest, appeared on the mast-head, as commander-in-chief of the whole legion. Raasay, on observing him, instantly foresaw the result; he, however, determined to sell his life as dearly as possible, and immediately commanded an attack upon the cats but, alas! it soon proved abortive. With a simultaneous effort the cats overturned the vessel on her leeward wale, and every soul on board was precipitated into a watery grave. Thus ended the glorious life of Iain Garbh Macgillichallum of Raasay, to the lasting regret of the brave clan Leod and all good people, and to the great satisfaction of the abominable witches who thus accomplished his lamentable doom.

The seventeenth-century anonymous document called *The Wardlaw Manuscript* has an interesting note on what appears to be a death warning or premonitory dream: 'One Alexander Mackleod in Lewes the night before had voice warning him thrice not to goe with Raasey, for all would drown in there return; yet he went with him being infatuat [drunk] and drownd with the rest.' The fact that the crew had been drinking heavily before they left may have been a contributory factor in the disaster, but black magic makes for a better story.

Unlike the MacLeods of Dunvegan, the Raasay Macleods chose to support the Jacobites in 1745 and sent a hundred men and twenty-six pipers to fight for the cause. After the disaster of Culloden, the family hid the fugitive Bonnie Prince Charlie on the island and aided his escape. For all this they paid dearly, with Government troops burning, looting, raping and murdering their way across the island. The last MacLeod chief became bankrupt in 1843 and sold up, emigrating to Tasmania. Raasay then passed through a number of different owners, some of them less than satisfactory, before being acquired by the Highlands and Islands Development Board in 1979. The present population is less than 200.

As given in John Gregorson Campbell's *Superstitions of the Highlands and Islands of Scotland*, various magical powers were ascribed to the King Otter. The white spot on its breast was the only place vulnerable to harm, and if a hunter shot and missed this target the large animal would bite the assailant to death. On Raasay the King had a jewel in its head, and anyone who possessed this precious stone was guaranteed good fortune and invulnerability in battle. Even a piece of the King's skin provided protection against bullets and ensured victory. Some Raasay women could change into seals, while at least one island man married a mermaid; when his wife discovered her fish-skin hidden in the barn she immediately took to the sea and was never again seen. John Nicholson's memoir of Raasay, *I Remember*, mentions the legend that many generations ago the people of Raasay had been tricked into eating meat from the each-mart, an animal that was half-cow and half-horse.

CLACHAN

For want of a better term Clachan is the capital of Raasay. Here were based the MacLeod chiefs, and their influence is everywhere. The key building is Raasay House, built in the 1740s to replace the mansion burned by Government troops to punish the MacLeods for supporting the Jacobite cause. In January 2009, ironically following an extensive refurbishment, Raasay House suffered severe fire damage and at the time of writing is a roofless shell. In *Highways and Byways in the West Highlands* Seton Gordon described a recess in the old house whose stone floor bore a stain that could not be washed out. The story went that the brother and sister of MacLeod of Raasay climbed up DUN CAAN. The woman spied a boat and said, 'If I wished to sink that boat I could do it.' Her brother jokingly invited her to do so – so she immediately pronounced several dread incantations to conjure up a storm that condemned all those on the vessel to a watery grave. Back at the house her brother, who was a doctor, told her she looked ill, and decided to bleed her ('bleeding', simply removing blood, was a medical cure-all in the old days; it was thought to remove the illness from the body). After a while he asked her what colour was the flame of the candle. 'Yellow,' she replied. After more bleeding, he asked again. 'Red,' was the answer. She was bled a third time, and on being asked the colour of the flame, said, 'Blue, and now I understand your purpose, which is to take my life.' She died from loss of blood, and thus the family honour was saved from being tainted with witchcraft.

The old pier on the shorefront, now adjacent to the new ferry terminal, backs onto a defended promontory known as 'the Battery'. This structure is a typical example of the small shore defences built by landowners when fear of invasion by Napoleonic forces was rife. The battlements enclose a small cannon now spiked with one of its own cannonballs, but the truly amazing sight is the statues that flank the Battery – an enormous pair of fish-tailed, full-breasted (and rather butch) stone mermaids. The story goes that the twelfth chief commissioned what he thought were modest-sized statues from an Italian firm. When the mermaids arrived they turned out to be enormous, and the bill precipitated the chief's bankruptcy.

One of a pair of gigantic butch
bare-breasted mermaids at
Clachan.

An unobtrusive square stone at the northern end of the Battery wall is a fragment of the base of a presumably medieval cross, which may have been one of the sanctuary markers of St Maol-luag's chapel (see below). The sloping rockface on the south side of the Battery, next to a shed, supposedly bears an incised cross, but I failed to find it (although admittedly my inspection was hampered by construction activity for the new ferry). This may too have been a sanctuary marker.

Several walks start at the information point near Borodale House hotel, and a leaflet can be picked up from reception or on the ferry. For those with limited time, the circular walk up Temptation Hill provides the best option, as it takes in several of the more important archaeological remains. Start almost opposite the hotel, where a stile on the west side of the Inverarish-Clachan road gives access to a short path into the souterrain of Uamh Nan Ramh, Oar Cave (NG 54953639). This splendid structure begins as a cleft between two parallel rocks and becomes an artificial passage covered with heavy stone lintels, a clever piece of engineering making use of natural providence. The limber can make it to the end and squeeze out through the terminal entrance. The souterrain, which has been cleared of rubbish in recent years, is Iron Age, although when Boswell and Johnson visited in 1773 it was used for the storage of oars, hence the name.

Return to the road and proceed north behind the wall of Raasay House to St Maol-Luag's Chapel (NG 54833664) built into the slope beside the road. An early Christian church dedicated to St Moluag was founded here around AD 569, although all the present remains are medieval or later. Of the three roofless structures in the graveyard, the largest is the former parish church, originally built in the early thirteenth century. The arch within the south wall is a tomb recess, but there is no record of who was buried here or if there was an effigy. Johnson and Boswell visited, and as the latter noted:

Inside the Iron Age souterrain of Oar Cave, Clachan.

Above: The ruined burial vault of the MacLeods of Raasay at St Maol-Luag's Chapel.

Left: The enigmatic sculpture high up on the burial vault. Its identity is unknown.

We here saw some human bones of an uncommon size. There was a heel-bone, in particular, which Dr Macleod said was such, that if the foot was in proportion, it must have been 27in. long. Dr Johnson would not look at the bones. He started back from them with a striking appearance of horror. Mr McQueen told us, it was formerly much the custom, in these isles, to have human bones lying above ground, especially in the windows of churches.

Over a century later Miss Gordon-Cumming was told tales of the Island of the Big Men, 'where huge bones of some extinct race of giants are still shown in the kirk.' South of the chapel is the family burial vault of the MacLeods of Raasay, with a small human head high upon the east wall. The building is dated 1839 and the carving was transferred from a medieval structure on the same site. Boswell thought this was a representation of the Virgin Mary, but no-one has any real idea who it is. Finally, there is the tiny mausoleum known as the Lady Chapel.

Martin Martin recorded eight carved stone crosses that stretched in an arc beyond the church. He regarded them as memorials for 'deceased ladies' but a survey shows them to be the markers of the church sanctuary. Anyone who passed into the sanctuary area was safe from persecution, at least for a time. The cross incised on the rock below the Battery may have been one of these markers, and the cross-base beside the Battery another. The Pictish stone (see below) may have been a third, another cross-base is beside the path in the forestry, and fragments of carved crosses have occasionally turned up in the graveyard.

Leave the church and proceed along the road a short distance to a Pictish stone carved with the 'tuning fork' and 'crescent and V-rod' symbols (NG54673677). The cross was probably added much later when the stone was reused as a sanctuary marker. The stone is not in situ, having been found about 100 paces from the cross by the pier in the early nineteenth century, when the road from the pier to Raasay House was being made.

Above left: The carved Pictish stone near St Maol-Luag's Chapel. The cross-of-arcs was added in the Middle Ages when it became a sanctuary boundary.

Above right: Raasay cemetery. In the foreground is a modern sculpture in memory of a German prisoner-of-war killed while working in the iron mine.

The scrambled but compelling ruins of Dun Borodale on Temptation Hill.

Above left: Clearly some creative people have time on their hands on Raasay. This road sign by Inverarish originally read 'The North'.

Above Right: More roadside jokiness near Inverarish. A toy koala is perched high on a eucalyptus tree – the koalas' food in their native Australia.

After the cross, turn right into the forest to follow the path up Temptation Hill. After passing the cross-base a road on the left leads up to the modern cemetery, outside of which is a memorial to a German prisoner-of-war who was killed in an accident. Contrary to the protocols governing POWs at the time, Germans were used to build the iron ore mine, railway and ancillary structures on Raasay. These industrial relics can now be visited by taking the Miners Trail and Burma Road, while the furnaces and hopper are next to Suisnish jetty. Back on the path, a signposted offshoot runs up to Dun Borodale (NG 55473633), a ruined but terrifically atmospheric broch surrounded by dark trees. The path continues by the isolated Free Church and thence to the road above Inverarish.

LOCH NA MNA

The path from the disused mine to Dun Caan passes along Inverarish Burn. In 1773 Boswell was being taken up the mountain by his guide, Malcolm, when they passed this small loch (NG 57913870):

> Malcolm told me a strange fabulous tradition. He said, there was a wild beast in it, a sea-horse, which came and devoured a man's daughter; upon which the man lighted a great fire, and had a sow roasted at it, the smell of which attracted the monster. In the fire was put a spit. The man lay concealed behind a low wall of loose stones, and he had an avenue formed for the monster, with two rows of large flat stones, which extended from the fire over the summit of the hill, till it reached the side of the loch. The monster came, and the man with the red-hot spit destroyed it. Malcolm shewed me the little hiding-place, and the rows of stones. He did not laugh when he told this story.

A more elaborate version appeared in *More West Highland Tales, Vol. II* by John Francis Campbell. The water-horse slayer was a smith whose daughter the monster had murdered, leaving behind only her heart and lungs on the lochside. The smith constructed a forge near the loch to hammer out large iron hooks, and a fire to keep them heated.

A sheep was roasted as bait, and when the water-horse appeared the smith and his son pierced its flesh with the red-hot hooks. In a curious coda, the corpse of the beast was said to have dissolved into 'star-shine'. Star-shine, also known as star-rot, is a mysterious and as-yet unidentified gelatinous substance sometimes found in fields. Country people sometimes believed it had fallen from the sky, specifically from the stars.

DUN CAAN

This extinct volcano, with its truncated shark's fin look, is the most obvious landscape feature on Raasay. In *Highways and Byways in the Western Highlands*, Seton Gordon claims some old stones in a corrie beneath the plateau mark the graves of Mackenzies from the mainland, killed by Raasay MacLeods in a clan stramash, but no one else has been able to find these alleged graves.

After hearing the Loch na Mna water-horse story, Boswell climbed Dun Caan and danced his version of a Highland jig upon the flat top. In *Redemption Song*, his biography of punk legend Joe Strummer, London journalist Chris Salewicz describes coming to Umachan, a deserted township in the north of the island, to find the house once occupied by Strummer's grandmother. The former lead singer of The Clash had planned to search for his roots, but died before he made it to Raasay. My goal had been to ascend Dun Caan, put The Clash on the iPod, and lurch in an ungainly fashion around the summit, thus honouring both Boswell and Strummer. Sadly a storm intervened and this ambition remains unfulfilled. In his later years Strummer supported various environmental initiatives, and Rebel's Wood, an area of forest dedicated to him, is near ORBOST.

SUISNISH

A distiller of homemade whisky was returning from his still at Suisnish when he passed an opening in a hill. Within lay a sumptuous feast, the guests attended by colourfully attired servants. Not wanting to miss out on a good thing, he invited himself in, and soon had eaten, drunk and danced himself giddy. He then decided to leave for home, and looked for a souvenir to show others. The obvious item was a tablecloth, so he snatched it, and soon found himself running from a gang of irate fairies. He reached home safely with his prize, and showed it to all and sundry, but was compelled to hand it over to Iain Garbh. According to the tale, which was collected by Mary Julia MacCulloch, the item was long a prized possession of the MacLeods of Raasay, but, unlike the Fairy Flag of DUNVEGAN CASTLE, the Fairy Tablecloth of Raasay did not achieve lasting fame. The fairy mound in the story may have been the prehistoric cairn that once stood on the roadside spot now occupied by Raasay War Memorial (NG55293545). Human bones were found here in 1841.

MacCulloch had another story of Iain Garbh. A girl resolved to win the heart of a young man who had no time for her, so she paid a wise man for a love charm. Part of the charm involved simply going up to the man and, without saying a word, kissing him (such an action may of course achieve the desired aim even without magic). Due to some sensory malfunction (did she have her eyes closed? Was it dark?) she found

Raasay War Memorial, Suisnish, built on top of a prehistoric cairn and fairy hill.

she had kissed Iain Garbh. The enchanted chief immediately declared he would make her his wife, despite being already married. According to the story, he did indeed divorce his first wife and wed the possessor of the love charm.

EYRE

A cul-de-sac road runs south from Inverarish through Suisnish to Eyre Point, where recent surveys have revealed an archaeological wonderland with sites encompassing several thousand years. The current tally stands at two chambered cairns, three round cairns, eight cairns with kerbs of stones, one small standing stone (NG57753432), four Pictish cairns (distinguished by their rectangular construction), three Viking boat burials, one unidentified mound, a fisherman's bothy, and some small pits. The chambered cairns are the most obvious prehistoric features – a substantial cairn is north of the road at NG57283405 while the burial cist of another can be seen north of the lighthouse at NG58053426. Most of the other structures are not immediately apparent, so start from the lighthouse and just wander around – you're bound to bump into something.

OSKAIG

In the 1920s an old woman from Oskaig, on the road north from Clachan, told Alasdair Alpin Macgregor that in her childhood she saw hundreds of fairies, gruagachs and brownies, and they were smartly dressed in white shirts, 'just like the gentry.'

BRAE

About thirty paces west of the road, and south of the path to Inver, is Storab's Grave, a barely-noticeable rectangular mound (NG56094166) close to the edge of the burn. In *Afoot in the Hebrides* Seton Gordon describes this as the grave of a Norwegian prince, killed while raiding Skye.

BROCHEL

Brochel Castle (NG58464627) is possibly the most thrilling castle in the area, an impregnable fortress built on an irregular stack-like rock. It is as if the castle and rock are fused, a (now-broken) digit projecting defiantly out into the Inner Sound, warning off all comers. It is not known when the castle was built, but the last inhabitant was Iain Garbh, who died around 1671. Sadly, the crumbling ruin is now very unsafe, and is fenced off. A short distance away are the fragmentary remains of a small chapel and burial place (NG58484630).

A little north of the castle a roadsign tells you you are on Rathad Cahuim, (Calum's Road). The roadside cairn bears this inscription:

> Calum's Road. This former footpath to Arnish – a distance of 1¾ miles – was wid-
> ened to a single-track road with passing places and prepared for surfacing by Malcolm
> MacLeod, BEM (1911-1988) South Arnish. He accomplished this work single-handedly
> over a period of ten years.

Calum MacLeod got so fed up waiting for the powers-that-be to build a proper access to Arnish that he did it himself, with only a second-hand book on road building as his guide. It's worth walking this section of road, with its inclines and difficult terrain, to appreciate the sheer scale of this heroic task. The full story is in Roger Hutchinson's splendid book *Calum's Road*. The Raasay roadsign pranksters have been active here again. A sign for 'bumpy road' has had a curly-tailed pig added ('pigs might fly').

TORRAN

A miniscule disused burial ground nestles against a rock at Cladh An Torrain, north of Loch Arnish (NG59414897). According to local tradition it was used for 'plague' burials of small children in the late nineteenth century. Good luck in finding it.

RONA

In 1579 George Buchanan wrote of Rona in his *History of Scotland*: 'In a deep bay it has a harbour, dangerous for voyagers, as it affords a covert for pirates, whence to surprise the passengers.' The pirates paid MacLeod of Raasay protection money to turn a blind eye to their nefarious activities, and were 'encouraged' to only attack ships belonging to the MacLeods' enemies. Pirates' Port is now merely called Acairseid Mhor, the Big Harbour. To the north is the deserted settlement of Acairseid Thioram, Dry Harbour. The schoolmaster here, Angus Murchison, was once told by two pupils that they had 'seen' a funeral procession. So clear was the vision that the boys could name the coffin bearers and the order in which they proceeded. Around two weeks later a young woman from Dry Harbour died, and the funeral proceeded exactly as described. The episode is in Alasdair Alpin MacGregor's *Over the Sea to Skye*.

MacGregor also gives the story of Leac Nighinn Righ Lochlainn, the Tombstone of the Daughter of the King of Denmark. The son of the King of Greece wooed and eloped with the daughter of the Danish King. The couple were pursued to Rona where the Greek prince was killed. The girl insisted the grave was made big enough for two, and she leaped into the earth beside her slain lover. The cairn is supposedly somewhere west of Loch Braig, which is at NG628598.

On the opposite side of the island to Acairseid Mhor is Uamh an Fhuamhaire, Giant's Cave, more usually called Church Cave (NG62705696). Here the islanders worshipped until the construction of the church at Dry Harbour in 1912, and well into the twentieth century children were still being baptized within the natural font of boulders (fed by drips from the cave roof). The vague path to it leaves the main track at Meall Acairseid and proceeds down the slope to the shore. The arch of the entrance leads into a space occupied by serried ranks of very low stones – the 'pews' – facing a flattish rock used as the pulpit. Sitting in this cave, you have a strong sense that church-going on Rona must have been a cold and damp affair.

The track to the south ends at An Teampuill, the roofless ruin of an exception- ally small medieval chapel, probably on the site of an early Christian hermit's cell (NG61645437). Adjacent is a blink-and-you-miss-it burial ground.

In 1913 David Rorie, writing in the journal *Folklore*, extracted some interesting bits and pieces from the official 'Report of the Highlands and Islands Medical Service Committee'. Paragraph twenty-one of the Report read: 'Primitive Customs and Habits. In some parts of the Highlands and Islands there still remains a belief in inherited skill and traditional "cures".' A man from Rona described how a person suffering from epilepsy was cured by burying alive a black cock beneath the spot where the patient had had the first attack. He also spoke of a woman with tuberculosis who travelled from Rona to the island of Scalpay, on Harris, where she was healed by a seventh son. Paragraph fifty-seven of the Report read: 'The persistence of the traditional 'cures' and superstitious practices in remote districts referred to in paragraph twenty-one is undoubtedly due largely to the want of medical attendance.'

SCALPAY

Teampull Fraing (NG62852816) is an utterly ruined church in a disused burial ground. A stone carved with a simple cross stands to the west. The dedication of the site is obscure, with suggestions including the unlikely (St Francis) or the utterly unknown

(St Frangaig). Near the centre of the island is a hill called Sithean Glac an Ime, the Fairy Hill in the Butter Bowl.

PABAY

In *Description of the Western Isles of Scotland Called Hybrides*, written in 1549, Donald Monro, High Dean of the Isles, described Pabay as 'a main shelter for thieves and cut-throats.' Things had not improved thirty years later, when George Buchanan stated the island was, 'infamous for robberies, where the thieves, from their lurking-places in the woods, with which it is covered, intercept the unwary travellers.' Otta Swire recorded a demonic tale of these thieves and cut-throats, which is very similar to another 'Taghairm' told of TOTE in Trotternish. The Pabay brigands roasted three cats alive on a fire built on the beach. Several minor demons appeared but the robber chief insisted that Lucifer himself put in a personal appearance. Eventually the big satanic cheese did appear to bargain with the chief. His minions would kill two of the bandits' sworn enemies – presumably lairds or Government officials who were pursuing them – but the price was two souls. This worried the bandits and an argument broke out. The Devil remembered the chief's boast that he and his men could storm the gates of Hell if they could find swords that did not melt, and offered to slaughter all the robbers' enemies if they agreed to fight in a pitched battle for their souls, 'here on the shore where swords do not melt.' The bargain was struck, and the demons set out to track down and kill their victims. When this task was accomplished the legion of Hell assembled on the beach and rushed at the brigands. In the battle that ensued all the humans were killed except the chief, whose sword had an apotropaic cross hilt. Suddenly a great black cat jumped on his arm making him drop the blade, and he was taken to his just deserts in a fiery place.

There is a tiny, utterly ruinous chapel at NG67362651, probably built on the site of an early Christian foundation, which has threaded itself into the local folklore. According to Donald Lamont's 1913 *Strath: in Isle of Skye*, the site was originally 'a Druidical grove', although this may simply be part of the misplaced enthusiasm for all things Druid-shaped at the time the book was published. Apparently the site was later Christianised by St Maolrubha (Maolrubha was also associated with Tobar Ashaig at BREAKISH). In Otta Swire's tale of the holy man who refused to bless the fairies (see KYLEAKIN), the priest concerned came from Pabay. The disused graveyard contains a strange semicircular structure whose low wall encloses a small circle of stones. The Ordnance Survey team did not notice it in 1876 and so it is probably a modern construction. It is therefore doubtful whether the name of 'The Altar' that has been applied to it has any meaning.

CROWLIN ISLANDS

The largest of the three islands, north-east of Pabay, bears a place name suggestive of an early Christian foundation, Camus na h-Anait, Beach of the (mother) Church. There is nothing remaining, no history, and no folklore.

NINE

THE MAINLAND: LOCHALSH

KYLE OF LOCHALSH – EILEAN DONAN – GLENELG – SANDAIG

> Glen Beag is a weird, eerie glen. Maybe this is due to the pervading influence of times
> pre-historic. The upper reaches of it have an atmosphere decidedly uncanny – nay,
> oppressive.

> Alasdair Alpin MacGregor, *Somewhere In Scotland*

This chapter covers those parts of the mainland that are easily visitable from Skye.
The main A87 from Kyle of Lochalsh runs alongside Loch Alsh and Duich, past Eilean
Donan, to Shiel Bridge, from where a hair-raising minor road leaves for Glenelg.
If the ferry is running (Easter to October, weather permitting) it is far easier to reach
Glenelg and Sandaig from KYLERHEA.

KYLE OF LOCHALSH

Here the railway line from Inverness terminates, and there is a small railway museum.
C.F. Gordon-Cumming noted that the locals knew the railway was coming for at
least three decades before it was built, because on several occasions people on the
coach-road at night had seen visions of it. They saw:

> … a great light coming towards them, and as it drew nearer they saw that it was a huge
> dark coach with fiery lamps – they could see no horses; only a great glare of flames and
> sparks, and it rushed past them at a place where there was no road, and vanished among
> the mountains.

Could there be some parallels here with the later phantom car of SLIGACHAN?
Apparently the apparition was seen so often that the coachman could no longer stand
the strain, and gave up travelling at night.

LOCH ALSH

Gordon-Cumming also added an episode to the expanding body of herring folklore
(see also DUNVEGAN and PORTREE). Two men drowned themselves in the loch, and so
the herring deserted the waters. After several years of hardship the fishermen kindled

two great bonfires on the places where the bodies had been washed ashore. Gordon-Cumming describes this as 'a sacrifice to the insulted herring' but it is not clear what, if anything, was sacrificed; perhaps the fires were merely intended to cleanse the tainted spots.

BALMACARA

In 1836 Lord Teignmouth described a recent case in which a young man was drowned near here. His mother consulted a seer, who told her that the body would be recovered. On the strength of this assurance she waded daily, waist-deep in the loch, searching for her son. After days, perhaps weeks, the waters did eventually give up the corpse.

KIRKTON

The white-harled nineteenth-century parish church by the roadside is built on a much older site going back at least to the Middle Ages. The original dedication was to St Comgan, the local patron saint (NG82872719). A warrior is carved on a medieval graveslab. Just to the north is the Hill of the Angels, a circular graveyard built on the site of a prehistoric dun (NG83142745).

EILEAN DONAN CASTLE

(Open March–October 10 a.m. to 6 p.m. daily, from 9 a.m. in July and August. Admission charge, no disabled access.)

Outside Urquhart Castle on Loch Ness, and Edinburgh's iconic fortress, this is probably the most photographed castle in Scotland, and its picturesque location on a bridged island poking out into the mountain-girt loch has made it the star of a number of films. The medieval castle was blown up by Government troops in 1719 as a reprisal for Jacobite activities (Spanish soldiers had been garrisoned there during the entirely abortive rising of that year, culminating in the Jacobite defeat at the Battle of Glenshiel). What visitors see today is a faux-medieval Edwardian baronial-style Romantic recreation built in 1912-32. The Clerk of Works for the reconstruction, Farquar Macrae of Auchtertyre, is said to have received the appearance of the new castle in a dream.

Although a vitrified Iron Age fort was visible until the reconstruction, the early history of the site is largely unknown. And into such a vacuum folklore flows abundantly. The sixth-century AD saint, Donan, is reputed to have had a cell here – and to have given the island its name – but no trace remains. Robert the Bruce is supposed to have taken shelter here during his years of wandering before defeating the English at the Battle of Bannockburn in 1314. Another monarch, this time the King of the Otters (see RAASAY), is buried here in a robe of silver. The Gaelic word for otter is Cu-Donn, and so it is easy to see how the legend has grown from the similarity between 'Donan' and 'Donn'. Another tale has a chief's son receiving his first drink from a raven's skull, and thus being able to understand the language of

Eilean Donan Castle today.

Eilean Donan Castle as sketched by Lt-Col. Murray for Morison's *Sketches of Scenes in Scotland* in 1834.

the birds. One day, his father asked him what the birds were chattering about. The unwelcome reply was that they were discussing how one day the father would wait upon the son like a servant. This angered the old chief, who promptly exiled the boy. After ten years of many adventures in foreign lands – often aided by his gift of avine translation – the son returned on a magnificent ship, laden with jewels and gold. Not revealing his identity, he called on the chief, who received the illustrious visitor with due honour, himself serving the young stranger at the table. Thus the prophecy was fulfilled, father and son were reconciled, and the talented youth was commissioned by King Alexander II to build Eilean Donan as a defence against the Vikings.

The known history of the castle from the thirteenth century onwards is the usual round of internecine hatreds and conflicts between neighbouring clans, or between members of the same family. Primary contenders were the Mackenzies, the MacDonalds, and the Earls of Ross. Kidnappings, sieges, executions, battles and injustices were par for the course. In 1331 the Earl of Moray, known for his bloodthirsty implementation of the law, came for a visit. When he arrived he was delighted to find the severed heads of fifty men adorning the castle walls – he said the sight was sweeter than a garland of roses. The miscreants had been executed especially for the visit, to demonstrate the Mackenzies' robust loyalty.

GLENELG

This section owes much to the Revd T.M. Murchison's article 'Glenelg, Inverness-Shire: Notes For A Parish History', published in the *Transactions of the Gaelic Society of Inverness* in the 1950s; this is the source for the stories unless otherwise indicated. The descriptions start from the jetty from the small car ferry at Kylerhea.

Glenelg is rife with strange stories and legends. The place name has (almost certainly erroneously) been derived as the Glen of Ealga, this supposedly being the name of the Norse princess said to be buried on the top of Beinn Na Caillich near Broadford. Glenelg was where a MacLeod supposedly killed a terrible bull using only his dirk (see Dunvegan Castle). The Fingalians pole-vaulted across the strait (see Kylerhea). In *The Haunted Isles* Alasdair Alpin MacGregor tells the tale of Mary MacPhee, a four-year-old girl who went missing one autumn evening in the mid-nineteenth century. The villagers searched for her all night in the pouring rain without success. Early the next morning Mary turned up, completely dry. She said she had spent the night in a big well-lit house inhabited by little people dressed in green, who danced merrily to the sound of bagpipes. At dawn they took her to the door and pointed to her house in the village. MacGregor was unable to locate this fairy hill, other than noting that Mary seemed to have come from somewhere in the direction of Glen Bernera.

A little before the track leading up Glen Bernera leaves the main road, there are two almost invisible mounds just north of the road (NG80542094 and NG80492096). Even though this is a field, the area is called Lomair nam Fear Mora (Ridge of the Big Men). Here, allegedly, were found the skeletons of two huge men, believed to be Fingalians. As with all stories of giants, the tale may have grown in the telling. Murchison's version is that, although the area was thought to be unchancy, a foolhardy farmer ploughed the area and turned up a human skull so large that it fitted over the head of the biggest man present. At this point, as is traditional with such tales, a terrible storm sprang up and, so as not to anger the powers-that-be any further, the skull was speedily re-buried. Otta Swire's *The Highlands and their Legends* (1963) claims several skeletons were dug up, and two were pronounced by a doctor as being the remains of men respectively 8½ft and 11ft (2.6m and 3.3m) tall. Crikey. As for the date when this happened, both M.E.M Donaldson (*Wanderings in the Western Highlands and Islands*) and Alasdair Alpin MacGregor (*The Haunted Isles*) plump for the 1890s, while Murchison says a witness was Revd Cohn MacIver, minister of Glenelg from 1782 to 1829. The persistence of tradition is so strong that it seems likely that human bones were indeed uncovered. However, we do not know when this occurred, what happened to the bones, and how big they were in reality. As ever, giants are big in folklore but minimal in archaeology.

A little to the north of the cairns, a large rock outcrop bears the 'Fairy Footprint' – prehistoric rock art consisting of cupmarks, grooves and a 'bar-bell' shape (NG80552110). At an unidentified spot in the Bernera area was Tobar Bhan (the White Well), a healing well containing a sacred trout. In *Somewhere in Scotland* Alasdair Alpin MacGregor described how the custodian of the well, Anne MacRae, who maintained the structure, sprinkled the approach with gravel from the shore, and gathered a medicinal herb called 'flower of the three mountains'. When Anne died, around about the year 1905, the trout disappeared. Perhaps it died because she was no longer feeding it, or possibly with the guardian gone the taboo on catching the trout no longer applied. The well and its location now seem to have passed out of memory.

The forest road up the glen will bring you to the walk up Glas Bheinn. Somewhere in this area in February 1986 forestry worker Charlie Greenless spotted a large fawn-coloured big cat. The encounter was in broad daylight. Later Greenless learned there had been several previous sightings in the area. (Source: Ron Halliday, *Evil Scotland*.) Just to the east of Glas Bheinn summit is Carn Cloinn Mhic Cruimein, the Cairn of the Clan MacCrimmon. Supposedly, eighty-one MacCrimmon warriors from Glen Elg are buried here, killed in battle by the Mathesons of Loch Alsh. There is no obvious mound, but fairy music has been reported.

Nothing worthwhile remains of the dun called Caisteal Mhicleod atop the hill behind Galltair (NG81552024). Despite the name, it was never a proper castle and was probably reused as a hunting lodge in the Middle Ages, the last occupant being Alasdair Crotach, who became MacLeod chief in 1480. The tradition is that the site was abandoned after a nurse accidentally dropped Alasdair's infant son out of a window and down the fatal precipice. The exact same story is told of DUNTULM CASTLE and many other locations further afield.

A footbridge from the road over the Glen More River gives access to the path to the starkly impressive and roofless remains of Bernera Barracks, an eighteenth-century fort built by the Government to guard the Kylerhea crossing during the Jacobite troubles (NG81521974). Some of the stones came from the brochs in GLEANN BEAG. There is no access into the interior. South of the Barracks, in the village, stands the simple parish church (NG81251926) on a much older site originally dedicated to the seventh-century St Cuimen. The graveyard has a good eighteenth-century tombstone decorated with the usual symbols of mortality – skull, hourglass, crossed bones, sexton's tools, mort-bells and coffin. Somewhere close by is – or was – the Well of the Wine, which may have been a holy well.

GLEN MORE

Alasdair Alpin MacGregor's *Somewhere in Scotland* is the key text for legends of this glen, along which runs the occasionally alarming road to Shiel Bridge. One of MacGregor's informants, John MacRae, told him about beliefs concerning the 'serpent-mound' near Scallasaig: 'the mound was in the shape of a serpent; and when the chief of the people would die, he would be buried in the head of the serpent.' The mound (which is definitely not serpent-shaped) was opened in the 1870s or 1880s, revealing a stone-lined cist and a cinerary urn apparently containing cremation ashes. The urn was temporarily kept at the manse, and while it was there some strange sounds were heard. The noises stopped when the urn was taken to Edinburgh. The scant remains of the cist can be made out by the roadside just north of Scallasaig farm (NG84842029). Apparently another mound was excavated at Cosag, east of Glenelg, but the local people were so alarmed by a great storm that they pressured the archaeologists to abandon the dig. As there is no other record of a cairn at Cosag this may be a confused version of the Bernera storm story. Between Scallasaig and Beolary is a large stone on the skyline which, according to the Brahan Seer, will one day topple and kill a man called John MacRae who will be riding on a white horse.

South of Suardalan bothy, the track from the end of the glen over to Glen Beag passes Loch Iain Mhic Aonghuis (John MacInnes' Loch, NG879162). John found a suspiciously fine horse by the lochside. Taking advice from a wise man, he vowed not to use it after sunset, but one day carried on working into the gloaming and the water-horse – for such it was – carried him beneath the loch. All that was found remaining of John MacInnes were his heart and lungs.

GLEANN BEAG

Two of the best-preserved brochs in Scotland stand 600 paces apart on the roadside. Access is easy (both are in the care of Historic Scotland) and these terrific Iron Age monuments are worth the drive from Skye alone. Of the pair, Dun Telve (NG82901725) is in the best condition, with one wall standing to about 30ft (9.1m) and the entrance, stairs and galleries between the walls still intact. Dun Troddan (NG83401724) was badly plundered in 1722 for the construction of Bernera Barracks, but you've still got a 23ft (7m) high section of wall, and a climbable stairway ascending atmospherically into the intra-mural gallery. Not surprisingly, the brochs were thought to be the palatial residences of Fingalian giants.

Further along the glen are the roadside Balvraid chambered cairn (NG84511662), hard-to-find cup-marked stones at NG84071667 and NG84961635, and Dun Grugaig,

a broch in not such good condition as its neighbours but still retaining a wall about
8ft (2.4m) high (NG85151591). Murchison mentioned an earth-house or souterrain at
Balvraid – he probably meant the chambered cairn – and claimed two stone circles
for the area, one lying near a cup-marked stone, and the other on the hill between
Gleann Beag and Glen More. No-one else has ever seen these circles, which are
probably misidentifications.

Murchison also tells the tale of a group of caterans from Lochaber who drove
away the minister's cattle from Gleann Beag. On their return journey they lost their
way and asked a stranger for directions. The stranger took them on a path which led
directly into an ambush set by the Gleann Beag men. When the thieves were secured
their guide revealed himself as the minister. MacGregor has a rather more robust
version, in which one of the caterans was wounded in a raid, and cared for by the
minister. When he left for home, the ungrateful thief drove away his host's cattle, but
got lost in the gloaming. Encountering a man he thought was a kinsman, he agreed
to exchange two cows for directions to Lochaber. The minister – for such was the
supposed 'kinsman' – took the thief to the edge of the precipice, and pushed him off.

SANDAIG

Here once lived the world's most famous otters, and their equally illustrious owner.
Sandaig was fictionalised under the name 'Camusfearna' in Gavin Maxwell's *Ring
of Bright Water* and its two sequels, *The Rocks Remain* and *Raven Seek Thy Brother*.
At Sandaig Maxwell lived with and studied his otters, wrote books (some of them
masterpieces), and lived a life that was both idyllic and infernal, often at the same
time. Maxwell was a complex character – aristocrat, adventurer, intellectual, introvert,
shark fisherman, naturalist and romantic (and apparently also bloody-minded and
difficult). Other than his own autobiographical books, the best guide to his creative,
challenging and chaotic personality is Douglas Botting's magisterial *Gavin Maxwell:
A Life*, while another excellent read is Richard Frere's *Maxwell's Ghost: An Epilogue to
Gavin Maxwell's Camusfearna*.

Maxwell brought his first otter, Mijbal (Mij) back from the marshes of Iraq. Mij's
death at the hands of a local workman is the heartrending early climax of *Ring of
Bright Water*. Maxwell then acquired two West African otters, Edal and Teko. In January
1968 Sandaig burned down, killing Edal. Maxwell and Teko then moved to EILEAN
BÀN. Both owner and otter died the following year. Other than the peace and the
beauty of the bay, nothing remains of Maxwell's west coast Eden except memorials –
a large boulder bears the inscription 'Gavin Maxwell b 15.7.14 d 7.9.69', while nearby
a plaque reads 'Edal, the otter of Ring of Bright Water, 1958-1968. Whatever joy she
gave to you, give back to nature'.

Maxwell's interest in 'sea monsters' is discussed in the section on SOAY, and in *Raven
Seek Thy Brother* he mentions that during the Second World War the carcass of some
unknown creature was found in the boom defence net off Sandaig lighthouse island
(Eilean Mór). Although EILEAN BÀN was allegedly haunted, Maxwell experienced
nothing strange there – a situation very different to Camusfearna, where he and
others directly witnessed several examples of poltergeist phenomena (as recorded

in *Raven Seek Thy Brother* and *Maxwell's Ghost*). At 10 p.m. one May night in 1964 Maxwell, Frere (his soon-to-be business manager) and Jimmy Watt (one of the youths who looked after the otters) were in the kitchen when all three saw a marmalade jar fly off a shelf and smash on the floor. Both Frere and Maxwell said 'Poltergeist!' The next day they found that a glass windowpane had been pushed some 5ft (1.5m) from the kitchen into Edal's enclosure outside; the putty had been left behind. Later Maxwell, alone in the kitchen, heard a rustling sound from the living room. As he came through he watched as a stack of LP records spread out like a pack of cards from a pile under a table, coming to rest in an orderly fan-like arrangement on the floor. Jimmy Watt witnessed a baby's plastic bottle, used for feeding animals, shoot out from a high shelf directly towards Maxwell's face before falling to the floor; Maxwell felt it had been deliberately aimed at him.

Maxwell and Frere floated the notion that the root cause was one of Maxwell's former assistants, whom Frere names as Brewster, although Douglas Botting calls Philip Alpin. The young man was staying about 5 miles away and was obviously very unhappy at the time. Maxwell thought the youth was unconsciously causing the phenomena through 'some projected part of his personality'. When Brewster turned up and Maxwell started to tell him about the recent incidents, both heard a loud crash from the coatroom. The laundry hamper had been flung from its table more than halfway across room, flying over two pairs of fishermen's thighboots. This was the last hurrah for the poltergeist, which never again disturbed the peace, although Brewster had another encounter with the supernatural on Eilean Bàn.

The key story of Sandaig, however, is the 'Curse of Camusfearna', a controversial episode that caused bitterness for years afterwards. In the bohemian London of the 1950s Maxwell forged an intense non-sexual union with Kathleen Raine, a poet inclined to mysticism. A few days after they first met Raine had a waking dream, a vision of a twelve-year-old boy asleep at the foot of a rowan tree whose branches bore white blossom and a blackbird. In her interpretation the boy was dreaming of the tree, bird and blossoms, and through his creativity bringing them into life. The boy, the creative genius, was, of course, Gavin Maxwell, and after this vision Raine believed they shared a special bond. She often talked of her semi-occult powers, and once performed a spell to heal Maxwell's pet bird, a golden-breasted fruit-sucker named Psuckah. From this and other episodes Maxwell, almost despite himself, tended to believe in Raine's magic.

The Maxwell/Raine relationship was often tumultuous. After a row at Sandaig, Raine stormed out of the house, and, unknown to Maxwell, returned to the rowan tree outside to pronounce the following words: 'Let Gavin suffer in this place, as I am suffering now.' When, many years later, Maxwell read this episode in the manuscript version of Raine's autobiography, it came as both hammer-blow and revelation. In the years since the quarrel he had suffered the death of his beloved Mij, the end of his short-lived marriage, the alienation and departure of his assistant Jimmy Watt, the decline in his health caused by a car crash, the ruination of his financial affairs, and the destruction of Camusfearna and the loss of Edal. It was now clear: all these horrors had been visited upon him by Raine's curse, of which he had previously been unaware. A few days after reading the manuscript he bluntly told Raine the truth that had now been revealed to him: through the curse she had destroyed him.

When *Raven Seek Thy Brother* came out in 1968 Raine was horrified to see that Maxwell had included the full story – the quarrel, his reaction to the manuscript, the 'curse' and its supposed consequences – and had effectively cast her as the wicked witch in the story of his life. The section in *Raven* reads, 'She had put her hands upon the trunk of the rowan tree and with all her strength she had cursed me, saying, "Let him suffer here as I am suffering".' Even as it was, this published version was toned down: before Raine had insisted on the change, Maxwell had originally inaccurately written that the wording of the curse was, 'Let him, and the house and all that have to do with it suffer here as I am suffering, for as long as he shall live.' These subtle but important differences in the wording of the 'curse' are teased out in Botting's biography. In particular, Maxwell's original words have a truly apocalyptic edge, which presumably reflects his feelings as the victim of a life-destroying curse.

While Raine's own works were essentially read only by the literati, Maxwell's books reached a wide audience, so the damage and insult Raine felt was huge, even if she was not directly named in *Raven* and only referred to as 'a poetess'. Raine had written the episode as just one more event in the emotional rollercoaster of her life: a hasty badmouthing to be later regretted, even deplored, but not meant to have any lasting impact. Maxwell, however, having learned of it many years later, made the connection with the catastrophes of his life. For Raine it was a throwaway moment, for Maxwell the covert cosmic force behind the annihilation of everything he held dear. Raine, the mystic, did not believe in her curse; Maxwell, the rationalist, did.

After the fire had swept through Sandaig, Richard Frere buried Edal under the adjacent rowan; the tree that Maxwell later learned was the prop for Raine's curse. Ironically, rowans were traditionally meant to guard against witchcraft. The tree has now died.

There is something about Maxwell's lucid prose and evocation of the wonders of nature that invites the reader to make a pilgrimage to Sandaig. The route is via a forestry track that leaves the Arnisdale road just north of Loch Drabhaig (NG783151). At the various junctions go left, left again, left over a footbridge, then right at two successive crossroads, to the beach. The easiest return is to retrace your steps, although an alternative steep route through the woodland exists – but first you have to cross the Allt Mòr Shantaig via a bridge that consists of just two ropes, one for the feet and the other above it for the hands. This exciting option is recommended for the adventurous (and those who recognise that one false move will result in a soaking).

One September day in 1979 author Jim Crumley was sitting alone by the mouth of the stream, musing on Maxwell and his books. To his irritation his solitude was interrupted by a party seeming to consist of a man, a boy and a dog running with an awkward gait. He could not see them clearly as they were silhouetted against the sun. The group passed out of view behind a low rise – but did not reappear. Eventually Jim went over to the rise, wondering if anything had happened. There was no trace of the trio, not even a footprint in the sand. With a shock he realised there was a once a time when the beach would have commonly been the recreation area for an adult man (Gavin Maxwell), a boy (Jimmy Watt or another of Maxwell's assistants, Terry Nutkins), and an animal running not like a dog but with the posture of an otter ... Weeks later he discovered he had been on the beach on the tenth anniversary of Maxwell's death. As Jim put it in *The Heart of Skye*, 'I felt as if he had tapped me on the shoulder.'

BIBLIOGRAPHY

HISTORY, ARCHAEOLOGY AND GENERAL

Adams, Douglas *The Meaning of Liff* (Pan; London, 1983)

Adams, Richard *The Adventures of Gavin Maxwell* (Ward Lock Educational; London, n.d.)

Anderson, Alan Orr & Anderson, Marjorie Ogilvie (ed. and trans.) *Adomnan's Life of Columba* (Thomas Nelson & Sons; London, 1961)

Armit, Ian *The Archaeology of Skye and the Western Isles* (Edinburgh University Press; Edinburgh, 2005)

Barnett, T. Ratcliffe *Autumns in Skye Ross and Sutherland* (Grant & Murray; Edinburgh, 1930)

Boswell, James *The Journal of a Tour to the Hebrides with Samuel Johnson, LL. D.* (Oxford University Press; Oxford, 1979 – first published 1785)

Botting, Douglas *Gavin Maxwell: A Life* (HarperCollins; London, 1993)

Buchanan, Robert *The Hebrid Isles: Wanderings in the Land of Lorne and the Outer Hebrides* (Chatto and Windus; London, 1883)

'B., J.W.' (Burgon, John William) 'On a cairn in the Isle of Skye' in *The Gentleman's Magazine* Volume XV, January 1841

Cameron, Alexander *The History and Traditions of the Isle of Skye* (E. Forsyth; Inverness, 1871)

Cockburn, Henry *Lord Cockburn Circuit Journeys* (David Douglas; Edinburgh, 1889)

Collingwood, W.G. *Scandinavian Britain* (Society For Promoting Christian Knowledge; London, 1908)

Cooper, Derek *Skye* (Queen Anne Press; London, 1989 – first published 1970)

Crumley, Jim *The Heart of Skye* (Colin Baxter Photography; Grantown-on-Spey, 1994)

Donaldson, M.E.M. *Wanderings in the Western Highlands and Islands* (Alexander Gardner; Paisley, 1920)

Ferguson, Malcolm *Rambles in Skye* (Chas. Murchland; Irvine, 1885)

Fisher, Ian *Early Medieval Sculpture in the West Highlands and Islands* (Royal Commission on the Ancient and Historical Monuments of Scotland; Edinburgh, 2001)

Forbes, Alexander Robert *Gaelic Names of Beasts (Mammalia), Birds, Fishes, Insects, Reptiles, Etc.* (Oliver and Boyd; Edinburgh, 1905)

———— *The Place Names of Skye and Adjacent Islands* (Alexander Gardner; Paisley, 1923)

Frere, Richard *Maxwell's Ghost: An Epilogue to Gavin Maxwell's Camusfearna* (Birlinn; Edinburgh, 1999 – first published 1976)

Geddes, Tex *Hebridean Sharker* (Herbert Jenkins; London, 1960)

Geikie, Sir Archibald *Scottish Reminiscences* (James Maclehose and Sons; Glasgow, 1904)

Gordon-Cumming, C.F. *In the Hebrides* (Chatto and Windus; London, 1883)

Gordon, Seton *The Land of the Hills and the Glens – Wild Life in Iona and the Inner Hebrides* (Gassell and Co.; London, 1920)

———— *The Charm of Skye: The Wingèd Isle* (Cassell & Co.; London, 1929)

———— *Highways and Byways in the West Highlands* (MacMillan and Co.; London, 1935)

———— *Afoot in the Hebrides* (Country Life; London, 1950)

Grenier, Katherine Haldane *Tourism and Identity in Scotland, 1770-1914: Creating Caledonia* (Ashgate; Aldershot, 2005)

Haswell-Smith, Hamish *The Scottish Islands: A Comprehensive Guide to Every Scottish Island* (Canongate; Edinburgh, 1996)

——————— *An Island Odyssey: Among the Scottish Isles in the Wake of Martin Martin* (Canongate; Edinburgh, 1999)

Hutchinson, Roger *Calum's Road* (Birlinn; Edinburgh, 2006)

Johnson, Samuel *A Journey to the Western Isles of Scotland* (Oxford University Press; Oxford, 1979 – first published 1775)

Lamont, Donald M. *Strath: in the Isle of Skye* (Celtic Press; Glasgow, 1983 – first published 1913)

Macculloch, J.A. *The Misty Isle of Skye – Its Scenery, Its People, Its Story* (Oliphant Anderson & Ferrier; Edinburgh and London, 1905)

Macgibbon, David and Thomas Ross *Castellated and Domestic Architecture of Scotland From The Twelfth To The Eighteenth Century* (David Douglas; Edinburgh, 1889)

MacGregor, Alasdair Alpin *Over the Sea to Skye* (W. & R. Chambers; London, 1926)

——————— *Somewhere in Scotland: The Western Highlands in Pen and Picture* (George Routledge & Sons; London, 1935)

——————— *Skye and the Inner Hebrides* (Robert Hale; London, 1953)

MacGregor, Alexander 'Highland and Island Scenery' in *Celtic Magazine* Volume IV (1879)

——————— 'Dunvegan Castle – A Gaelic Poem with Notes' in *Celtic Magazine* Volume IV (1879)

——————— 'History of The Macdonalds, and The Lords of The Isles' in *Celtic Magazine* Volume V (1880)

——————— 'The History of The MacLeods' in *Celtic Magazine* Volume Xlll (1888)

MacLeod, Fred, T. 'Notes on the Relics Preserved in Dunvegan Castle, Skye, and the Heraldry of the Family of MacLeod of MacLeod' in *Proceedings of the Society of Antiquaries of Scotland* Volume 47 (1912-13)

MacLeod, R.C. MacLeod of *The MacLeods of Dunvegan: From the Time of Leod to the End of the Seventeenth Century* (The Clan MacLeod Society; Edinburgh, 1927)

Martin, Martin *A Description of the Western Islands of Scotland Circa 1695* (Birlinn; Edinburgh, 1994 – first published 1703)

Maxwell, Gavin *Harpoon at a Venture* (House of Lochar; Colonsay, 1998 – first published 1952)

Maxwell, Gavin (ed. Austin Chinn) The Ring of Bright Water Trilogy – *Ring of Bright Water, The Rocks Remain, Raven Seek Thy Brother* (Viking; London, 2000)

Miers, Mary *The Western Seaboard: An Illustrated Architectural Guide* (Rutland Press; Edinburgh, 2008)

Miket, Roger and David L. Roberts *The Mediaeval Castles of Skye and Lochalsh* (Birlinn; Edinburgh, 2007)

Miller, Hugh *The Cruise of the Betsey: Or, A Summer Ramble Among the Fossiliferous Deposits of the Hebrides* (Gould & Lincoln; Boston, 1859)

Ministers of the Respective Parishes, *The New Statistical Account of Scotland* Volume XIV Inverness–Ross and Cromarty (William Blackwood & Sons; Edinburgh and London, 1845)

Mitchell, Sir Arthur (ed.) *Macfarlane's Geographical Collections* (The Scottish History Society; Edinburgh, 1907)

Morrison, Alick *The Chiefs of Clan MacLeod* (Associated Clan MacLeod Societies; Edinburgh, 1993)

Monro, Sir Donald *Description of the Western Isles of Scotland Called Hybrides* (published with Martin Martin, op. cit. First published 1774)

Murchison, T.M. 'Glenelg, Inverness-Shire: Notes For A Parish History' in *Transactions of the Gaelic Society of Inverness* Volume 39/40 (1942-1950)

Nicholson, Alex. 'The Isle of Skye' in *Good Words* magazine, 1875 (ed. Norman MacLeod)

Nicholson, Alexander *History of Skye* (MacLean Press; Portree, 1995 – first published 1930)

Nicholson, John *I Remember – Memories of Raasay* (Birlinn; Edinburgh, 2002 – first published 1989)

Oldham, Tony *The Caves of Scotland; Except Assynt* (Tony Oldham; Bristol, 1975)

Raine, Kathleen *Autobiographies: Farewell Happy Fields, The Land Unknown and The Lion's Mouth* (Skoob Books; London, 1991)

Reed, Laurance *The Soay of our Forefathers* (no publisher or date)

Ritchie, Graham & Harman, Mary *Exploring Scotland's Heritage: Argyll and the Western Isles* (Royal Commission on the Ancient and Historical Monuments of Scotland; Edinburgh, 1985)

Salewicz, Chris *Redemption Song: The Definitive Biography of Joe Strummer* (HarperCollins; London, 2006)

Sillar, Frederick C. and Meyler, Ruth M. *Skye* (David and Charles; Newton Abbot, 1973)

Sinclair, Sir John (ed.) *The Statistical Account of Scotland* (EP Publishing; Wakefield, 1983
– originally published 1791-1799)

Smith, Alexander *A Summer in Skye* (P. Nimmo, Hay, & Mitchell; Edinburgh, 1885)

Stirling, A.M.W. *Macdonald of the Isles – A Romance of the Past and Present* (John Murray, London, 1913)

Stott, Louis *The Waterfalls of Scotland* (Aberdeen University Press; Aberdeen, 1987)

Suffling, Ernest R. *Epitaphia: Being a Collection of 1300 British Epitaphs Grave and Gay, Historical and Curious* (L. Upcott Gill; London, 1909)

Teignmouth, Lord (Baron John Shore Teignmouth) *Sketches of the Coasts and Islands of Scotland and of the Isle of Man*, Volume 1 (John W. Parker; London, 1836)

Watt, Robert A. *Glossary of Scottish Dialect Fish and Trade Names – Scottish Fisheries Information Pamphlet Number 17* (Department for Agriculture and Fisheries for Scotland; Aberdeen, 1989)

MYSTERIOUSNESS

Adams, Norman *Haunted Scotland* (Mainstream Publishing; Edinburgh, 1998)

Bassin, Ethel *The Old Songs of Skye: Frances Tolmie and her Circle* (Routledge & Kegan Paul; London and Henley, 1977)

Bennett, Margaret 'Balquhidder Revisited: Fairylore in the Scottish Highlands, 1690-1990' in Peter Narváez (ed.) *The Good People: New Fairylore Essays* (Garland Publishing/The University Press of Kentucky; Lexington, Kentucky, 1997)

Black, Geo. F. 'Scottish charms and amulets' in *Proceedings of the Society of Antiquaries of Scotland* Volume 27 (1893)

Briggs, K.M. 'Some Late Accounts of the Fairies' in *Folklore*, Volume 72, No. 3 (September 1961)

Britten, Emma Hardinge (ed.) *Ghost Land, Or, Researches into the Mysteries of Occultism* (Published for The Editor; Boston, Mass. 1876)

Byrd, Elizabeth *A Strange and Seeing Time* (Robert Hale; London, 1969)

Campbell, John Francis *More West Highland Tales*, Volume 2 (Birlinn; Edinburgh, 1994 – first published 1960)

Campbell, John Gregorson *Superstitions of the Highlands and Islands of Scotland* (James MacLehose and Sons; Glasgow, 1900)

———— *Witchcraft and Second Sight in the Highlands and Islands of Scotland* (James MacLehose and Sons; Glasgow, 1902)

Campbell, Elizabeth Montgomery and David Solomon *The Search for Morag* (Tom Stacey; London, 1972)

Dinsdale, Tim *The Leviathans* (Routledge & Kegan Paul; London, 1966)

———— *Project Water Horse: The True Story of the Monster Quest at Loch Ness* (Routledge & Kegan Paul; London, 1975)

Dorson, Richard M. 'Sources for the Traditional History of the Scottish Highlands and Western Islands' in *Journal of the Folklore Institute*, Volume 8, No. 2/3 (August 1971)

Eberhart, George M. *Mysterious Creatures: A Guide to Cryptozoology* (ABC-CLIO; Santa Barbara, 2002)

Evans-Wentz, W.Y. *The Fairy-Faith in Celtic Countries* (H. Froude; London and New York, 1911)

Farquhar, Angus (ed.) *The Storr: Unfolding Landscape* (Luath Press; Edinburgh, 2005)

Frazer, James G. 'Notes and Queries – Witchcraft in Skye' in *Folk-Lore Journal*, Volume 4, No. 3 (1886)

Furlong, David *Working With Earth Energies* (Piatkus; London, 2003)

Gould, Charles *Mythical Monsters* (W.H. Allen & Co.; London, 1886)

Gregor, Walter *Notes on the Folk-Lore of the North-East of Scotland* (Folk-Lore Society; London, 1881)

———— 'Notes and Queries' in *Folk-Lore Journal*, Volume 1, No. 7 (July 1883)

Guthrie, E.J. *Old Scottish Customs Local and General* (Hamilton, Adams & Co.; London, 1885)

Halliday, Ron *Evil Scotland* (Fort Publishing; Ayr, 2003)

Henderson, Robert *Scottish Keeriosities* (Saint Andrew Press; Edinburgh, 1995)

Hunter, Michael (ed.) *The Occult Laboratory: Magic, Science and Second Sight in Late 17th-Century Scotland* (Boydell Press; Woodbridge, Suffolk, 2001)

Insulanus, Theophilus (= Revd D. McLeod) *Treatises on the Second-Sight* (J. Wylie & Co.; Glasgow, 1819 – first published 1763)

Kerr, Cathal 'Fishermen and Superstition' in *Celtic Magazine* Volume XIII (1888)

Lang, Andrew *The Making of Religion* (Longmans, Green, and Co.; London, 1898)

MacCulloch, Mary Julia 'Folk-Lore of the Isle of Skye' in *Folklore*, Volume 33, No. 2 (June 1922), No. 3 (September 1922) and No. 4 (December 1922); and Volume 34, No. 1 (March 1923)

Macdonald, Alexander 'Medical Spells and Charms of the Highlands' in *Celtic Magazine* Volume XIII (1888)

MacDougall, J. *Waifs and Strays of Celtic Tradition, Argyllshire Series. No. III: Folk And Hero Tales* (David Nutt; London, 1891)

McEwan, Graham J. *Sea Serpents, Sailors and Sceptics* (Routledge & Kegan Paul; London, 1978)

MacGregor, Alasdair Alpin *The Haunted Isles or, Life in the Hebrides* (Alexander Maclehose & Co.; London, 1933)

———— *The Ghost Book* (Robert Hale; London, 1955)

———— *Phantom Footsteps* (Robert Hale; London, 1959)

Macgregor, Alexander 'Ancient Mythology and Modern Superstitions' in *Celtic Magazine* Volume III (1878)

———— 'The Government Factor and the Widow's Cow' in *Celtic Magazine* Volume V (1880)

———— *Highland Superstitions Connected With The Druids, Fairies, Witchcraft, Second-Sight, Hallowe'en, Sacred Wells And Lochs, With Several Curious Instances Of Highland Customs And Beliefs* (Eneas Mackay; Stirling, 1901)

Mackenzie, Alexander 'The Prophecies Of The Brahan Seer, Coinneach Odhar Fiosaiche' in *Celtic Magazine* Volume II (1877)

MacKenzie, Donald A. *Footprints of Early Man* (The Gresham Publishing Company; London, 1909)

———— *Scottish Folk-Lore and Folk Life: Studies in Race, Culture and Tradition* (Blackie & Son; London and Glasgow, 1935)

Mackenzie, William 'Gaelic Incantations, Charms, and Blessings of The Hebrides' in *Transactions of The Gaelic Society of Inverness*, Volume XVIII (1891-92)

MacKinlay, James M. *Folklore of Scottish Lochs and Springs* (William Hodge & Co.; Glasgow, 1893)

Maclagan, R. C. 'Ghost Lights of the West Highlands' in *Folklore*, Volume 8, No. 3 (September 1897)

Matheson, Norman 'The Apparitions and Ghosts of the Isle of Skye' in *Transactions of the Gaelic Society of Inverness* Volume XVIII (1891-92)

Michell, John & Rickard, Bob *Unexplained Phenomena: A Rough Guide Special* (Rough Guides; London, 2000)

Mitchell, J. and J.N. Dickie *Philosophy of Witchcraft* (Murray and Stewart; Paisley, 1839)

Morris, Ruth and Frank Morris *Scottish Healing Wells* (Alethea Press; Sandy, 1982)

O'Donnell, Elliott *The Screaming Skulls and Other Ghost Stories* (Four Square; London, 1966)

Oudemans, A.C. *The Great Sea-Serpent: An Historical and Critical Treatise* (Luzac & Co.; London, 1892)

Rannachan, Tom *Psychic Scotland* (Black and White Publishing; Edinburgh, 2007)

Rauszer, Rhona *The Light Fantastic: Skye Folk Tales and Fantasies* (Polygon; Edinburgh, 2005)

Rorie, David 'Folk-Medicine in the Report of the Highlands and Islands Medical Service Committee' in *Folklore* Volume 24, No. 3 (September 1913)

———— 'Chamber-Pots Filled with Salt as Marriage Gifts' in *Folklore* Volume 45, No. 2 (June 1934)

Scott, Sir Walter *Letters on Demonology and Witchcraft* (Wordsworth Editions/The Folklore Society; Ware/London, 2001 – first published 1830)

Skeat, Walter W. 'Snakestones and Stone Thunderbolts as Subjects for Systematic Investigation' in *Folklore* Volume 23, No. 1 (March 1912)

Stewart, Alexander Nether *Lochaber: The Natural History, Legends, and Folk-Lore of the West Highlands* (William Paterson; Edinburgh, 1883)

Squire, Charles *The Mythology of the British Islands, an Introduction: Celtic Myth, Legend, Poetry, and Romance* (Blackie and Son; London, 1905)
———————— *The Mythology of Ancient Britain and Ireland* (Constable & Co.; London, 1909)
Stewart, William Grant *The Popular Superstitions and Festive Amusements of the Highlanders of Scotland* (Aylott and Jones; London, 1851)
Swire, Otta F. *Skye: The Island and its Legends* (Birlinn; Edinburgh, 2006 – first published 1952)
———————— *The Highlands and their Legends* (Oliver & Boyd; Edinburgh, 1963)
Thompson, Francis *The Supernatural Highlands* (Luath Press; Edinburgh, 1997)
Underwood, Peter *Gazetteer of Scottish Ghosts* (Fontana; London, 1974)

NEWSPAPERS AND MAGAZINES

Aberdeen Press & Journal 29 October 2001, 22 January 2002
Daily Mail 8 February 2000
Daily Record 29 October 2001
Daily Express 31 October 2008
Daily Telegraph 28 August 2001; 18 January 2002; 1 February 2002
Guardian 1 February 2002; 28 October 2008
Scotland on Sunday 20 January 2002
Sunday Mail 20 January 2002
Sunday Express 21 December 1986
Sunday Times 14 January 2007

WEBSITES

Centre for Fortean Zoology: www.cfz.org.uk
Dunvegan Castle: www.dunvegancastle.com
Eilean Bàn Trust: www.eileanban.org
High Pasture Cave: www.high-pasture-cave.org
The Lodge at Edinbane: www.the-lodge-at-edinbane.co.uk
The Modern Antiquarian: www.themodernantiquarian.com
Royal Commission on the Ancient and Historical Monuments of Scotland (Canmore): www.rcahms.gov.uk
Skye Serpentarium: www.skyeserpentarium.org.uk/
Sleat Local History Society: www.sleatlocalhistorysociety.org.uk
Staffin Community Trust: www.staffin.net

INDEX